A PROPER JOB

A
PROPER
JOB

by

BRIAN AHERNE

Illustrated with Photographs

Houghton Mifflin Company Boston

1969

To Hazel Littlefield Smith
and a pussycat

Foreword

EUROPEANS in the U.S.A. get along splendidly with a few words of English and the thickest of accents, but Englishmen have the misfortune to speak the same language, or what seems to be the same language. If it were not so, both the Americans and ourselves would no doubt be constantly delighted by the similarity in our points of view; as it is, we are constantly mystified to find that the words we speak do not necessarily mean the same things, and when we find that they are often not even spelled the same, mystification can turn to irritation.

The Englishman who, like myself, resides in the U.S.A. for a long time, makes an effort to compromise this difficulty and finally comes to feel that he is linguistically suspended halfway across the Atlantic, suspect on both sides. I have therefore not attempted to adopt, in the following narrative, either English or American idiom. The resulting confusion is an indication of the state of my mind where nationality is concerned. All I can say is that I regard myself as an Anglo-American.

BRIAN AHERNE

Contents

viii   *Contents*

Illustrations

ACT I

ACT I

Scene 1

Worcestershire — Where the Sauce Comes From

D AMN!" said my father. "What a thing to happen!"
Just when everything in life was going so well, too.
Tall, dark, and handsome, he stood in his rose garden at eleven o'clock on a bright, May morning. Behind him was The Pleasaunce, a beautiful, half-timbered English country house which, as an up-and-coming young architect, he had designed and built himself, some miles south of Birmingham, in Worcestershire. Over the wall, built of old bricks and covered with espaliered fruit trees, lay the kitchen garden with its profusion of vegetables and fruits, gooseberries, raspberries, red and white currants, all carefully tended by two gardeners and full of promise for the summer. In the stables stood his pony and trap and his shiny new de Dion Bouton car, with its novel two-cylinder engine, acetylene headlamps, and chain drive. Beyond the orchard, now covered in spring blossom, rose the gentle green fields of Bell's Farm, whose ancient and beautiful buildings could just be seen, peeping through the surrounding trees. He heard the contented hum of his bees as they passed to and fro in the sunlight. He saw his peacocks preening their gorgeous feathers on the lawn, and he saw the topiary of which he was so proud, the neatly clipped yews that lined the grass walks. It was a magical morning, that second day of May, and he

should have been very happy — and now this had to happen! He looked grimly at the nurse who stood smiling before him in her stiff, starched uniform. Another son! This was hard to bear. Both he and Louise had wanted only a daughter when they had the boy Patrick, and this time somehow they had both felt certain she would come.

"Damn!" said my father again, and he went in to comfort his wife.

It was later in the day that Gag arrived. She was my mother's mother, although we never thought of her as a grandmother. For one thing, she never looked like it; she just looked like Gag to us. This was clear to Patrick from the first moment he saw her; pointing a baby finger at her, he cried, "Gag! Gag! Gag!," and so she remained. The widow of Town Councillor William Thomas, a respected Birmingham lawyer, she had been a good Victorian wife and mother but, after the death of her husband, she suddenly, and quite unaccountably, became gay and flighty. She wore a red wig, dressed smartly in bright colors, loved to put half a crown on a horse and always seemed to have a gentleman admirer, usually with a large mustache, a checked waistcoat, and a flower in his buttonhole, who would sit in her drawing room, contentedly sipping brandy and water while he laughed at her jokes. I remember the mustaches and the smell of brandy because the gentlemen would often give me an uncle-ish peck on the cheek, which I didn't like. As I grew older they would tip me half a crown, which I liked better.

Now, when Gag found the grieving parents refusing even to look at me, she took me instantly into her arms. "Well I like him!" she said, and in her arms I stayed all my young life. There were moments when this devotion irritated my parents acutely; the first occurred at my baptism in the parish church.

"What name is this child given?" asked the parson.

"William!" said Gag firmly.

My father started forward. "No!" he cried. "Brian de Lacy!"

The combatants glared at each other across the font. The parson, deeply shocked by this unseemly hassle, gave them a horrified glance, threw a few holy drops on my face, made a hurried Sign of the Cross, and mumbled, "I baptize thee William Brian de Lacy!"

As for me, I remained silent and my mother said I smiled. Despite my rather frosty exterior I have always been good-natured. My father, however, was not to be defeated by his mother-in-law; stalking into the vestry, he signed the Registry, omitting the name of William, and thus I became William in the eyes of Gag and the Church but not in those of my father and the State.

In the next decade Gag and I were constant companions. We would visit seaside resorts "for the bracing air" and inland spas "to take the waters." I shall never forget those waters; they spouted from jets in Victorian pump rooms and tasted horribly of sulphur and other noisome chemicals. The most serious business of the day was our regular walk along the promenade in the morning to consult the cab drivers about the day's racing events and maybe pick up a tip from them; it seemed somehow that the cabbies' association with horses should endow them with special knowledge, and there was nothing that Gag loved better than to put a couple of shillings each way on a secretly tipped outsider. In the hotel dining rooms Gag taught me table manners, and in the privacy of our room I practiced shaking hands, bowing from the waist, and how to open a door for older people. We were very popular with the other guests, she with her jolly ways, her bright colors and her red wig, and I with my old-world manners. We ate five-course "table d'hôte" meals of soup, fish, entreé, sweet, and cheese, followed by fruit or perhaps a "savoury," that curious English invention composed of soft herring roes or sardines on toast and the like, the purpose of which was to induce a thirst at the end of the meal and so assist the port wine trade, which had become so important in England in the nineteenth century after the Peninsular War. If ever my appetite flagged, Gag would lean across the table and whisper encouragingly, "Eat it up. It's all paid for!" and I would obey. To this day I can never bring myself to leave anything on my plate, hungry or not. We walked and we played simple games together, and when she took her after-noon nap I would play contentedly by myself in the hotel gardens until she awoke for tea, at which of course we ate bread and butter, jam, crumpets, perhaps, and cakes, just to keep us going till dinnertime. In all the years I never heard a cross word from her — nor indeed from my parents — and our only point of conflict arose from her natural feminine love of window-shopping. As she stood looking at something that had caught her fancy, I would tug at her long skirts and say earnestly, "Come on, Gag — hold on to your purse!"

On the dark day when she died in her little house on the Malvern Hills, twenty-four years after she had first taken me in her arms, there was a dapper old gentleman sitting in her parlor, sipping brandy and water.

"How is Louisa?" he asked the doctor huskily. "Can't you give her somethin' to keep her goin'?"

The doctor sorrowfully shook his head.

"I wish to God I could give her a winner!" he sighed.

Down under the world, in Melbourne, Australia, I came to the stage door of the Kings Theatre and found a cable from my mother: "Darling Gag passed away today." Passed away? Not from me, for she stays always in my heart.

My brother Patrick and my sister Elana were born as I was, at home in The Pleasaunce, attended into the world by Dr. Rennie, who came in his dogcart, driving a spanking horse and wearing a shiny top hat in which he kept his stethoscope. Doctors don't come to the house these days; one has to go to their offices, and they drive another kind of horsepower. In my youth there was a constant procession of horses down our drive, the coalman with his great Clydesdale pulling a dray, the chimney sweep with his rods and brushes strapped to the back of his pony, the milkman with his float, the baker, whose van was drawn by a pair of grays between whose feet ran a proud spotted dog — a "coach dog" — and all the others who supplied and maintained the house. The butcher and the fishmonger drove up in their traps between nine and ten to get their orders for the day and drove back again to deliver in time for luncheon, though we lived several miles from our village of King's Norton.

In summer my father walked two miles every morning to the terminus of the new electrified tramline which took him into Birmingham, but in winter the gardener drove him in the governess cart, harnessed either to Polly the pony, who shied at each passing vehicle, or to Jenny the donkey, who solemnly turned into each gate she saw and had to be turned around, with much beating and cursing, and led out onto the road again. Along New Street Birmingham, he rode on horse buses, still driven by Dickensian coachmen dressed in many-caped coats and handling long whips. At the street corners he saw crossing-sweepers, whose job it was to clear the street of horse manure.

Horses, coachmen, crossing-sweepers, and chimney sweeps, lamplighters, organ-grinders, and muffin men, lavender girls, and Breton onion men, footmen, governesses, nursemaids, kitchen maids, housemaids, and curates; all are gone now, but all were familiar to my father, who saw the internal com-bustion engine abolish the horse and high factory wages abolish the servant. Curates seem just naturally to have faded away. If he also saw contraception abolish the big family, my father was not aware of the change, for such things were not even thought about by his parents, and the Pater and the Mater were two fixed guiding stars, to whose example he was bound, I suspect, not so much by love as by a strict sense of Victorian family discipline. They had pro-duced ten children — ten, that is, who lived — for, as was not uncommon in those days, there were a number who didn't. Seven sisters had accustomed him to the presence of lots of women in the house and led him to expect many daughters of his own. The arrival of his first son, Patrick, was a pity, but that of his second, Brian, was an annoyance that was hardly erased when his daughter Elana was born two years later.

One might assume, from the size of their family and their Irish name, that the Pater and the Mater were Catholics, but oddly they were Plymouth Brethren. I don't know why or when they embraced this curious and bigoted sect, but they did so with fervor and their narrow religion became the ruling passion of their lives.

William Ahern, whose father was a Fellow of Trinity College, Dublin, came to England as a private tutor, but when he married Miss Patterson and started his large family he went into the City, where he displayed financial acumen and rose to become Secretary of the Investment Trust Corporation, a position occupied today by his grandson, one of my many cousins. At some point, he bought a hideous gabled house on the beach at Pevensey Bay in Sussex, to which the family went in summers until they moved there permanently, and this he named, in the pompous fashion of the period, Tower Holme. It was a smallish house, always filled to capacity with Aherns. There was no gas or electricity, no bathrooms, and water only from a well under the kitchen which had to be pumped daily up into the cistern in the attic. As a child, I used to watch with awe while the Pater in his shirt sleeves "put one hundred strokes on the pump" in the morning before trimming and filling the oil lamps; later I did these tasks myself.

Tower Holme was to become the Mecca of the younger Aherns who became so numerous that to this day I have difficulty in sorting them out. Crowded sometimes three in a bedroom, we spent long, magical holidays playing on the shingle beach, swimming, and hunting for eels and mushrooms on the marshes, though, of course, never on Sunday, for that was the Lord's Day, and we must all put on sober expressions and our best clothes and walk three miles across the fields to church, morning and evening. I came to think of the Lord as a sort of angry, vengeful old man, looking much like the Pater, who had made us imperfectly and blamed us for it. I never could understand why he sought to correct his errors by sending his son down into the world to be crucified, but I would never have dared, at any age, to ask my grandparents to explain these matters. "Little boys should be seen and not heard," we were told, and we believed it. There were prayers, and grace before and after meals, and the curate came on Wednesday afternoons to hold a prayer meeting in the parlor, perhaps on the theory that the goodness generated on Sunday could not be expected to last the week.

Both the Pater and the Mater were terrifying, almost biblical, figures to us, he towering majestically over the family with his great beard and stern expression, she very small but equally impressive, with an aquiline nose and sharp reproving eye. In an age when the powerful influence of Queen Victoria still dominated the thinking of English people, they were true products of their time, good and kind, but stern and inflexible if their rules of conduct were broken. The Bible lay always beside their small double bed, and they read it aloud to each other every night before retiring. On Sunday afternoons, after the gargantuan joints of roast beef, one at each end of the long table, had been carved, and the many dishes and plates passed from hand to hand up and down, and finally all cleared away, the Pater would lie face downward on the dining room table reading his Bible. The door would be shut, and those doing the washing up in the kitchen must speak softly and refrain from any noise that might disturb him. The Mater would take her nap, and this was the moment for the bravest among us to take a quick, surreptitious dip in the sea, risking cramps by going in so soon after the roast beef, and woe betide us if either of them should rouse and glance out of the window, for this was the

Lord's Day, and He would frown on such self-indulgence.

At the age of seventy, the Pater became so exercised about the meaning of certain passages in the Old Testament that he taught himself Hebrew with a postal course and translated them for better understanding. The bulky envelopes arrived with others bearing strange foreign stamps which came from missionaries in dark corners of the world to whom contributions had been sent. It mattered not at all that there was no money to send the children to school; they educated each other at home, and only Aunt Eunice, the youngest, received any formal education. My father taught himself to paint in oils and to play the violin. Aunt Eunice taught herself to play the harp, Aunt Dorothy Honora produced a fine contralto voice and became an ardent follower of the infidel Bernard Shaw. All of them learned how to care for a baby, for it seemed there was always a baby, and not one would have dared to ask for money for anything but the church collection. The result was a family of strong individualists, people who brought themselves up and formed their own tastes and opinions, uninfluenced by the conventions of school life or the teaching of others. Vehement artistic and political discussions, strong personal likes and dislikes, deep emotions, all testified to Irish blood and unconventional upbringing but were perhaps inadequate preparation for life in the outside world. Just as there were no servants, because they were unnecessary, so there were no friends for the young people in that eccentric family, for friends were superfluous among so many, and indeed would have been hard to find in Pevensey. When my father in later years suggested to his mother that she invite a young man or two to the house to meet the unmarried girls, she replied firmly, "If there is a husband for one of the girls, the Good Lord will send him," and somehow she was right, for in the end only two remained unmarried. When, however, shortly after their golden wedding, the Good Lord took her William away, she was not reconciled to His wisdom, but grieved day and night for the ten more years that she lived, and even the Bible, which lay always on her bed, did not comfort her.

A few days after the Pater's death, Aunt Bessie asked her mother for money to pay the grocer, to be told that she had none. What about the bank account? There was none. My father was appealed to. He interviewed the Investment Trust Corporation, who scoffed at the idea that their secretary could leave nothing. Why, they said, not only had he drawn a very handsome salary, but he of all people in the City of London had had unique opportunities to make money in the investment market for many years! The Mater was questioned. Yes indeed, he had brought his salary home in cash every month and poured it into her lap, saying, "This is yours, my darling." Investments? "Certainly not!" she said. "Your dear father would have thought it sinful to take money which he had not earned!" To invest and care for other people's money was his job, and he had been superlatively good at it, but his conscience would never have allowed him to do such things for himself, for he truly believed his Bible which told him that the love of money was the root of all evil, and that usury is sinful. Well then, where had all the salary gone? "To Missions to the Heathen, of course, as your dear father wished!" To the great credit of the directors of the Investment Trust Corporation, it must be said that they made an allowance to the widow and the unmarried daughters for the rest of their lives, but my aunts had always to be wary and watch the mail, because if the Mater laid hands on a pound it was likely to be posted off at once to some missionary in darkest Africa or the Solomon Islands.

How strong is the influence of heredity as opposed to environment? I plump for heredity. I can see in myself elements of both my father and my mother, and not always those elements which I admired. I hear my mother speak, I see my father move in me, and I am often fascinated and amused to observe where I conform to, and deviate from, the pattern of their lives, though their lives were, in later years, isolated and sad, while mine has been cosmopolitan and exciting. And so I speak briefly of them now.

At the age of nineteen, my father left home. There was nothing else to do. One of his brothers got a local girl "into trouble" and was shipped off to Africa, never to be heard of again; the other married suddenly and mysteriously, possibly for the same reason. Lacy was left with all his sisters, with no education, no friends, and no prospects, but with an untrained aptitude for drawing and painting. He saw an advertisement for an architect's apprentice in the Midlands city of Birmingham at a salary of £1 a week, packed an old cardboard suitcase and left home. The Pater gave him £5 with which to start life and went off to a prayer meeting, not seeming to realize that poor Lacy was singularly ill-equipped to face the world. Intensely shy and introverted, he had a cold, imperious manner that belied a gentle and generous nature. Never having had any friends, he had no idea how to set about making them, and indeed seemed to repel advances from others. Heaven knows what agonies of loneliness he must have suffered during those early years in Birmingham,

which he spent in a basement room, eking out his existence
by copying building plans at night — "taking in the washing," as it used to be known among the architects' appren-
tices.

Occasionally he would catch sight of the Pater, who used
to visit an old clergyman friend in Birmingham. The two
would be walking slowly along the pavement or standing,
oblivious to the passersby, wrapped in discussion of some religious matter, sometimes pounding with their canes —
walking sticks, as they were called — to emphasize a point.
Apparently the Pater never thought to look up his son, for
that was not the purpose of his visit, nor would Lacy dream
of interrupting the debate. Such actions would have been
embarrassing, and even slightly suspect, in the Ahern family.

I don't know how he eventually came to meet my mother,
or summoned up the courage to speak to her when he did, for
they were a most ill-matched pair, and remained so all their
lives. Small, golden-haired and very pretty, Louise was viva-
cious, full of gaiety and charm, and adored by everyone. It
seems quite natural that she was always known as "Lulu."
She sang and painted passably, played the mandolin, danced
"the Skirt Dance" which, performed in a voluminous pleated
skirt, was all the rage then, and she was passionately devoted
to the theater, a passion which was to influence her whole
life, and mine too. Always she wanted to act, or to be in a
theater in any capacity, before or behind the curtain, but in
those days it was thought hardly proper for ladies to go into
the profession, and her father, a kind and intelligent man,
resolutely opposed the idea, so she turned her energies and
her undoubted talents to the amateur stage.

How often in my life have I met women who are possessed

by the same urge. Most men who become actors do so either because, like myself, they couldn't get a job at anything else or because, as I firmly believe, they are attracted by the prospect of long mornings in bed. With women, it is different; they seem driven by an overpowering urge to express themselves, to dress up, to stand in the limelight, and to be the center of attention. I have known actresses great and small who would ruthlessly cut ties with home, husband, and children, who would cast aside anyone and anything, and endure any hardship, loneliness, and distress if only they could get a chance to act. What is this demon that possesses them? It offers no chance of satisfaction or of compromise. I have seen very young girls filled with elation and wracked with despair, and I have seen great stars, after a lifetime of fame and fortune, feeling just as deeply. These are the real actresses, the stuff that both stars and character women are made of, quite inexplicable to ordinary people, and this passion is not based upon anything so slight as vanity; it is a deep, enduring need, and God help the man who gives his heart to such a woman, for the need never leaves them.

I can pay no greater tribute to Lacy and Lulu than to say that they lived out their lives together in amity and kindness and I never heard a harsh word spoken between them, but how great was the compromise they both made I can scarcely guess. Certainly Lacy could at first have had no idea at all of what he was getting into. During the long, lonely ten years in his basement, while he slaved to learn his trade, he had tended more and more to live in an introspective dreamworld. He looked in the mirror and saw his dark, handsome, aristocratic face, his long black hair, aquiline nose, and steady eyes, and he dreamed that his descent was

noble and that it was this that set him apart from other men.
Who were these common Birmingham manufacturers, with
their money, their fine clothes and jewels and their brash self-
confidence, but mere jumped-up "Brummagem Tykes," unfit
to associate with him, let alone to be his friends? It was a
consoling thought. He searched the public library and
wrote to Dublin for information about the Aherns, but unfortunately it was not as encouraging as he hoped. As far as
both he and I have been able to gather, the Aherns were genuine bog Irish from County Cork, and this did not satisfy
him. He wrote down his name, William Lacy Ahern.
Ahern? He tried the other spellings, A'Hern, O'Hern,
Ahearn, O'Heran; all looked disappointingly tribal. What
about Aherne? Yes, there was something about that extra "e"
which seemed to give the name more style. Still, he was not
satisfied. There was the question of lineage. A descendant
of the ancient Irish Kings, of course, with Brian Boru as ultimate ancestor, but even they were only ignorant, fighting
kerns, not really noble. He looked again — William Lacy
Aherne — and there he saw it, in his own name; *Norman*
Irish, that was the explanation!

In the eleventh century, William the Conqueror sent an
army to conquer Ireland under the command of Count Hugo
de Lacy, one of the great Norman nobles who had fought
with him at the Battle of Hastings. It was the de Lacys who
erected the castle of Trim in County Meath, the ruins of
which still stand and are the property of Lord Dunsany, who
was kind enough to show them to me. The de Lacys built
the famous Pale around Dublin, beyond which all civilization was reputed to stop. Why, Count Hugo and King William had even stepped ashore at Pevensey when they in-

vaded England in 1066! It must be true, it *shall* be true,
thought Lacy who, in that moment, became de Lacy;
William de Lacy Aherne, it looked good. When, shortly
after, William became Willoughby, and de Lacy became part
of the surname, it was even better — Willoughby de Lacy
Aherne!

The heady wine of his newly discovered aristocracy acted
as a tonic to my father. He took a one-room office and put
out his shingle, "de Lacy Aherne, Architect." His stiff collars
grew higher, his stiff cuffs longer, and his manner more
haughty than ever, but for the first time in his life he understood himself, and in his isolated way he was happy.

Forty years later I asked him to make me a family tree. He
looked at me sternly and said, "Your ancestor was Count
Hugo de Lacy," and that was that. I forbore to tell him that
the title became extinct in 1238, or that I knew that the coat of
arms, which he kept locked in a cupboard and displayed only
on special occasions, was designed by himself and registered
with the College of Heralds for a small fee. His red lion ram-
pant on a field of gold pleased him more than the "pelican in
her piety," which denoted an Ahern, though I find it odd that
he should have abandoned the family motto *Per ardua
Surgo*, through adversity I rise, which should have suited
him, as it suits me.

Although as children we were constantly reminded of our
noble ancestors, only two were actually named to us: Count
Hugo, whose head was chopped off with an axe by a jealous
husband, who jumped from behind a tree as the gallant
count was strolling with the lady one evening outside the
castle of Denbigh in North Wales, and General Maurice de
Lacy, whose unexplained services to Queen Catherine of

Russia were said to have been rewarded by the gift of vast estates at Grodno in Poland. Count Hugo's headless effigy may be seen over the ruined gateway of Denbigh Castle, and proof of the existence of General Maurice used to exist in the form of a yellow press cutting from the London *Times*, appealing for the whereabouts of heirs to the fabled Grodno, though I doubt whether my father ever had the nerve to answer this. I once asked my mother if he did, and she replied no, because the Pater did not approve of getting one's name in the papers.

Our parents were very reticent about themselves, and, unlike American children, we never knew their ages, their birthdays, or the date of their wedding anniversary. We would have thought it presumptuous to ask. When they died they were cremated with nobody present, and their ashes scattered in the garden of the crematorium. While they lived, they were to us simply Mum and Dad, ageless and changeless, and it never occurred to us to discuss their personal lives with them; we would not have thought it proper, any more than we would have thought it proper to ask them about sex, though this subject fascinated us, as it does all youngsters in their early teens. I shall never forget my embarrassment when my headmaster, as I was about to leave my preparatory school at the age of fifteen to go to public school, called me into his study and told me that my father had asked him to have a talk with me on the matter. Naturally, I possessed a great deal of highly inaccurate knowledge, but feigned ignorance, and was dumbfounded when he continued, with many pauses and much unnecessary clearing of the throat.

"Your father thinks you should know, before you go to

your public school and associate with older boys — er — how babies come. Well — er — there are certain — er — parts of the human body which are different in man and woman. I think you — er — know what I mean. Well, in order to produce a baby, a certain — er — connection has to take place between them. [Hastily] What that connection is we needn't go into now, but — er — well, anyway — if an older boy comes up to you and asks you if you know how babies come — er — well, my advice to you is to knock him down! That will be all for now, Aherne." I thanked him and withdrew, covered with embarrassment, both for him and for my father.

As I said, I do not know how, or where, Louise and Lacy met. It seems incredible that they should have met at all, and even more incredible that they should have attracted one another, unless it be true that opposites attract. I suppose that, like electricity, a magnetic field was created by the juxtaposition of positive and negative. Anyway, it was some time before she dared to speak to her mother about her strange admirer whom, in fact, she hardly ever saw, though she heard him, groaning with jealousy and despair, on the other side of the hedge as she and her partner sat in the garden at the dances, to which of course he was never invited. Finally, a meeting for tea was somehow arranged, not at home in case Lulu's father, Mr. Thomas, should appear unexpectedly, but at a rendezvous in town.

As Gag and Lulu strolled along with their big lacy hats, their leg-of-mutton sleeves, and their parasols, Gag saw an interesting sight approaching: a tall intensely serious young man in a silk top hat, black frock coat, and striped stovepipe trousers, all obviously rented, his stiff collar inordinately high, his cuffs equally long, a cane in his hand, a flower in his buttonhole, and a strained expression, combined of fear and formality, on his face.

"Why this must be he," said Gag, and then, "Good gracious! Where's he gone?" For he had disappeared, suddenly and completely, just at the moment he raised his hat. The ladies looked anxiously around and then heard a groan at their feet. There he lay, at the bottom of an excavation in the pavement which yawned unnoticed right before them. Lulu gave a cry of horror. Lacy scrambled out, retrieved his squashed top hat and broken cane, climbed from the pit and ran, losing himself in the crowd, hoping no doubt to lose himself forever.

When Gag told Mr. Thomas about his daughter's strange and unsuitable admirer he cannot have been pleased, but he behaved with the fortitude and sagacity which might have been expected from a lawyer, a connoisseur of good port, pretty women, and fine horses, a Town Councillor of the City of Birmingham, and a member of the Watch Committee, whose function it was to watch over the morals of Birmingham's citizens and protect them from temptation. He had a serious talk with Lulu in which he pointed out the unsuitability of such a match. His son Bob, a charming no-good rascal, had been a grief to him in many ways, and he looked to Lulu, the apple of his eye, to do the right thing. Lulu, however, had a good shot in her locker, which now she fired: she had given up, she said, her ambition to be an actress solely at her father's behest, and this time her wish must prevail. That golden hair, those baby blue eyes, that small retroussé nose — "Ah, Miss Lu," her nurse used to say, "you was behind the door when the noses was give out!" — that delicate appearance concealed a determination which could be called upon if need be. Mr. Thomas compromised. He invited Lacy to luncheon.

Sunday luncheon at The Spinney was a serious affair. Following Morning Service at Moseley Church — Church of England, of course — there was church parade in which the families walked or drove home, raising their hats formally to each other and stopping to chat en route. For this was an age of reason, of civilization, peace, and order, and when the Boer War broke out, it was at first only regarded as a dashing and unusual adventure for the young volunteers. It was a specially good opportunity for Lulu, for there were concerts and plays in the Assembly Rooms to raise money to send comforts to the troops, into which she threw herself with delight. Her specialty was a dramatic recitation of Kipling's poem, "The Absent Minded Beggar."

> *When you've shouted "Rule Britannia," when you've*
> *   sung "God Save the Queen,"*
> *When you've finished killing Kruger with your mouth,*
> *Will you kindly drop a shilling in my little tambourine*
> *For a gentleman in khaki ordered South?*
> *He's an absent-minded beggar, and his weaknesses are*
> *   great —*
> *But we and Paul must take him as we find him —*
> *He is out on active service, wiping something off a*
> *   slate —*
> *And he's left a lot of little things behind him!*
> *Duke's son — cook's son — son of a hundred kings —*
> *(Fifty thousand horse and foot going to Table Bay!)*
> *Each of 'em doing his country's work*
> *(And who's to look after their things?)*
> *Pass the hat for your credit's sake,*
> *   And pay — pay — pay!*

And pay they did. Those who paid over five pounds got a kiss for their money.

All this excitement only added fuel to Lacy's passion. It made the poor fellow burn with jealousy. When he arrived at the Spinney on the day of the luncheon he was also paralyzed with fear. He had never been to a party, never heard the light, worldly conversation of people like the Thomases and their friends, and furthermore he felt himself to be on trial before the family of his adored one. Nobility of descent was a poor substitute for *savoir faire,* and though Gag tried her best to put him at ease, alas he couldn't think of a thing to say. He frowned and looked dignified, and died a thousand deaths inside. It was even worse when the ladies rose and left him with the gentlemen. The port appeared after the coffee, in crusted and cobwebbed bottles, and was opened and tasted with ceremony; a drop rolled on the tongue, sometimes even a sniff of the bouquet, was enough to tell these connoisseurs the year of its origin. Of course, only the great vintage ports were drunk, but they were discussed and analyzed at length and the ritual lasted until the late afternoon. Nuts were on the table, but nobody would have dreamed of spoiling the palate by smoking even the finest cigar, and cigarettes of course were unknown. The conversation, which ranged over politics, sports, the newfangled motor cars, and kept women, was interlarded with shocking jokes which staggered him. It was not only the fumes of the port that made his head reel on his long walk home to his lonely room.

It was some months after this experience that the return match took place, and Lulu was permitted to accompany him on a visit to his family. Now it was her turn to be staggered. The Aherne girls, several beautiful and all unusual, were dressed in "sensible," but shabby clothes, sensible walking shoes, thick woolen stockings, and sensible dresses made of heavy dark materials, high at the neck and long in the skirt. They stared at Lulu, in her light summer dress, all buttons and bows, flounces and frills, as if she were someone from another planet. They examined her pink and white complexion with awe. "Do you think she paints?" they whispered to each other. They were congealed in the presence of such chic and femininity. After grace, supper was eaten in solemn inhibited silence, and Lacy, remembering the gaiety and chatter of the Thomas household, cudgeled his brains for some agreeable topic. Finally he leaned toward his eldest sister.

"Bessie," he said, "why do you do your hair like that? Lulu says it looks terrible!"

But the sisters were intelligent and sensitive girls, and by the next evening had gained enough confidence to talk to their guest, in a shy and rather formal way. Dorothy even obliged with a little Bach on the piano after supper, while the family sat gravely in high-backed antimacassared horsehair chairs to listen. This gave Lulu her cue; running upstairs, she came bounding down again with her mandolin, brought for just such an occasion, and launched into song. She sang:

> *Gently the troubador waltzed round the waterbut*
> *Singing "My own true love, come down to me,"*
> *Softly a brickbat dropped on his coconut.*
> *The old man was watching in the big pear tree!*

followed by "Ta-Ra-Ra-Boom-Deay!" at the conclusion of which there was a stunned silence.

Lacy stole an anguished look at the Pater, who sat immobile, staring glassy-eyed at the Jezebel before him. It was the Mater who saved the day. "Well, my dear," she said at last, "of course, it is very, very shocking." Then she leaned forward and smiled a little. "But perhaps we could hear that one just once more?" she asked. They heard it of course, and also,

> *Has anybody here seen Kelly,*
> *Kelly from the Isle of Man?*

and "Knocked 'Em in the Old Kent Road."

A girl with less determination, or less in love than Lulu, might have given up the romance after that visit, but the Thomases saw with resignation that there was no hope of that. Mr. Thomas sighed, gave in, and put up the money for Lacy to build a row of suburban houses on speculation, and these, though too gabled and ornate for our modern taste, were so admirably planned and built that they sold like hotcakes, made a fair profit, and established the name of de Lacy Aherne as a rising young architect.

And so, in the course of time, the princess married her prince, and I should like to finish their scene as the fairy tales do, by saying that they lived happily ever after, but retrospection hardly warrants such a conclusion. Lacy and Lulu lived more than forty years together and experienced the hopes and disappointments, the uncertainties, anxieties, and griefs, and the occasional gleams of fugitive happiness, that seem to make up the strange pattern of the life of mankind. They thought their lives were humdrum and dull, but I know they went through very deep waters and suffered much; it was their kind hearts and upright characters that supported them and brought them some measure of peace in the end — though more than once I heard Lulu refer to the institution of marriage as "Holy Deadlock."

Scene 2

All the World's a Stage

THERE were men working on the roof. We were coming home from the seaside, and as we entered the gates in a growler, the horse going clip-clop, clip-clop, faster as he saw the end of his journey, I looked out of the window and saw them. My father said this was impossible as I was only two years old at the time, but I distinctly remember seeing them. They were putting the tiles on the roof of the new wing, which my father had designed with a nursery and bedrooms for the children above and a great ballroom below; it seems great in my memory, but looks quite small now, though the beautiful polished dance floor, "swung on chains" they said, is still there. To this ballroom came the children from the country round, with their nannies and their mothers, every Saturday afternoon to a dancing class, conducted with decorum by Mrs. Rice. Here we learned to bow and curtsy, to enter and leave a room with grace, and to dance the polka, the one-step, the waltz and the Lancers. When I played Higgins in *My Fair Lady*, nearly fifty years later, I waltzed with ease and pleasure, thanks to Mrs. Rice's correct teaching, while my poor understudy struggled unsuccessfully for weeks to learn. In the ballroom, too, we took piano lessons, grappling with quavers and semi-quavers and practicing endless scales. Most of all we enjoyed "dressing-up nights," when Lulu opened her theatrical trunk and we draped ourselves in scarves and hats and makeshift costumes, and danced about the room to the strains of a gramophone, imagining we were ballet dancers and actors. No one enjoyed this more than my mother.

The arrival of my sister two years after myself must have pleased my parents very much, but alas it did not cement their happiness. The quiet, easy country life, the beautiful surroundings, and the prosperity and elegance of their lives were not enough to satisfy Lulu. She saw herself resigned to the endless production of children, like her mother-in-law before her, and she pined for her old love, the theater. She would spend hours in her room before a full-length mirror, rehearsing parts that she longed to play, watching her expressions and muttering the lines. "Don't disturb your Mum; she's rehearsing," our governess would say, and this was a ritual which was perfectly understandable to our childish minds; after all, we did the same things ourselves on dressing-up nights.

In those days, women were inclined to lose their figures when they bore children, and to Lulu, the actress, this was a deep and genuine fear. It was not until very late in his life that my father told me that it was at this time that she refused to have any more children or to have any further physical contact with him. On their honeymoon in Wales they had bought a beautiful antique double bed, on the wood back of which was carved "Come, gentle dreams, the hour of sleep beguile," and for thirty years, until we had all left home and they moved into separate rooms, they slept under these words, divided by an invisible barrier which remained always unknown to us and unforgiven by my father.

It is not bad luck, as they so often believe, but ignorance that mars men's lives, and poor Lacy's knowledge of the world was almost nil. He knew no women except those of his own family and he had no men friends, nobody to turn to. Right and wrong were as clear as day and night to him, and any doubts could immediately be resolved by looking at the example of his parents. He knew nothing of planned parenthood, and the idea of a mistress would have shocked him to the core. "Besides," he said to me in his old age, "Your mother was much too jealous. She never let me even look at another woman!" He knew no way of coping with his situation other than to retreat into silent bitterness and resentment. He lost all ambition and all interest in his work, his house, his garden, and the good things that life had given him. Of course he had always been a regular churchgoer, and there is no doubt that now he needed spiritual help desperately. In the absence of psychiatry, it was the custom in those days to go and have "a little frank talk with the Vicar." It seems likely that his distress and his religious unbringing may have prompted him to do this, and I have wondered whether the result may not have been as unhelpful as my own frank little sex talk with my headmaster, some years later. Anyway, he stopped going to church around this time and, to my knowledge, never went again. Indeed poor Lacy never did anything much again; he went on strike, he gave up, he sat down.

Lulu must also have been desperately unhappy, for she was sensitive, loving, and kind, but she too was a prisoner of her own ignorance. Fortunately for her, she was at this moment offered a strong helping hand by the unexpected appearance of a Fairy Prince, who came to her rescue.

It was a lovely summer's morning and I was riding my birthday present, a red tricycle, up the drive when I saw him riding toward me on a spirited, well-groomed horse. Jumping off my own humble steed, I ran to hold the reins while he dismounted and went in to see my mother. His name was Barry V. Jackson, and he was a wealthy bachelor with a keen interest in the theater. He had come to ask my mother to join him in forming an amateur dramatic company, to be known as The Pilgrim Players, which would play Shakespeare and classical English plays in the surrounding countryside. She was instantly on fire with the idea. Together with John Drinkwater, a local insurance salesman who was later to become a famous poet and playwright, author of *Abraham Lincoln, Bird in Hand,* and other successful plays, they formed their company, which played in gardens, church halls, and barns all over Worcestershire and Warwickshire in the summers and gave a dozen performances in the Edgbaston Assembly Rooms in the winters. They staged their own productions, making their own costumes and scenery. Many were the performances, and many of them rained out, that I saw as a boy of *As You Like It* or *Midsummer Night's Dream* in a sylvan setting, the audience seated on the lawn while the actors made their entrances and exits through the bushes.

The first play I ever saw, at the age of four, was one of the first ever written in the English language, the old morality play *Everyman,* in which my mother played Luxury; it was done on the chancel steps of St. Jude's Church, Birmingham, where the Reverend Arnold Pinchard, a picturesque priest of theatrical inclinations, was happy to welcome the Pilgrim

Players. This was followed by *The Interlude of Youth,* another morality play, in the same setting. At the Assembly Rooms, I saw Shakespeare's *King John,* after which for nights I would wake in terror as I dreamed of the boy Arthur, pleading with his jailer Hubert, who has come to put his eyes out with a red-hot iron. I had a different impression of the theater when Gag took me to see a musical comedy called *The Milkmaids,* in which I loved the pretty girls of the chorus, a taste that has never left me. My playgoing career was thus launched with variety and excitement.

In 1912, Barry Jackson considered the company good enough to turn professional, and he used his money to build and endow a beautiful modern theater, the Birmingham Repertory Theatre, which was far ahead of the times in design. The floor of the auditorium was raked so steeply that the head of the person in front was level with the viewer's knees; there was no charge for cloakroom or programs, a string orchestra played unseen in the pit during intervals, free coffee was served at the bars, exhibitions of costume and scenery design hung in the foyer, and everything was done for the comfort of the audience. Behind the curtain, the equipment was such as had never before been seen in England; Schwabe-Haseit lighting and a cyclorama were installed there years before they appeared in London, and accommodation for the actors was as good as anything one finds in most American and British theaters today. Mr. Jackson established a policy of the finest plays and productions at low prices; nobody was paid more than a living wage at the "Rep," but everybody had a chance to gain wonderful experience. Ibsen, Chekov, Galsworthy, Strindberg, Wilde, Shaw, Synge, the new Irish, German, and Spanish playwrights fol-

lowed one after the other in Birmingham, at a time when the
London stage was still locked in the nineteenth-century tra-
dition. Many of the actors of our day got their training and
many subsequent Broadway and West End successes began
there. *The Farmer's Wife, The Barretts of Wimpole Street,
The Apple Cart, Bird in Hand,* and *Back to Methuselah* are a
few that were first performed at the Rep.

When Barry Jackson was knighted, it was an honor upon
which, for once, the whole profession could agree. He retired to live at Malvern, in a house which my father designed
for him, and his name will go down in theatrical history as
that of a brilliant, charming, and dedicated man of the theater who used his money wisely and well, displaying a high
standard of taste and intelligence without, as far as I am
aware, making enemies or incurring serious personal criti-
cism. He died in 1961.

It was a great day for my mother, and curiously enough
for me too, when she joined the Pilgrim Players, but when
they became a professional company she could not find it in
her heart to desert her family, nor would my father have allowed it; but she would go down from time to time to play
some suitable part and she took us to see almost every production that was done at the Rep. I used to go up to the box
office in my school cap, and the manager, Bache Matthews,
would hand me with a fatherly smile free tickets for myself
and my friends. I think perhaps those years were responsible
for my occasional complaint that the theater has nothing
new to show me.

It was while the Pilgrims were still an amateur company
that I made my first appearance on the stage, the date of
which is given by that astonishing publication, *The Stage*

Year Book, as the 5th of April, 1910. The play, *Fifinella,* written by Barry Jackson himself, was a fantasy for children. The scene in which I appeared was "The Palace of the Dream Merchant." The dream merchant was an imposing character in oriental robes who sat like a Pasha on an elevated throne and gave out rewards and punishments, in the form of gold and silver tinsel balls, to the children who came before him, one by one, to relate their doings of the day. As the last and smallest of the good children, I was taken on his knee, and I can remember even now the smell of whisky that engulfed me, a smell which I was long to associate with actors and have all too often recognized since. I had only one line, but it brought the house down. I said, "It was so small, so very small. I took a fly from a spider's web," and I lisped.

The dancing lessons continued, and I became the star pupil, doing a Russian dance, with much stamping and pirouetting, dressed in white satin with a white egret feather in my cap. Russian dances were all the rage, for the great Diaghileff Ballet had just burst upon the Western world, and when they opened at the Palace Theatre in London the enthusiasm was tremendous. My mother took me on a special excursion train up to town for a matinee, and I saw Pavlova, Mordkin, Nijinsky, Karsavina, and the rest from the balcony, from which we nearly fell with excitement. The memory of that brilliant exhibition of the art of dancing is to me still so vivid that I am today a tough critic of the ballet.

It was only a few months later that she took me up to town again, this time to stay for the night. She had secured an appointment for me to give an audition of my Russian number to Fred Farren, ballet master at the Empire Theatre.

I duly came out on the huge bare stage, a piano tinkled somewhere off in the wings, and I did my stamps and pirouettes awkwardly, as the boards were very rough and quite different from the smooth, polished floor at home. Farren beckoned to my mother and murmured a few words to her, and then I heard "next please!" and I was scuffled off the stage and out to Lyons for a cup of tea. The boy needs side-practice, he had said, and he recommended Italia Conti's School for stage children. We went to visit Miss Conti, whose class was held in a basement room beneath the Bay Malton public house in Great Portland Street, and there I understood for the first time what side-practice was, for there was a row of youngsters holding onto a bar placed around the walls and lifting their legs sideways in what seemed to me a most unnatural manner.

I have often, since then, wondered what could have induced my parents to leave me, a little boy of ten who had never been away from home, in London alone, but they did. I suppose my mother's theatrical frustration must have impelled her to push one of her children on the stage, and my brother being too recalcitrant and my sister too young, she fixed upon me. I didn't mind at all; to me it was just a lark. My father was instructed to find me lodging, which he did by inserting an advertisement in a London paper. This was answered by two maiden ladies by the name of Veale, who lived in a dilapidated house in Ladbrook Grove, and it was only after I was installed there that I discovered that, despite their name, the Misses Veale were strict vegetarians. They fed me a diet of nut cutlets and date roasts, eked out with watery potatoes and brussels sprouts, and they were kind to me in their fashion, though they knew nothing about chil-

dren. They used to take me to Theosophist meetings in
Bloomsbury on Sunday nights, and I heard Mrs. Annie
Besant lecture there, but the only part of it that meant anything to me was the lemonade and cakes after the meeting,
for it seemed I was always hungry. I had a season ticket on
the underground which made me feel very grown-up, and I
went daily to Miss Conti's classes, where I dutifully kicked
my legs sideways and learned to recite "The Charge of the
Light Brigade" with emphasis on broad vowels, rather than
the narrow ones of Birmingham.

The wintry, dark and wet streets of London were strange
and sad to a little boy from the country, and I was often
lonely and unhappy, but as Christmas approached we all became very busy with preparations for the West End production of *Where the Rainbow Ends,* a play for children which
Miss Conti produced annually for Sir Charles Hawtrey, the
famous actor-manager. This was the second year, and for
many succeeding years it was performed for a short season at
Christmas. The sensation of the piece was an entrancing
little girl named Mavis Yorke, who played the Will o' the
Wisp in a small, silvery voice and danced like a bit of thistle-
down. Gracie Seppings danced "the Spirit of the Lake" and
mothered us all backstage. Reginald Owen, now a distinguished movie actor but then a handsome young man with
wavy golden hair, played Saint George in shining armor and
fought a clashing swordfight with James Carew, Ellen
Terry's husband, as the Demon King. An unpleasant youth
with large ears, too much assurance, and the name of Noël
Coward, played William the pageboy. Noël claims that he
can only have been four years older than I, and that he cannot remember me, but I remember him all right. I sent my

cherished autograph book in to Owen and Carew, who signed it, but the page was ruined for me by a large and unwanted "Noël Coward," scrawled across it. I wish I could find it now.

We, who were listed in the program as "The Italia Conti Chicks," had all to go into court to secure permission to work at nights. The magistrate regarded us and shook his head sadly.

"They look very young," he sighed. "I am sure it will be long past their proper bedtime," and we little pros were alarmed at the prospect of losing our jobs, but after Miss Conti's lawyer had made an eloquent appeal, coupled with an agreement that we should all lie down and rest in the intervals, permission was reluctantly granted and we breathed again. The salary was £1.12.6 a week, which my father invested in Chinese government bonds for me. Eight years later I was able to buy an old motor bike with the proceeds, which amounted to £16. It is lucky I didn't hold those bonds longer.

Toward the end of the season, I began to feel very peculiar, and Gag came up to London to inspect me. She called a doctor, who diagnosed malnutrition, and indignantly she took me back home, where she lavished attention on me. I was sent as a day boy to an excellent school, where I enjoyed the games and began to be happy, but my mother was not quite defeated. The next Christmas, hearing from Miss Conti that they could use me for a speaking part in *The Rainbow*, as we all called it, she whisked me up to London and I started to rehearse, but I had had enough of being an actor. I wanted to be like the other boys at school and I would not pay attention or learn the lines. I was fired, Harold French took over the part, and we returned sadly to Birmingham. Poor Lulu felt as if her last chance was gone, but I shall always think of it as a lucky day for me; there is something a little sad about theatrical children, who live in a world of unreality, becoming clever in some ways but remaining ignorant in so many others. If successful, they rarely carry it into adult life, and if not, they feel badly used; they are like hothouse flowers, artificially stimulated in an exotic atmosphere, but apt to wither if transplanted outside.

And now came a great change in the lives of us all. A series of heavy blows struck my father and ruined the fortunes of the family. The death of Mr. Thomas had bereft him of the capital with which he had built speculative houses, and the manner of our life had left him with little or no money saved. He was forced to work simply as an architect who is engaged on a commission basis, and because he had no degrees or qualifications other than his talent, the better jobs were not offered to him. For a few years he had made a little by retaining ownership of the land upon which his clients' houses were built, and charging an annual ground rent for it, but Lloyd George's Land Act of 1911 specifically forbade the practice. Shortly after that, old Squire Lane, whose family had owned the adjoining estate for centuries, died and his heirs sold the property to a lunatic asylum; my father tried to sell The Pleasaunce, but found no takers, and in the end was forced to sell for a nominal sum to the asylum authorities. He sold his car, his horses, and much of his beloved antique furniture, and we moved into a small house in the suburb of Moseley. A name for it, so essential in England, was hard to find, for it seemed so insignificant a dwell-

ing after the Pleasaunce — just a house really — so that
was what it was finally called, "Maison," these French
names, I suppose, being a sort of echo of our Norman an-
cestry.

In 1914 the Great War broke out, and all building, except
that necessary to the war effort, was officially stopped, and
remained so for four years. We began to learn the hard lessons of genteel poverty. Every year or so, we sold our house
and moved to a cheaper one, and each time the neighbor-
hoods became more dilapidated and depressing.

Somehow, with such small assistance as Gag could provide, we were kept at school. The few pounds that my
mother could pick up from time to time at the Rep, or from
speech lessons which she gave to impossible youngsters for
an occasional five shillings, did not go very far, and my father, burdened with anxiety and still unhappy in his relations
with his wife, sank into misery. He was not the type of man
who could turn to other work, and he had no friends to en-
courage and support him. He would take the penny tram,
which wound slowly through the slums down to the city in
the morning, and spend a few hours sharpening pencils,
making sketch plans, or reading old architectual magazines.
My mother would beg him to stay in town for lunch, but
either he had no money or he was afraid to enter a café
alone, and he always arrived home rather sheepishly, at one
o'clock. After lunch he dozed by the coal fire for half an
hour, and then went off on his tram again, or perhaps to inspect some little repair job on a building, but he was back for
tea, and, come what might, was always in bed by nine
o'clock.

The cold, dark, smoke-laden atmosphere of Birmingham,

with its eternal drizzling rain, the horrors of the war, and the
very real privations which we all suffered in England from
the effects of the German submarine campaign were additional trials. He was called up by the Army, but sent home
because he was one day over age. What we would have done
if he had been taken I can't imagine, for my mother was not
the type to undertake a job, unless it was acting; she would
have thought it beneath her as a member of the upper class,
and she believed firmly in the class system. "N.O.C.D.," she
would whisper to us of a stranger (not our class dear), and
of course we soon learned to recognize the "G.U." (great unwashed).

We knew nothing of our parents' distress, only knowing
that we could not have a new cricket bat or pair of football
boots when we needed them, that our clothes were hand-me-
downs from relatives, that we had to ride many miles on our
old bicycles to school in all weathers, instead of going on the
bus which cost money, and that our allowance was twopence
a week instead of the two shillings the other kids got. At my
school the boys were given a glass of milk and a biscuit during the mid-morning break, but this cost five shillings a term,
so I could only watch them enviously. The police were in-
sistent that bicycles should carry both front and back lights,
and it was obligatory among boys to have an acetylene head-
lamp and oil tail lamp; for me it was a choice between a four-
mile walk home through the dark, wet winter night, or
stealing carbide and oil from other boys' lamps. I once nar-
rowly escaped being caught by the head boy, for I could not
discover how to put his lamp back together again in the dark.

English schoolboys are naturally frightened of public
opinion and, to disguise their fears and distract attention

from their own shortcomings, they can be very cruel to others. Turn the spotlight of attention on another, expose him to derision, and you are, at least temporarily, safe yourself, and so in disguising my poverty I became adept at subterfuge. American boys, it seems to me, are on much easier and friendlier terms with each other, perhaps because Americans are so intensely interested in education and do so much for their children. Such a thing as a Parent-Teachers Organization was unknown and unheard of in the England of my day. I doubt if my father would ever have thought of speaking to Mr. Cholmondely (pronounced Chumly), who taught us Latin and Greek and how to keep a straight bat on the cricket field, and who deplored a split infinitive, or to Monsieur Legrand, who taught us French with an impeccable accent and coached me in the leading parts of the French plays at the annual concert.

I was a dreamer and never a bright boy, but I had an inquiring mind and was anxious to learn. I alone was interested in my school reports, for my father never looked at them, though he groaned over the bills three times a year. "If this goes on," he would say to us, "there is only one thing for it. We must all go to the Workhouse!" We didn't know just what the Workhouse was, but we were terrified by the threat. Like his father before him, he took no interest in his children's education. He was once persuaded to go to the annual prize-giving at my sister Elana's school and came back exclaiming, "Thank God my daughter has no brains! Why, all the girls who won prizes had buck teeth and wore glasses!"

As for Lulu, such things bored her; she would have preferred that we spend our time learning a recitation, a new

dance, or how to play some musical instrument. Until Patrick and I became old enough to rebel, she dressed us in the
style of Little Lord Fauntleroy, with long curls, black velvet
suits, tussore blouses edged with lace, pale blue sashes with
big bows on the side — Pat's was always wrecked within ten
minutes — and silver buckles on our patent leather shoes.
"Artistic," such costumes were called, and we loathed the
word. School took us away from her and changed us from
the gay young Bohemians that she dreamed of into ordinary,
scrubby little boys. Dressing-up nights were no more, there
was no money to entertain or to go out, no television and few
movies in those days, nothing to divert a bored and restless
spirit except a penny book from the library, a dull daily
newspaper and perhaps a simple family card game. Poor
little Lulu must have felt the bars of her prison close upon
her, but she remained true to herself; even in the bleak
depths of our poverty, she kept a housemaid and never went
in the kitchen, washed a dish or made a bed. She also kept
our beloved Miss Halden, always known as Hor, who came to
us originally as a governess and stayed on for seventeen
years, bringing us up firmly and teaching us the three Rs,
making and mending the family clothes, cooking and helping
in the house, giving us all Christmas and birthday presents
— all for forty pounds a year and one day off a month. My
mother constantly complained of these underpaid, ill-used
helpers, saying, as she rang the bell for some further service,
"Well, what can you expect from people of that class?"

At fifteen, I was the oldest and biggest boy in the school
and won every event in the Sports Competition with embarrassing ease. My headmaster wrote suggesting that the time
had come for me to leave, and my father was not sorry to

think that he was to be relieved of the burden of school bills at last, but I had my own ideas about that; I wanted an education. Choosing a third-rate public school — I use the words in the English sense — at which I believed the requirements were sufficiently low for me, I sat for and won a small scholarship, and this news I now broke to my family. My parents were aghast, but felt obliged to look the place over. They returned in dudgeon. "It's a dreadful place!" cried my mother. "Why, I saw two *black* boys there!" Actually I suppose they were Indian princelings, who often came to England to be educated, but this was enough for her. In desperation, I persuaded them to interview the headmaster of Malvern, a first-class public school in Worcestershire. He at first protested that I was too old, but after Lulu turned her charm on him, he agreed to accept me as a day boy.

Two problems now faced my parents: how to pay the school fees which, while modest for a day boy, were still beyond their means, and how to find a dwelling place for me. My father solved the first by selling his treasured boyhood stamp collection, Gag the second by volunteering to move to Malvern to take care of me.

In addition to its famous school, Malvern is a "Spa," now of a certain faded elegance but once frequented by rich Victorians, who came to drink its tonic spring waters and to enjoy its bracing air, its lovely hills and its wide views of the Severn and Wye Valleys. Its quiet Victorian streets are lined with genteel stucco houses which have gradually been converted into hotels and boardinghouses for elderly people, and in one of these Gag and I had furnished rooms. Our landlady, a large, ample woman named Mrs. Williams, bul-

lied us almost as much as she bullied her husband and
daughter, two pale characters who eked out their existence
belowstairs, answering the bell and scurrying up and down
with trays and mops when required.

Poor Gag, when nearly seventy, had been knocked down
by a man on a bicycle and had fractured her hip. An incom-
petent doctor had failed to diagnose the injury and she never
walked again, hopping pitifully on crutches which she could
never learn to use, or being pushed in a bath chair for the
rest of her life. It was my duty to push her out when I could
get time, but as almost every waking hour was filled with
classes or compulsory games, and I had two hours' homework
to prepare every evening, we did not get out very much and
when we did we could not go into the town unless I had a
signed pass from my housemaster, who could not well understand the necessity for such gallivanting. When I returned
home for the holidays, Gag was left to the mercy of Mrs.
Williams and had to beg for the services of Miss Williams to
push her out occasionally.

Our wartime ration books provided coupons for our
weekly rations of meat, butter, sugar, tea, jam, and other ne-
cessities, and we would divide these portions in half with the
utmost care, watching each other closely.

In the long cold winter evenings we sat by our tiny fire of
rationed coal briquettes, Gag dressed perhaps in an orange
plaid tweed skirt and red sweater, and I in the uniform of a
public-school boy, striped trousers, black coat and waistcoat,
stiff collar and black tie. I would do my sums and learn my
lessons while she, in the manner of ladies of her era, would
knit, sew, and play patience. When my books were put away
we would play draughts — checkers, as it is called in Amer-

ica — halma, and simple card games, at all of which she invariably beat me; or she would tell me stories of her youth, of "the swells" she had seen driving in their carriages in Birmingham, or of relatives such as Great-uncle James, who was so fat that he had a semicircle cut in the dining room table to enable him to sit close, or of the Royal Family, whose doings were an endless source of interest to her.

Considering the great difference in our ages, we were very companionable and I think she must have been desperately lonely when I cheerfully waved goodbye and went home at holiday times. When I left Malvern, she was completely alone, and although I went to see her on occasional weekends the circumstances of my life took me inevitably farther away from her. Alas, this is the general way of young people, who cannot sacrifice their lives to the old — except, of course, in Catholic countries like Italy and Ireland, where grandmother lives in her eldest son's house and usually dominates the family. There seems to be no happy solution of this problem.

At Malvern I was, like other boys, thoroughly frightened and regularly beaten, but managed to survive the humiliation of being a day boy who lived with his grandmother; I also managed to squash certain dark rumors that I had once been a chorus girl. The dark shadow of the war hung over my school days. Our masters were the medically unfit and the over-age. In one class, I had a "dugout" colonel, trying inadequately to do his bit for the war effort, and in another, a mistress — hitherto unheard of in an English boys' school — struggling to keep order and to teach English literature. Food was sparse and dull, no sugar, sweets, or chocolate, nothing in the Grub Shop but ersatz coffee and dry little cakes made of maize flour. We were always hungry, always cold, and rarely dry.

On the whole I am not sure that I am in favor of the English public school system, which has been for so long a pillar of the British Empire. The rigid training given us was designed to turn out young men of a definite pattern, gentlemen who could be relied upon to behave correctly, to keep order, dispense British justice, and to change every night for dinner, even if alone in a steaming jungle, remote from civilization. Until the second decade of this century it achieved its purpose splendidly but, though English affairs are still largely managed by men wearing the old school tie, the vast social changes and the necessity for specialized, technical education have shaken The System. Only recently I received a form letter, warning Old Malvernians that they should review any bequests they might have made in their wills. Nationalization of the public schools, which means seizure by the government, would, said the letter, mean seizure of their funds, too, just as it had when the hospitals were nationalized.

The war dragged on. Every term the older boys left to go into the armed forces, and it seemed only a few weeks before we heard their names read out by the headmaster on the Roll of Honor at the conclusion of Sunday evening chapel service. To be on the Roll of Honor in America it is only necessary to serve, but in England you have to be killed and the boys who, after a brief training, were sent out to the muck and carnage of the trenches were killed by the thousand. Once, in Rheims Cathedral, I saw a small plaque on the wall which read "To the glory of God, and to the memory of one million dead of British blood who lie in Flanders fields." How soon they were forgotten!

There was a particular shortage of young officers and the War Office felt that, trained for leadership as we were, the public school boys were ideal material for the job of scrambling out of a trench ahead of the men, waving a sword, and gallantly leading the way through a hail of machine-gun bullets toward the forest of enemy barbed wire. The Germans naturally concentrated their fire on these poor chaps and few of them lived long, so a scheme called the Officers Training Corps had been devised to ensure a steady supply of replacements. Three times a week we all paraded in uniform, learned the Manual of Arms, drilled, and attacked or defended the Malvern Hills. I hated every minute of it but rose to the rank of corporal, and by good luck the war ended before I reached the call-up age of seventeen and a half. At the same time I managed to scrape through the London Matriculation examination, a feat of which I have always been proud, and my father, feeling that enough was enough, took me away from school and set me to work tracing plans in his bare little architect's office.

It is hard for a young man to work for his father. I thought his architecture old-fashioned, while he thought me a stuck-up young prig. Both of us were partly right. On my nineteenth birthday, I suddenly realized that I was bored — bored by the trivial tasks in my father's office, by poverty, by my family, and by dismal, dirty, depressing Birmingham. I felt I must get out and do something, but what? Become an actor, urged my mother, but I had had enough of that. I saw the shabby, impoverished actors whom she sometimes brought home to tea, listened to their boasting of their little triumphs and thought that, deprived of lights and make-up, they were only half men, still playing childish games on dressing-up night, a little ashamed of the past and deeply

afraid of the future. I wanted something more of life, though
what, I hardly knew. I told myself that I wanted a proper
job, with scope — that was it — with scope for my abilities.
I was always an inveterate reader and my head was full of
dreams. I wanted to live in the sunshine, to know great men
and beautiful women, to experience a grand passion, to appreciate great art, to walk on top of the world and to see it all
before I died. Curiously enough, I have done all these
things, but not by the route that I now chose.

Possessed by the idea of finding a job with scope, I decided
to go to Liverpool and get into shipping, which I felt was a
great and exciting business in which there must be room at
the top. To me there was something romantic about the sea,
and ships sailing all over the world. My head was full of
Conrad, Kipling, and Masefield. One day, like my father before me, I packed an old cardboard suitcase with my few
belongings and left home. Like his father before him, he
gave me five pounds, saying, "I'm sorry, old chap; that's all I
have."

I daresay he was not sorry to see me go, for I was not his
favorite child. I made him feel uncomfortable and my love
for him was tinged with the impatience and intolerance of
youth. He was always kind to me, and never raised his hand
to me in my life, but I had not, like my brother and sister,
spent my years at home, having been away most of the time,
either with my grandmother or at school. After I left, I never
again spent a full week at home.

Scene 3

Liverpool and Love

THE VIEW from the dirty window of a third-class railway carriage on the train between Birmingham and Liverpool is dismal on a wet afternoon in November. The squalid, hideous towns of the Black Country, Tipton, Walsall, Wednesbury, Wolverhampton and Stafford, the factory chimneys, the slag heaps and the rows of slum streets passed endlessly by in the gathering darkness. At that time many of those streets were unpaved, and littered with refuse among which half-starved children, with rags of filthy clothing and no shoes and stockings, fought and played. Four times a day "The Bulls," or steam sirens, went off at the factories, summoning and dismissing the toilers. In the Black Country it was a great diapason of sound, one note being followed a split second later by another, perhaps half a tone higher or lower, and another and another, with finally a deep bass bellow from the last. For one minute they would blow, and we, who would hear them distantly at home, would say, "There go the Bulls," and set our watches by them, noting as we did so perhaps that Cadburys was a second late, or Nettlefolds two seconds early.

As I stared gloomily out of the train window I could visualize the insides of some of those factories, the century-old, low-ceilinged rooms, lit by flickering gas jets and grimed with dirt, clamorous with the thud and stamp, the roar and whine of machines, and the loud flap-flap of transmission belts; I could smell the chemicals and the human sweat and feel the hot breath of the fetid air that met one at the door. Cleanliness, electricity, air conditioning, cafeterias, sports facilities and all the other amenities that are taken for granted today were not even dreamed of then. I can't help feeling that it was the influence of the U.S.A. with its concern for the rights of man, and its dedication to change and progress, that has helped to abolish the old miseries. When in 1914 Henry Ford first paid his workmen a minimum wage of $5 a day, increased to $6 in 1919, he struck a blow for humanity whose echoes still ring round the world. It is strange that the great nineteenth-century captains of industry could not realize that if you pay a man a decent wage he can afford to buy more goods, and so in the end your business will prosper; it took many years of struggle on the part of the labor unions to bring this truth home to them. The introduction on a wide scale of the American credit system has also improved the living standard of the average man immeasurably, though it is only recently that I have come to realize it, the struggles of my youth having left me with a horror of debt and a yearning to accumulate some savings, however small, to protect me from the wolves of want whom I heard howling ever at my heels, so that I have always, like Mr. Micawber, scrupulously balanced income and outgo. Unfortunately, this has turned out to be the wrong way to make money in the modern world, where fortune seems to be based upon some mysterious policy of financing and refinancing, borrowing and spending one's way upward.

It was dark by the time I lugged my suitcase out of Lime Street Station and as I was poorer by the price of the rail fare

I could not think of a hotel. I went into a café and fortified myself with a cup of tea, the Englishman's standby, and as I munched a Bath bun I asked the waitress where I might find a room. She told me the most likely neighborhood and pointed out the tram, one of the many small dirty white ones that swayed and ground all over the city in those days. When I got off it was raining heavily, and both I and my suitcase were soon thoroughly soaked. I trudged along the street, looking at the ROOMS TO LET signs and assaying their probable cost. At the third try I settled on a small bedroom and sitting room, kept by a severe-looking landlady and sparsely furnished with stiff black horsehair furniture and a brass bedstead. I went to sleep with the sound of distant steamers hooting in the fog of the River Mersey, a sound which was to become very familiar to me during the next two years.

The following morning I went to the office of a cousin of my mother's, a kind gentleman whom we called Uncle Ernest. The sign on the door described him as a Turf Commission Agent; I found that he was in fact a bookie, a bookmaker who did not visit the racecourse but took bets by telephone in his office. There were telephones all around the room, and two young men answering them, while Uncle Ernest sat at an old-fashioned rolltop desk, writing figures in a ledger. In no time at all I caught the spirit of the place and offered to put two bob on a horse.

Uncle Ernest sat me on a chair beside him and put his hand in a fatherly manner on my knee. "Now listen to me," he said, "I have a wife and two kids, I have a nice little house in Wallasey where I hope you will come and stay for the weekend, I have a little car in which we will go for a drive, I pay my bills, and my family lives comfortably. Where do I

get the money for all this?" He tapped my knee to emphasize his words. "Out of mugs like you!" he said. I put my
two shillings back in my pocket, and he took me out to lunch.
His words surprised me, for Gag's example had encouraged
me to think that backing horses was a normal function of
life.

The businessmen of Liverpool, like businessmen everywhere, ate hurried sandwich lunches in smoke-filled basement cafés, and it seemed that everybody, at the place we
went to, was interested in the game of dominoes. Uncle Ernest sat down opposite a red-faced man wearing a bowler
hat, a dominoes board was produced, and three mugs of ale
with three ham sandwiches were set before us. After a brief
introduction, in which my uncle told the red-faced man that
I was looking for a job, they set the board, lit their pipes, and
settled down to play in silent concentration.

I was nineteen, very tall and very thin, gawky and shy. My
wrists and ankles stuck out of my threadbare suit, which I
knew was too small for me. I didn't drink the ale; I had
never touched alcohol. I was hungry as usual, and the sandwich seemed very little. I was frightened by the crowd of
confident, talkative men around me. I felt lost and alone.
What could I do? Where could I go? When the few coins in
my pocket were gone, what was to become of me? Had I
known it, I must have appeared very like my father at the
same age.

The red-faced man triumphantly added his last domino
to the line and turned to me. "Would you like to go to West
Africa?" he said. I stared at him in amazement. "Here, take
my card." And he wrote something on it. "Go and see Colonel Rea at the Commonwealth Trust on Water Street. Eight-

een months' tour of duty, six months' leave, four hundred a
year and free quarters and medical care. Not bad!"

Not bad indeed! These were the days after the war when
ex-officers of famous regiments were standing in the streets
selling pencils, and youngsters like myself, with nothing but
a London Matriculation certificate behind them, could
hardly aspire to £400 a year, right off the bat as it were.
Add to this the prospect of travel, of long leaves and free
perquisites! My heart sang as I ran up the steps and down
Water Street. Africa! The very name thrilled me. Mungo
Park, Dr. Livingstone, Stanley, Kitchener, Rhodes — and perhaps Aherne, the white bwana, ruling the natives with a firm
but kindly hand, exploring the jungles, shooting the dangerous Falls of the Upper Zambesi, discovering diamonds, putting down uprisings of the wild Fuzzy-Wuzzies, and maintaining always the upright justice and authority of the
British Raj!

I think I rather expected the walls of the Commonwealth
Trust office to be hung with spears and assegais, long leather
shields and plumed headdresses. I would not have been
surprised if the clerk who attended me had worn a solar
topee. In actual fact it was a rather dreary-looking place,
with a counter running the length of the main room, behind
which a number of shabby-looking clerks and typists sat or
stood at desks. I presented the card of the red-faced man,
together with one of my own printed with my name, Mr. B.
de Lacy Aherne, and after a short wait was ushered into the
presence of Colonel Rea.

Among the German possessions in West Africa which were
seized during the war was a company called the Basel Mis-

sion, which combined missionary work with some profitable trading and had depots up and down the Gold Coast. By some process of which I am ignorant, an English company was formed to take over the assets of the old Basel Mission and to use its profits for the benefit of the natives. The missionary work disappeared, and the Commonwealth Trust devoted itself to the two-way trade of buying copra, palm oil, and cocoa beans from the natives and selling manufactured goods of all kinds. The company was controlled by some government agency, and our bosses would occasionally rush up to London with reports and statistics, but for us the twin peaks of authority were Colonel Craik and Colonel Rea.

Colonel Rea was a small, cocky, sour little man with balding head and spectacles. His idea of running an office was to bark at the workers as if it were a parade ground, and he was cordially disliked, but I must say he was always pretty decent to me, and once even let me off for the day to go to the Grand National, saying, "Well, I suppose when I was your age, I would have wanted to go." It was Sergeant Murphy's year, and I won a week's wages on him. The colonel now took me in to meet his superior, Colonel Craik, a rather stupid but easygoing man who must have hated being in business and longed for the life of the regiment. They looked at me and questioned me closely, displaying, I thought, more interest in my health than my qualifications, which was all right with me. Finally they said they would consider the matter and let me know.

A few days later, I received a letter saying that they thought me too young and inexperienced to send abroad, but were willing to take me into the office and train me until such time as they felt I was ready to go, at a salary of £3.10.0 a

week. Of course I accepted at once. I sat down and wrote
my mother a long letter, telling of my triumph. She replied
lovingly, wishing me luck and telling me to buy a new suit,
which she would pay for, but she said she was still sorry I
had not chosen to be an actor.

It might be that, looking back at those two years in Liverpool, they would seem almost a dream to me, but in point of
fact they are a harsh reality compared to the middle years of
my life in California which, untroubled by any change of climate throughout the year, slipped by almost unnoticed with
ever-increasing momentum. In Liverpool the damp, cold,
fogs, rains, and winds, which came sweeping up the Mersey
from the Irish Sea, made even the Birmingham winter seem
mild. I would awake while it was still half dark, breakfast by
gaslight, and run for standing room on the tram. On a table
in the outer office stood a book in which one signed one's
name, and promptly at 9 A.M. Colonel Rea strode three paces
from his room, drew a strong red line below the latest signature, and slammed the book shut. Latecomers signed sheepishly below the line, and after three slips were called into the
guardroom for a sharp reprimand. I was the worst offender,
particularly after I got the current craze for dancing and
stayed up till two and three in the morning; this phase was
yet to come, however, as for the first months I knew nobody.

During the days I worked at bookkeeping, posting ledgers
from the journals that store managers sent home each month
from the Coast. It was tedious work, hour after hour, and I
am not sure that I ever really understood the double-entry
bookkeeping system. My companions in the office were
products of the secondary and board schools, only half-edu-

cated, very poor, and limited in their horizon. A wife and
kids, a visit to the pub, and maybe one day a motor bike and
sidecar: these were the limits of their ambition. They were
kind to me, but a bit leery of my gentlemanly ways and my
public school education which put me in another and unfamiliar class; in the main the classes respect each other but do
not mingle in England. We are not democratic, in the American sense of the word, but our much-maligned class system
has endured for centuries, and we understand it. I find this
difficult to explain to Americans, whose whole way of life is
based upon the belief that all men are created equal. I tell
them that every Englishman has two families, his own and
the Royal Family, but the Royal Family is an ideal family, to
which he likes to look up with respect. This is why the action of the Duke of Windsor was such a shock to English
people, and why they have been so concerned over Princess
Margaret's marriage to a commoner. They just don't want to
think of their royal father and mother, and brothers and sisters, as being the same as themselves, and they want to look
up to the classes which they imagine to be above them. It
had been dinned into us at home that our aristocracy, while
setting us above the lower and middle classes, obliged us to
behave well to less fortunate folk, and never to make them
feel uncomfortable, but nevertheless I suspect that the clerks
at the Commonwealth Trust would have been relieved to see
me shipped abroad.

The evenings I spent reading by the gas fire, after eating
the landlady's dinner, usually mutton stew and potatoes. Toward the end of the month I would read in bed, because I
would run out of shillings to put in the gas-fire slot, and at
the same time I would run out of money for lunch and have

to go without for the last two or three days, making up for it
by attacking the mutton stew at nights. On Saturdays we
were free at one o'clock. I was still not far from my school
days when I had become accustomed to a lot of games and
exercise, and I wistfully looked at the local Cricket and Tennis Club, but this was obviously beyond my means, so I in-
vented my own diversion for Saturday afternoons, going
down to the docks where I stared at the ships and watched
the sailings of White Star and Cunard liners to America, the
Blue Funnel Line to the Far East, or Elder Dempster to
West Africa. I would dream of the day when I too would sail
down the river to foreign parts, and I would give myself a
foretaste of that delight by taking the ferry down to New
Brighton at the entrance to the river. On one of these excur-
sions I saw that the famous actress Mrs. Patrick Campbell
was playing Ibsen's *Hedda Gabler* in the theater on the end
of New Brighton Pier. I bought a cheap ticket to the matinee and went in. I have read that it was one of her great
parts, but I was theater-wise, and she did not impress me.
She was by then too old and too fat for the part, and she
played it wearily, as if she knew that she was only playing a
matinee on the end of the pier to an audience of twenty
people. Years later I was to see her play *The Matriarch,* in
London, in which she was more worthy of her great reputation.

I have often thought of that little experience, when I have
been playing in "the sticks," or on some cheesy little radio
program and I have never allowed myself to do less than my
best, or to do anything which, as Hamlet says, "cannot but
make the judicious grieve, the censure of which one must in
your allowance o'erweigh a whole theatre of others." Years

later, in Hollywood, the name of Mrs. Campbell came up for a part in a picture, but a memory of her throwing away Hedda Gabler came to my mind and I suggested another actress. Her published letters have since told us that she was in desperate financial need out there; she would hardly have believed that she lost this part so long before, on the end of New Brighton Pier.

My lonely life in Liverpool was brought to an end when my guardian angel suddenly awoke and presented himself once more in the guise of my Uncle Ernest's friend, the man in the bowler hat. It seemed he had a daughter, not too attractive I am afraid, who needed an escort to take her to a tea dance, a form of entertainment then very popular with the young because it was cheap, needing only a bare floor and a gramophone with some dance records. He must have remembered the lanky youth he had befriended in the coffee house, and he wrote me a note in care of Uncle Ernest. Of course I was only too glad to escort his daughter, but it was the only time I did so because I met there a pretty girl who invited me to go with her to the next dance of the Sixty Club at the Adelphi Hotel, the smartest rendezvous in Liverpool. I was very excited, not only to go dancing, but to meet a pretty girl, which was a new and fascinating experience for me. I had one pretty cousin who once came to visit us for a few days, but otherwise I knew nothing whatever about girls. The strict seclusion of school life was almost matched at home, where we were too poor and too exclusive to entertain.

At the monthly dance of the Sixty Club it was necessary, I heard, to wear a dinner jacket, which of course was not in my wardrobe, but I thought of my mother's offer to buy me a suit; after all, I didn't have to tell her it was a dinner jacket. I found I couldn't tell her at all, because I knew very well she had no money to send me, so I cleverly had one made by a tailor, having read that tailors are used to giving long credit. It was nearly three years before I paid that bill, but in the meantime I wore the suit on every possible occasion, for I caught the dancing craze. I fell in love with a sweet and gentle girl named Leonie Mayall, and together we went dancing wherever we were invited and whenever we could afford it; we went to lunch dances, tea dances, dinner and supper dances, or just danced at the many halls that opened where entrance was only a shilling or two, and we were very happy. Leonie's mother was a jolly widow who ran a private nursing home, and she was very good to me. I think perhaps she thought of me as a possible son-in-law, and so I might have been if I had possessed any money, but penniless young men cannot think of marriage, and I was far too reserved to discuss my poverty. At Christmas I bought Leonie an umbrella, cheap from one of the wholesalers who supplied the Commonwealth Trust, and I put on the card "A present for a good girl." I blushed and could have fallen through the floor when her mother, tongue in cheek, thanked me for her nice present. Of course, I had no other for my girl, and was too shy to explain, so that Christmas Day was a misery for us both. I got another, and presented it shamefacedly a week later, but the lunches were very thin that month.

I am always grateful to my rich friends when they advise me how to save money: always buy the best they say, it is cheaper in the long run to buy the best, to patronize the best hotels and restaurants and drive the best cars; I am sure they mean to be helpful, but I can give them a few tips too, gathered painfully and from long experience. Hats, for instance: never wear a hat, for it will cost you money in cloakrooms. Don't take taxis if there is a bus, and don't take a bus if you can walk; the grandest butler will have no cause to doubt you if you mention that you have left your car just round the corner. Don't smoke, and don't drink. Not only are these habits costly, but sooner or later you will have to treat others. Wear colored shirts, not white, with two detachable collars so that the shirt will last a week. Don't buy newspapers and magazines; pick them up in trams and offices. Never, on any account, eat in a restaurant, but if you are forced to do so, go to a counter and don't sit down, or you will have to tip a waitress. Accept hospitality only from the rich, who don't expect you to ask them back. Above all, don't get married!

By chance I met a member of the Liverpool Green Room Club, one of the best amateur dramatic societies in the country, and soon found myself one of its leading lights. I played in *The Cassilic Engagement*, A. A. Milne's *The Romantic Age*, and other things, with some success, and learned to get up and act upon a stage, which was to stand me in good stead later. Their plays ran for a week each, and were extremely well done. They had a director who taught me the value of variety of tone and change of pace in a dialogue, and that when playing in costume a gesture must come from the shoulder rather than from the elbow. He helped me to throw aside constraint and to feel free, to take command of the stage when necessary. These lessons I have never forgotten.

Few people seem to realize the tremendous fun that can be got out of the amateur theater. Like most "do-it-yourself" projects it can bring great interest and satisfaction. All over America millions of people sit and stare at silly little plays on the television screen, from which they can have no reward but the passage of time. It only takes a little initiative to get a few friends together, choose a play which they like, read it and rehearse it in the evenings, and even paint scenery, make costumes, and devise lighting. "Four boards and a passion" are enough for a play, and the simplest beginnings will suffice. The Pilgrim Players and the Liverpool Green Room were both composed of charming and attractive people, all united by the same interest. Why don't more do it? The word amateur is French for "a lover of"; a lover of the theater, what could be more admirable? I often tell young people, who gush about their longing to act, to go and do it. Why do they all think they must be paid for it, and why should an audience be expected to pay to see untrained would-be actors practicing on the stage? My mother's life was enriched by the Pilgrims, and I myself gained happiness and rewarding experience from the amateur theater.

Occasionally, if somebody paid, Leonie and I would go to the professional theaters. We saw, from the gallery, Gertrude Lawrence, whom I knew to be, like myself, an old pupil of Italia Conti, in the musical comedy *Oh Kay!* We saw Edith Day and Pat Somerset in scenes from *Irene,* Matheson Lang in *Mr. Wu,* and Martin Harvey in *Oedipus Rex.* On my twenty-first birthday I looked for a show at which we could celebrate, and could find nothing but the opening of a musical with the unpromising title of *Stop Flirting,* starring a couple of unknown young American dancers, Fred and Adele

Astaire. I could not buy seats in advance because my birthday is May 2 and the Commonwealth Trust only paid us at
the end of the month, but I felt confident that my godfather,
Mr. Foster, would send me a check because he had always
come through with a few shillings on previous birthdays and
I felt that my twenty-first was his big opportunity. He sent
me a present instead, a book called *Self Help*, by Samuel
Smiles. When I read it, twenty years later, I thought it helpful, but not at that moment. On the great night we climbed
to our hard and distant seats in the gallery and resigned
ourselves to disappointment, but with the first notes of the
overture we sat forward, and from the time the curtain rose
we spent an evening of delirious enchantment. "Oompah!
Oompah! Oompah!" we sang all the way home, dancing like
Fred and Adele along the street to the astonishment of
passersby. It was a glorious twenty-first.

These nightly activities had now become the main interest
of my life. I no longer thought of work, of making my way in
the world, of becoming a captain of industry; I thought instead of the intricacies of the tango, then introduced by Ru-
dolph Valentino, or of my new part with the Green Room
Club, and I mooned a lot over my girl. The office became a
necessary evil, a boring round of posting books, checking
lists, decoding commercial cables, writing checks, and doing
odd jobs. I did them conscientiously but without interest,
and I might have gone on like that indefinitely if one day
Colonel Rea's bell had not summoned me to the guardroom,
where he told me they had a position for me overseas, and I
should be ready to sail in a month's time. He seemed a little
surprised when I asked for a week to think it over, but
agreed. The fact was that I had met some of the fellows who
had come home on leave. Their skins were suspiciously yel-

low, and their hands, when they borrowed a pen from me to sign their names on some paper, shook in the most alarming way. I had begun to realize why such a point was made of "free medical care" at the initial interview, and why six months' leave was offered at the end of an eighteen months' tour of duty. I had even diffidently asked one of these men what it was like on the Coast. "Don't bother to go," he replied. "Just go down and throw yourself in the Mersey."

I went home for the weekend and consulted my parents. "Go to London and get a job in the theater," urged my mother. "You must do as you wish old chap," said my father, as he retired to bed. I returned to Liverpool very perplexed. If I refused, I would be out of a job, with no money and no prospects, and if I went, what would become of me? Now that I was happy in my private life, I liked Liverpool. I had a wonderful girl and good friends; what would I do alone again? It was a turning point in my life, and as I answered the bell when the week was up and went into Colonel Rea's office, I had no idea which road I would take.

"Well, Aherne, what have you decided?" he asked.

I turned and looked out of the window. There, beyond the great tower of the Liver Building, I could see the Mersey river, going straight down to the sea. A Blue Funnel liner was at dockside, preparing to sail, and I could see her masts and funnel above the rooftops. Seagulls were floating gracefully against the gray backdrop of the sky. I felt momentarily suspended in space while I stood there and the seconds slipped by in silence. As I stared mutely at the blue funnel, a wisp of white steam broke sharply from it, and the deep roar of the ship's siren reverberated in the room. When it stops, I thought, I must speak. The sound died away. I turned and saw him staring at me. I gulped and stiffened my back. My voice sounded unreal as I said, "No, thank you, sir. I don't want to go."

For a moment he looked very angry.

"I must say I am very disappointed in you," he said. "Considering the time and trouble we have spent on your training over these two years, it seems hardly right for you to behave like this!"

"I am very sorry, sir," said I.

"Very well," he snapped. "You will receive your salary at the end of the month. After that, we shall of course have no use for your services."

"Yes, of course," I said. "Thank you, sir. I'm sorry," and I went out. I never spoke to him again.

The end of the month came all too soon. Desperately I asked everyone I knew for a job, but it is one thing to be a young man with a settled position, quite another to be an out-of-work suppliant with no means and no qualifications, and I could sense the doors closing on me. I interviewed a couple of men in my old love, the shipping business, but both solemnly assured me that shipping was down the drain and offered no hope at all. It seemed that every business was in the same sorry state. I decided to take my month's salary and go to London, where at least I had an uncle who might help me.

I felt sad to be leaving Liverpool, whither I had come with such high hopes, and particularly sad to be leaving my girl, whose gentleness and understanding touched me deeply. I knew it was best for her that I leave her, for marriage was impossible, but as I walked back to my rooms on that last night I remember holding on to a lamppost in the deserted street and crying my heart out.

Scene 4

Turning Point

Once again it was a dark and foggy November night, when I came out of a station into the roaring traffic of a strange city, and once again I carried in my hand my old green cardboard suitcase. I didn't ask anyone where to go, London seemed too vast; I just walked straight ahead. I had enough vague knowledge to realize soon that I was walking into Bloomsbury, where I had read the poorer artists and Bohemian set lived, and this seemed good to me. Halfway down Gower Street I saw a house with a red front door which had a card in the window saying "Rooms to let." The landlady, whose hair was so red that it almost matched her door, showed me a third-floor back room, poorly furnished and with the inevitable shilling-in-the-slot gas fire. I took it for a few shillings a night, paid in advance. My spirits had revived, for I was young, and I was feeling again that life was a great adventure. I sat down to my nightly custom of writing a letter to my girl. I did not know that right next door was the Royal Academy of Dramatic Art, where so many aspirants to a theatrical career came for training, but if I had known I would not have cared, for I had no money to go there, and anyway I was not interested in the theater as a business.

What I was after was still what I thought of as "a proper job," something that I could work at with pride and a sense of achievement. The proper job, however, was even more elusive in London than it was in Liverpool. I saw my uncle, who asked me to lunch in the city and was very nice, but knew of no jobs suitable for me. I spent several hours a day in newspaper offices in Fleet Street, combing the advertisement columns, but very few jobs were offered in those days, and all seemed to require qualifications that were not mine. I wrote to answer several, and waited anxiously for replies that never came. The days, and at last the weeks, slipped by and my little store of money dwindled almost to vanishing point. I prayed to God every night, as I had been taught to do, and my daily correspondence with Liverpool sustained me with affection, but it seemed my guardian angel was sleeping.

The English winter brings darkness very early, and it was nearly dark about four o'clock one wet December afternoon, as I stood on the pavement in Leicester Square. I hummed to myself an old song I used to hear the pierrots sing on the sands of Eastbourne. They called themselves pierrots, but actually the leading juvenile wore a straw boater, blue blazer, and white flannel trousers as, with monocle in his eye and gold-headed cane under his arm, he sang:

> *"Leicester Square, Leicester Square!*
> *What will they do when they miss me there?*
> *Who'll set the fashions in Regent Street,*
> *What will become of the Strand and Belgravia?*
>
> *Leicester Square, Leicester Square!*
> *When I've gone over the sea.*
> *I know I can do without London,*
> *But can London do without me?"*

The trouble was, I had not gone over the sea, and London could obviously do without me very well. I watched the crowds as they passed. Soon all the people would be leaving their jobs and catching a tube or a bus home. Everybody seemed to have a job but me. How did they get them? Where did they start? My hands were in the pockets of my thin old macintosh, for I did not own an overcoat, and I had no gloves, and I was very cold and hungry. My right hand closed upon a few coins, all I had left of my store. I counted them again, though it was not necessary, as I knew well they amounted to four shillings, a sixpence and four pennies, four and ten in all, perhaps enough to warrant a cup of tea and a sandwich at Lyons Tea Shop. But what would I eat tomorrow, and where would I sleep? My guardian angel, in whom I always had such faith still seemed to be sleeping soundly. In my left pocket I felt a piece of paper, and I took it out and looked at it again. In my mother's writing I read "Akerman May, theatrical agent. Remember Mrs. Silverthorne."

"If you can't find a job," she had said, "go and see Akerman May. Perhaps he can help you. Tell him I once met him at lunch with a Mrs. Silverthorne. The personal touch is sometimes good."

I went to a telephone book and looked up his address, and found that his office was just round the corner. I knew I could act, and had no doubt whatever that I could get a job in the theater, but I didn't want it. Never mind, it would only be temporary, and would give me a chance to look for a proper job. I found a dirty entrance and went up creaking old stairs to a door which bore the legend "Akerman May and Vincent Erne, Theatrical Agents." Inside was a plain bare room with faded pictures of actors on the walls and a

few hard chairs, on two of which sat a couple of women of
uncertain age, one of whom had dyed yellow hair and a
great deal of make-up. I sat down shyly and waited. After
a few moments a glass panel in the wall slid sideways and a
girl looked out. "Yes?" she said to me. I got up and handed
her one of my cards, Mr. B. de Lacy Aherne. "I should like
to see Mr. Akerman May please," I said. "You'll have to
wait," she said, and closed the panel. I sat down again. A
couple of old posters on the wall announced touring companies of plays, in which the name of Akerman May was fea-
tured as an actor. As I was looking at them silently the two
women whispered together, and finally the dark one leaned
toward me.

"Excuse me," she said politely, "but may I ask if you are in
the profession?" "Yes," I said, with as much de Lacy hauteur
as I could summon.

"Well, my little girl," she said, indicating the faded blonde,
"has an act on the halls, and we are looking for a tall man.
We thought perhaps you would be right for it. If you are at
liberty, perhaps you would care to consider it?" "No, thank
you very much," I replied. "You see, I am a legitimate
actor."

"Oh, I understand," she said, and we lapsed into silence.
This was my first professional offer.

The sliding panel had slowly opened and I became aware
of a man peeping at me, and then it quickly closed again.
Soon the girl came to the door and beckoned me in. I felt
embarrassed at being called to the inner sanctum first, but in
I went.

Akerman May was a large, jovial man with a leonine head,
a shock of curly hair, bushy eyebrows, twinkling eyes, and

the vibrant voice of an old actor. His partner, Vincent Erne, was small, pale, and self-effacing. May did the talking, and I remembered the conversation as if it were yesterday.

"Well, young man, so your name is Aherne, eh? What can I do for you?"

"I thought perhaps, Mr. May, that you might know of a part in a play that might be suitable for me."

"Can you act?"

"Oh, yes, I think so." This with confidence, for I really did think so.

"Oh! You do, do you? Well, where have you acted?"

I caught Vincent Erne's eye regarding me shrewdly, and I could not lie. I spoke of Italia Conti, fudged a bit about the Birmingham Repertory Theatre and dilated upon my work with the Liverpool Green Room Club. "That's not the same as being a professional," he said. I decided the time had come to introduce the personal note.

"My mother asked to be remembered to you. I believe she once had lunch with you and a Mrs. Silverthorne." His eyes widened.

"Ah!" he said, and then after a pause, "Unfortunately, I married Mrs. Silverthorne!" This was getting me nowhere, and I hastily remarked that I knew that he himself had been an actor. I don't know how he thought I knew it, but he seemed very pleased.

"One night," he said, "I went out on the stage and I couldn't remember a God-damned word of my part. I decided the time had come to stop being an actor and become an agent!"

I laughed politely as he turned and whispered to Mr. Erne. Then he got up and came round the desk to me.

"Tell me," he said, "can you run?"

"Yes."

"Can you run fast?"

"Yes."

"Well, run like bloody hell to the Savoy Theatre and tell Mr. Courtneidge I sent you!" I turned to the door.

"Wait!" he cried. "What salary will you ask him?"

I gulped. "Eight pounds a week," I replied.

"*Eight pounds?*" He lowered his voice mysteriously. "Do you know what a boxer does when he faces his opponent in the ring?"

"No."

"He shuts his mouth, like this!" And he clamped his jaw shut. "So when Mr. Courtneidge asks your salary, say 'Eight pounds!' — and shut your mouth tight!"

I turned, ran through the outer office, past the music hall ladies and down the stairs. I ran like bloody hell to the Savoy Theatre.

Robert Courtneidge, the father of the great comedienne Cecily Courtneidge, was a manager of the old school who ruled his theater with a rod of iron. One of his greatest successes was an artificial little comedy called *Paddy, The Next Best Thing* which was made by the performance of an elfin, Irish-American actress with large, roguish eyes, named Peggy O'Neill. This had run at the Haymarket for over 800 performances, and now, a year or so later, Courtneidge was planning a short Christmas revival at the Savoy, with Herbert Marshall as the male lead. Miss O'Neill was doing the play out of town, and the part of Jack O'Hara, her brother, was open for London. Courtneidge offered to pay my fare to

Birmingham, where it was playing the following week, if I would agree to study the part and, when I felt ready, go on and give a trial performance which he said he would come down to see. In these days of theatrical unions, such a proposition would be unthinkable, but it seemed fine to me, for I had no doubt whatever that I could play Jack O'Hara, or anything else, superbly. Moreover, it was heaven-sent luck that the play was in Birmingham, where I could live at home and would not have to keep myself. I accepted a third-class return ticket and was off. My guardian angel was awake after all!

My mother was away somewhere, a most unusual thing for her, and I shared the silent house with my father, who came dutifully to the Theatre Royal on Thursday night when, after a few hours rehearsal with the understudies, I went on as Jack O'Hara. I replaced Colin Clive, later to thrill London and New York with his superb performance as Stanhope in *Journey's End*, and, like the dear fellow he was, he lent me his clothes and make-up. I learned in two minutes the truth of Mr. May's remark about amateur acting, and I found the attack and the pace of the professional company tremendously exciting. I felt for the first time the electric thrill that can come from playing with a fine actress, for Peggy O'Neill was an expert comedienne; she could pick up a scene, toss it in the air, turn it this way and that, extract every glint of color from it, and throw it away as she pounced on the next, so that the poor thin material seemed to glitter. I was thrilled by the experience, and felt sure that Mr. Courtneidge would be delighted with me. I rather think I expected him to burst into my dressing room, contract in hand, on that Thursday night, but when Friday passed and Satur-

day came with no word, my spirits sank. I went down to the
theater about eleven, and found the stage manager sorting
mail.

"Did Mr. Courtneidge come to see me on Thursday?" I
asked him.

"No, he came last night."

"Last night! Then he didn't see me! Did he say anything
about me?"

"No."

I groaned. Oh, why had I gone on so soon! Why had I
been so proud to do it on Thursday, not waiting till Friday!
My hopes crumbled into despair. I felt ill-used, betrayed,
and I turned away so that he shouldn't see the tears in my
eyes. I was only a boy, and this was too much to bear.

I suppose there is something about the job of a stage manager that gives him sympathy with actors. He stands in his
corner through every performance, following every word
and noting every little thing that happens, he is alert with
voice and hand to help in any emergency, and the true professional stage manager comes to love his company, and to
be their guide, counselor and friend. This little man, whose
name I don't even remember, was the first to show this to me
and there have been many since. He did not actually put his
arm around my shoulder, for that would not have accorded
with our British reserve, but he made me feel he did so, by
saying gently, "Why don't you go and have a talk with Miss
O'Neill? She is staying at the Grand Hotel."

I went hastily to my father's office and asked him for a
pound. I hated to do it, but I was desperate. I bought a
large box of chocolates, and ran to the Grand Hotel.

Miss O'Neill was in a dressing gown, eating her breakfast

before the matinee, when the card was brought to her, *Mr. B. de Lacy Aherne,* and she was regarding it in perplexity as I entered, chocolates in hand.

"Oh, it's you!" she said.

As I poured out my story, her large violet eyes regarded me sympathetically over her coffee cup. She seemed to be touched by the chocolates. She told me that as far as she understood, the part had been cast in London. "But you did think I was all right, Miss O'Neill?" I asked. She gave me her sudden enchanting smile.

"Gee, kid," she said, "I thought you were swell!" She thought a moment and then got up and held out her hand. "I've got to get ready for the matinee now," she said, "but don't you give up. Just stick around!"

As I waited for the lift, I heard behind me "Psst!" She was leaning out of her door. "Stick around!" she whispered, and waved encouragingly.

The solemnity of rehearsals at the Savoy was evidence of professionalism to me, for I would hardly have thought Peggy O'Neill needed a week out of town and two weeks' rehearsals when she had already played it 800 times, but Mr. Courtneidge was a serious worker. His manager had told me on arrival that I was engaged to understudy both Jack O'Hara and the lead, played by Herbert Marshall, at a salary of four pounds a week, and I was thankful for the job. The young actor who had been engaged in my place seemed to me very bad indeed, and Mr. Courtneidge wrestled long and hard to get what he wanted from him. Now and then Miss O'Neill passed behind my chair and whispered, "Stick around!" insistently in my ear. On the third day my chance came. They were rehearsing a scene between the two stars, which dragged on through the long afternoon. There seemed no possibility of anybody else working that day, but we were all there, until my supplanter and two of the girls sneaked off across the street for a cup of tea. No sooner were they gone than Mr. Courtneidge decided to abandon that scene and do another. Where were the actors? The roof went off. The terrified stage managers scurried in search of the delinquents, and we all sat in silence until they were found.

"What have you been doing?" asked Mr. Courtneidge, in a voice of thunder.

"We were just having a cup of tea, sir."

He permitted himself a gleam of wintry humor: "Did you examine the tea leaves in the bottom of the cup?" "No Sir." "Pity — you might have seen that you were going to have trouble with a dark man!"

We all laughed a little too loudly and rehearsal went on, but Mr. Courtneidge became even harder on the young actor, until the poor fellow could do nothing right. I saw Miss O'Neill whispering energetically in the directorial ear, and I was not surprised, and quite ready, when rehearsal was abruptly stopped and I was called upon to read the scene, nor was I surprised when that same evening I was asked to sign a contract to play Jack O'Hara and understudy Marshall, at a salary of £8 a week.

And so, eleven years after my first appearance in London, I again appeared upon the West End stage. The morning after our opening I set out once more to look for a proper job.

The wish to find some more reliable means of support than the business of acting was, as I have said, implanted in me at a very early age, and has never left me. Even now, with a long and successful career behind me, I can never overcome the feeling that each job comes to me only by chance, and the fear that I shall never get another. It is, I suppose, a fear that haunts all actors, whose employment ceases with the completion of each job and whose popularity is dependent upon the availability of suitable parts, fashions in the entertainment world, and so many other uncertain factors. I once secured an interview with the great actor-manager Sir Gerald du Maurier, famous for his naturalistic acting. Many actors tried to copy his method, but came to grief, not realizing that his was the art which conceals art, and that while he appeared to do nothing, every tiny effect was studied and carefully worked out. Gladys Cooper once told me that if he so much as entered on the wrong foot he was thrown for the whole scene.

I went for my interview to the stage door of the St. James's Theatre, which had housed so many of his great successes, and after a short wait was ushered into his dressing room. He was taking off his make-up after the matinee and was no doubt in a hurry to get off for his dinner before the evening show. After a few perfunctory questions and a sharp inspection of me in his mirror, he turned in his chair and said abruptly, "So you want to be an actor, eh? Tell me — have you a private income?"

I was rather taken aback, and at the time I thought it a cynical and unpleasant thing to say to a youngster in his profession, but he may have had good reason because, though of course I could not realize it, his own career was even then beginning to diminish and a few years later he died a poor man.

Du Maurier was one of the last of the great actor man-

agers, the greatest having been Henry Irving, of whose
Lyceum Theatre I have heard said it was like going into a
cathedral. While not as impressive as that, it was in my
youth excitingly glamorous to go to the St. James's to see du
Maurier, to His Majesty's to see Beerbohm Tree, to the Playhouse to see Gladys Cooper, to The Queen's to see Seymour
Hicks, or the Garrick to see Martin Harvey on one of his rare
London appearances, and their companies provided steady
employment for actors. The famous old actor Horace Hodges
told me that his first two engagements in the theater were
twenty years with Wilson Barrett and twelve years with
Fred Terry, this being possible because they were constantly
traveling. One year would cover a London season, the next a
provincial tour, and America, Canada, South Africa, Australia, New Zealand, and even the Far East might all be toured
before they played London again. But when I came into the
theater the actor managers were already losing their fight
against rising costs and the popularity of the motion picture,
and businessmen were taking over management who could
not allow sentiment to influence the choice or casting of
plays.

Paddy, The Next Best Thing was a pleasant engagement,
but was planned to run only six weeks, and beyond that lay
the void again, so I busied myself looking for a job. I almost
landed one as assistant to the London representative of a
group of Liverpool manufacturers, a lobbyist he would be
called in Washington, but I lost it at the final interview,
when I was asked, "What is your speed?" The Commonwealth Trust had not taught me stenography. It was Mr.
May who found me my next job, before I was halfway
through the first, a short tour with the celebrated actress Vio-

let Vanbrugh, playing her son in a melodrama called *The Flame,* which had been translated from the French. In this I followed Ralph Forbes who had made a hit in the part in London.

The famous Vanbrugh sisters, Violet and Irene, had always been idols of my mother, not only because they were fine actresses but also because they were reputed to have been the first genuine ladies to take up the profession, and my mother felt that, had it not been for the opposition of her father, she might have done the same. Prebendary Barnes of Exeter Cathedral had shown a little more understanding than Lawyer Thomas of Birmingham, for he had given his suppliant daughter Violet, a hundred pounds and permission to go to London to try her fortune, stipulating only that her old nurse should accompany her and that she should return if and when the hundred pounds was spent. Violet's nurse was the traditional English "nannie," that special member of the family whose firmness, kindness, integrity, and selfless devotion molded the characters of generations of English young people.

And so the day came when Violet found herself, at the age of nineteen, installed in furnished rooms in Baker Street. Excitedly she began to write to people in the theater world. The days passed, and so did the hundred pounds, with no result, until finally the last sad day of all came. Nannie was packing to go home, letters had been written, the cab ordered, the train tickets to Exeter bought. Violet was kneeling before the fire to dry her hair, which Nannie had washed for going home, drinking a glass of port which Nannie had prescribed for a cold in the head, and sobbing her heart out.

Suddenly there was a ring at the front doorbell.

"Now who could that be?" Nannie grumbled as she got to her feet. The bell was rung again impatiently.

"All right! All right! I'm coming!" said Nannie.

A moment later she burst into the room looking as if she had seen an angel, as indeed she had. "Oh, Miss Violet!" she gasped. "Get up! Get up at once! Miss Ellen Terry is downstairs!" She made a dive for the glass of port and hid it behind a flower vase, and before Violet could move, Ellen Terry, the greatest actress of her time, the Queen of the Lyceum Theatre, Sir Henry Irving's leading lady, and the beloved of all beholders, came rustling into the room.

"My dear!" she cried. "Are you the little girl who wrote to me? The one from Exeter? I am so sorry I haven't answered, but you know we are rehearsing for Sir Henry's new production and I have so much to think of that it just went out of my head, but I was driving down Baker Street and I saw this number and I suddenly thought: That's where that little girl lives who wrote me such a nice letter! So I stopped my carriage and jumped out. You must forgive me, my dear, but I am afraid I am very forgetful. What was it about? Is there something wrong? What can I do to help?"

Violet was stunned. She tried to dry her eyes and to arrange her hair as she stood there, speechless. Finally she gasped "Oh, Miss Terry!" But Miss Terry suddenly looked at the clock.

"Oh, my goodness!" she cried, "I shall be late for rehearsal if I don't run, and Sir Henry would *never* forgive me! Now I'll tell you what we'll do. . . . Pop on your hat and come in my carriage and tell me all about it on the way to the theater!"

As the horses clip-clopped down to the Lyceum, Violet

poured her heart out and Miss Terry listened with deep concern.

"We must think of something," she said. "You can't go
home yet." And as they got out of the carriage she whispered gleefully, "Sir Henry doesn't allow anybody in the
theater during rehearsal, but I'm going to hide you!" And so
Violet spent seven hours that day, lying under the seats in
the front row of the balcony, hearing but not seeing the rehearsal. She was stiff, hungry, and tired by the time Miss
Terry came to get her, but Miss Terry was full of beans.

"My dear, I've got it!" she cried. "I've been thinking and I
know what we're going to do! We'll drive to Baker Street
now and get your things and we'll tell Nannie to go home,
and then you will come and stay with me. I will write to
your father at once and explain everything. Everybody
comes to my house, and if we ask enough people somebody is
sure to give you a job!"

And this is what they did, and one day Sir John Hare, a
famous actor-manager, smiled and said "Yes, young lady. I
think perhaps I can help you." And he did, and so Miss Violet Vanbrugh started her career. In her turn, she befriended
me, guiding and advising, giving me love and understanding
until she died. My mother was right; she was indeed a genuine lady. I have been asked countless times to be godfather
to the children of my friends and have always regretfully refused because I have not felt myself to be a good enough
Christian, but I now confess to one godchild: Violet Vanbrugh's grandson, who lives in faraway Australia.

The week before our tour of *The Flame* closed, there was a
"week out," which means a week with no booking, and I
went back to London and saw Mr. May. There was a new

play coming to the Playhouse Theatre, he said, called *White Cargo,* which was expected to run a year. It had been a sensational success in New York, but the London managers had shied away from it as being too raw for English taste; it had also been thought impossible to get by the censor. An old American actress by the name of Ida Molesworth had stepped in and bought the rights and had succeeded in persuading the Lord Chamberlain to pass it. Mr. May thought it a certainty. They were now casting the parts, among which was a small one in the last act which he thought suitable for me. I was to go down and see the stage manager, Wallett Waller, who, he warned me, was a rough diamond. "Make him laugh," he said, and I tried in vain to think of something funny as I went.

At the Playhouse I found a small group on the stage who appraised me carefully. Miss Molesworth, a formidable woman with a strict eye to business, outlined the plot, which concerned a group of men in a small jungle outpost in West Africa where they collected rubber for the company, quarreled and drank in the steamy heat, slept with black women and slowly disintegrated, their health and their characters undermined by damp rot, like their houses, clothes, and furniture. This story had for me familiar elements, and I made some chance remark about the Commonwealth Trust that brought a laugh from Waller. Franklin Dyall, a fine if somewhat florid performer, was to play Weston, the central character; Horace Hodges, one of the great old actors, was the doctor, and Mary Clare the Negress. I knew enough about the theater to know that this was a magnificent cast.

After I read the part with Waller he looked at Miss Molesworth. "What about the other one?" he asked. "Yes," she said, "I was thinking of him for Langford." They gave me the script and sent me to a dressing room to read it.

What I read was one of the greatest parts for a very young man that I have ever known. Arriving in the first act just as his predecessor is being carried out delirious on a stretcher, Langford startles the wretched castaways by his freshness and youth, his immaculate white clothes and his absolute and rather priggish assurance that he will continue to maintain the standards of home in that filthy, steaming, diseased atmosphere. Slowly, loneliness, lack of feminine companionship, heat, and a bitter feud with Weston undermine him. "I'll be all right when I'm acclimatized," he says bravely, but as time goes on there are terrible quarrels, outbursts of hysteria, and fits of weeping. The great climax to the second act occurs when Weston attempts to stop Langford marrying the black trollop. The last act passes through disgust, degradation, and sickness to Langford's final exit on a stretcher. "Poor bloody fool!" sighs Weston, as he casually poisons Tondelayo, the girl. Enter another young man in white, full of confidence. "I'll be all right when I'm acclimatized," he says.

"God Almighty!" roars Weston. Curtain.

The great range of emotion and the slow change of character were hard problems for a young actor, but I was on fire to play it, and I told Miss Molesworth so; my frankness probably cost me money, but I didn't care. We settled for £12 a week, and I returned to Miss Vanbrugh with the contract to play Langford in my pocket.

Thus, from the moment I decided to try for a temporary acting job, I had three engagements that followed each other without a week's interval, and totaled nearly three years, and

all this due to Akerman May. I wish I could say that we
continued our pleasant and, to me, profitable association, or
that I could feel proud of my part in it. The customary
agent's commission was 10 percent for ten weeks, or one
week's salary, and Mr. May therefore received eight plus ten
plus twelve, or a total of £30 for my three years' work. Naturally, he felt this inadequate and asked me to sign a long-
term exclusive contract with him. This was against my nature, for long-term commitments were, and still are, anath-
ema to me, and I refused. He was extremely angry and
wrote me a furious letter in which he accused me of ingrati-
tude. Shortly afterwards he died, leaving me burdened with
one of those regrets that weigh upon the mind heavily and
uselessly through life.

Rehearsals of *White Cargo* were difficult. Miss Molesworth hired no director, preferring to save money by relying
on her memory of the New York production. She reproduced
exactly the simple set and furnishings, even to the backdrop
which, owing to the fact that the play had been done "on a
shoestring" in New York, was an old and quite unsuitable
one taken out of storage. We used to groan about the damp,
steamy heat of the jungle while gazing out at a view of the
Arizona desert, dry as a bone with only a couple of cactus
visible on the horizon. As far as I know every production of
White Cargo that was ever done faithfully reproduced this
backdrop, and nobody ever complained. When it came to
the action, Miss Molesworth's memory was not so exact, and
if it had not been for Waller, the stage manager, I don't know
how she would have got the play on.

I was to learn something about the ways of actors in these
rehearsals, for Franklin Dyall never took his hat and coat off,

mumbling the lines inaudibly until he came to our cues. At dress rehearsal he was suddenly transformed by make-up and clothes, and on the opening night his performance burst upon us, and a tremendous performance it was, delivered with fire and force, with command of voice and gesture, such as I had not encountered before. Fortunately, I was very secure, and the challenge served only to excite me and sharpen my powers, or I might have been blown off the stage. Horace Hodges told me that this was a trick sometimes employed by the older actors of his time in the belief that it gave them some sort of advantage, but I imagine it would take very great talent and confidence. A modern director would never permit it.

Our opening was a brilliant one and received an ovation such as I have rarely seen in the theater. My mother was in front and it was probably the happiest night of her life. Next day the press raved about the play and performances. I became overnight a theatrical sensation. On the way to work in the evening, I saw from the top of my bus the *Evening Standard* posters, shouting in red at every corner "VIOLET VANBRUGH'S DISCOVERY!" Naturally, I wondered what it could be, so when I got off I bought a paper — and found that it was myself. My mother, of course, bought every paper, and started a scrapbook for me which I dutifully kept for a few years until it bored me, and indeed it would have been difficult to find notices such as these for *White Cargo:*

— Mr. Brian Aherne is a young actor with a very great future. His adroitness and his restraint are very remarkable . . .
— Mr. Brian Aherne gives a really great performance as Langford . . .
— Mr. Brian Aherne showed the process of decline from being

a fine young Englishman to a half-drunken, lazy creature,
with a vividness altogether admirable . . .
— Mr. Brian Aherne, who appears to be a very young man,
plays the part of Langford with a subtlety and excellence
that would do credit to a far more experienced actor . . .
— Mr. Brian Aherne, displaying an astonishing technique for
so young an actor, went most credibly to pieces . . .

I must confess that, with the arrogance of youth, I secretly
regarded all this as no more than my due, but I was in any
case feeling very happy, and for a different reason: on the
afternoon of the opening, I had at last found a job! I had
persuaded a man who sold cars in Brook Street to hire me as
a salesman; this was a job which I felt I could do by day while
acting at night and which would support me after the play
closed. When I returned to my room after this interview, to
rest before my performance, I found a black cat sleeping on
my pillow and knew at once that good luck would attend my
new job. It didn't however, because when my boss discovered that I could not turn up on Wednesday afternoons,
owing to my matinees, he changed his mind, and sadly I had
to pass the job to my brother.

I had suffered under Miss Molesworth's direction in two
places, when she forced me to play scenes in a way which I
felt to be totally wrong. Two days after the opening we were
called to rehearsal and presented to the author, Leon Gordon, whom we had never seen before. A dark, rather satur-
nine American, who spoke little but to the point, he cor-
rected some movements and then beckoned to me. "Coupla
things," he said, and changed both scenes exactly as I had
wanted. I glowed with satisfaction, but did not dare to catch
Miss Molesworth's eye. After an hour he left, and I never
met him again. He was later successfully sued for plagia-

rism, but I read the book on which the suit was based and thought the decision unjust. *White Cargo,* at that time, was a brilliant piece of theater craft; its construction, characterization and dialogue were all done by a master hand. Horace Hodges, a successful playwright himself, used to stand watching in the wings night after night. "Whoever wrote this play," he said, "knows about the theater." As far as I can gather, Leon Gordon never wrote another, and became a movie producer in Hollywood, where years later he died, still a fascinating mystery to me.

I now began to learn the hard lessons that a long run teaches an actor who has any conscience about his work: the strict discipline, the unremitting care of one's personal health, the constant vigilance against inattention, or boredom, or any tendency to overplay. Horace Hodges, for whom I had profound admiration and with whom I formed a lasting friendship, had to warn me on several occasions that I was developing a tendency to go overboard, to color some scenes too highly, and it was from him that I learned the value of restraint. It is hard to realize, until one has done it, the grinding toil and the nervous strain of playing a big part on the stage eight times a week. Sometimes on Saturday nights one feels it is impossible to crawl out there and go all through it again, but I always remember Hodges telling me that for the audience it is the first and only performance, and they must never suspect otherwise, and for me every night is still the first. I was to receive advice of another kind from Mary Clare, a wonderful actress and easily the best who ever played the part. "Save your money!" she used to say earnestly to me. "Then you won't be forced to accept bad parts!"

I was learning other lessons, too, about life, of which I was so abysmally ignorant. I began to draw apart from Leonie my sweet girl friend in Liverpool, and to form an attachment with a charming young actress, and this caused both Leonie and myself much distress, but was hardly to be wondered at, for we were parted both by distance and interest, and I was now a part of the London theater world.

For the time being I gave up looking for another job, because I realized my performances were about all I could manage. I had to sleep late in the mornings, but on occasion would go out to "the Bullfrogs," "The Fifty-Fifty," or some little theatrical hangout for bacon and eggs and dancing after the show and there I would see other youngsters in the theater — Laurence Olivier, Ralph Richardson, Maurice Evans, Henry Kendall, John Gielgud, Reginald Gardiner, all soon to make their mark, Ivor Novello radiating warmth and charm, and Noël Coward with his entourage in black turtleneck sweaters, being very witty and worldly wise, frightening me with their talk. I was still my father's son, withdrawn and introverted off the stage, and given to much daydreaming. "The absent-minded beggar," my father used to call me, and with reason. I think he was rather startled by my success, and it was hard for him to share my mother's enthusiasm. He stayed in Birmingham and I rarely saw him.

I was now disturbed a number of times by events which I did not in the least understand. Various older and charming gentlemen would turn up at the stage door, either with or without introduction, and after speaking warmly about the play and my performance, would invite me out to supper, or to lunch, and I, feeling flattered by this attention, would go, to find myself in a peculiar atmosphere and sometimes among very peculiar people who made me feel uncomfortable. I couldn't understand why these encounters disturbed me, for they usually took place in first-class restaurants and famous clubs, where I was made much of. I felt ungrateful. I tried to be polite and nice but would find myself involved in little jealous scenes and curious unspoken intrigues which passed right over my head. I was hopelessly ignorant of the ways of the London world, and it never even occurred to me that homosexuality existed beyond the confines of a boys' school; indeed I still, after a lifetime in the theater, find it hard to believe. John Van Druten once remarked to a friend of mine, "Brian feels about homosexuals the way most people feel about ghosts; he just can't believe they exist!" and it is true, though I don't actually care what poeple do with their private lives so long as they do not infringe upon my own. "It doesn't matter what you do in the privacy of your chamber," said Sir George Arthur to me, "but don't do it in the street, in case you frighten the horses."

Scene 5

London Life and Silent Pictures

T HE MAXIMS of Sir George Arthur have proved a sore trial to both my wives. "I don't want to hear any more about your dear old friend Sir George Arthur!" my former wife, Joan Fontaine, used to say to me testily, but the older I grow the more I come to appreciate his wisdom. A small Victorian gentleman of the old school, he was formerly an officer in the Household Cavalry, and had been for some years private secretary to Lord Kitchener, whom he idolized. He combined adulation of royalty with a passion for the theater, spending his days in the writing room of the Carlton Club, turning out books of reminiscences and royal biographies which nobody read, and his evenings in the front row of the stalls, dressed immaculately in white tie and tails, his large white mustache quivering with excitement as he followed the play. He had been the friend of Sarah Bernhardt and Lucien Guitry, and spoke impeccable French, and he was the friend of all young people in the theater. In appearance he reminded me of nothing so much as the White Rabbit in *Alice in Wonderland*, as Sir George looked at his watch and cried, "My goodness, I shall be late for the Duchess!," diving into the tube for South Kensington, where he and his gentle wife gave small but very select dinner parties, mainly composed of theatricals and minor royalty. Once a month he scurried up a back stairway in Buckingham Palace to have tea with Queen Mary in her room. She loved to hear the latest gossip of the town, but quickly pushed him out if she heard the King coming.

Sir George served as a sort of one-man liaison between the worlds of the theater, letters, and the army, and many were the great names I met at little lunches in his Club. Galsworthy, Kipling, Arnold Bennett, H. G. Wells, Edmund Gosse, Maugham, Sir William Birdwood, General Haig, Marshal Foch, and many others, must have been surprised to find themselves meeting young actors they had never heard of; actresses were asked to tea in the Annexe.

I used to hear fascinating conversation at Sir George's lunches.

"I can never understand," said Kipling to me, "how it is that my little verse 'If' has become a sort of tract that people hang on the bathroom wall, for actually I wrote it in admiration of the life of George Washington."

"Sit down, young man," said Dame Madge Kendal, a *grande dame* of the theater, the violets in her bonnet nodding as she beckoned to me. "I wish to speak to you." She glared at the theatricals chattering gaily round the tea table. "In my young day," she said, "we were ladies and gentlemen from eleven to eight and actors and actresses from eight to eleven. Nowadays, it seems to me, we are actors and actresses from eleven to eight, and ladies and gentlemen from eight to eleven!"

"Well, young fellow," said Winston Churchill as he spied a book in my hand, "what are you reading?" "*The Decline and Fall of the Roman Empire,* sir." "What volume?" "Volume four, Chapter twenty-three," said I, glancing at it. He nodded.

"Ah, yes, that's the one that begins 'About this time a religion began to penetrate within the boundaries of the Roman Empire . . .'" He waved his cigar and continued to quote. "But Mr. Churchill," I cried astonished, "you seem to know it all!" "I should," he remarked casually, "I've read it three times!" I spoke of Gibbon's tremendous style, and of the way in which the long sentences seemed to unroll majestically, ending with a flip, like the sound of a roll of carpet being thrown down. "Pooh!" he snorted, "A mere literary trick! Every sentence ends in the genitive." "Does it?" "Do you mean to say you've read four volumes and not noticed that?" He got up and left me in disgust.

"Dickens?" said Prince Arthur of Connaught. "Yes, of course, I knew Dickens. Member of this Club." "What was he like, sir?" "Who, Dickens? Oh, a bit of a snob!"

When the Allied War Council invested him with Supreme Command, Marshal Foch told me, they warned him that the situation was so serious that it might shortly be necessary to give up either Paris or the Channel Ports. They asked how long he would need to examine the alternatives and give his decision. "Je vous dirai maintenant," said the Maréchal with a dramatic gesture. "Je livrai ni l'un ni l'autre! Je vais attaquer!"

"The only difference I have been able to observe since the introduction of popular education," murmured Lord Curzon, "is that rude words are now written on fences one foot lower than formerly."

It was Sir George Arthur who explained to me that there are three types of conversation, the first dealing only with personalities and little happenings of the day, the second with current events on the national and international scenes, and the third with abstract ideas. Women, he said, are rarely capable of the third.

Sir George disliked using the telephone, preferring to send out a stream of little notes to his friends, which he would often leave at the door, marking the envelope "by hand." He never spoke of "*The Times*," always "*The Times* newspaper," and in general he made as few concessions as possible to the twentieth century, but his willingness to understand the problems of young people was unfailing. I once asked him how he came to have so many young friends, and he replied, "If a man of my age likes young people and wants to have them around him, he must be prepared to give and to understand, and he must expect nothing from them." He gave much to the people of my generation in the theater; we gave him affection in return.

White Cargo had slogged along for a year when I received an offer to appear in a silent film at the Stoll Studios in Cricklewood, on the outskirts of London. It was suggested that I work there from 9 to 5, and from 9 to 12 on matinee days, but I would have to be at the studio by 8:00 A.M. for make-up. I went out one day to be interviewed by the studio manager, an excitable Semitic gentleman with a Cockney accent and the name of Joe Grossman. His eyes bulged and he had a nervous tic which made him continually twitch his head to one side.

"Naow listen ter me Brian," he said, "I want ter 'elp yer, see? This is a great part boy (twitch). It'll put yer were Ronald Colman is terday! But don't yer ask too much money boy (twitch). There's plenty of other actors yer know, an they're all dyin' ter play this part (twitch). 'Ow much money are yer askin' boy?"

I had no idea. I hadn't thought about it. Vaguely I knew they got a lot of money in pictures, but what was a lot? I began to wish I had signed that exclusive contract with Mr. May.

"How many weeks would it be?" I asked.

"Three," and he eyed me apprehensively.

I took a deep breath. "Forty pounds a week!" I said.

It was as if he had received a severe electric shock. Springing from his chair, he rushed round the desk, and I thought for a moment he was going to hit me.

"Jesus Christ! Wot do yer think this is — a bloody El Dorader?" He rushed to the door and flung it open. "Outside!" he shouted, pointing dramatically, "I said outside!"

I slunk out from my first encounter with a film magnate, feeling rather dazed. A few days later, he was on the phone to me. " 'Ello Brian," he said affably. " 'Ow are yer boy? When are yer comin' in ter sign this contract Brian?" He was all right, was Joe Grossman, and I actually became very fond of him in time. He had a passion for fires, and was always rushing about on fire engines and practicing fire drills at the studio. In doing a fight scene with Cyril McLaglen, brother of Victor, I once had to aim a blow at the camera lens, and in my enthusiasm I struck the camera a glancing blow, cutting my knuckle open. Joe was delighted with the opportunity to dive into his fire kit and practice first aid on me, and he made such a mess of it that I bear the scar on my knuckle to this day.

The picture offer necessitated a difficult interview with Miss Molesworth, who was strongly opposed to my undertaking extra work. In this, of course, she was right, but I was impelled partly by the glamour of the idea and partly by the fact that £ 12 a week did not go very far in London, and she had refused to give me a raise. I minimized the amount of work, though actually I hadn't the faintest idea what was entailed, and in the end she reluctantly gave me permission. It might have been better for me if she had refused, for I found myself getting up at 6:00 A.M. to catch a bus out to Cricklewood, working all day in heavy make-up before un-shielded Kleig and Cooper-Hewitt lights in the studio, or many miles out in the country on location, getting back into London just in time to grab a sandwich before going into the theater. I became so overtired that, though I would go straight home to bed after the curtain fell, I was often unable to sleep at all and lay wide awake until 6:00 A.M., when I had to catch my bus. Matinee days were the worst, and though the picture company said they tried their best not to use me those mornings, they never seemed able to manage it.

I hated the work. Make-up in those days was sticks of #5 Leichner greasepaint and heavy lipstick, which we applied so thickly that we looked like clowns and could scarcely move a muscle of our faces. "Thicker, thicker!" cried the cameraman. My still pictures look like bad French post-cards. At one time my eyes were burned by the Kleigs and I suffered violent headache and streaming eyes for several days. My performance in *White Cargo* must have been affected, but it seemed easy and relaxing to me after the grinding torment of a silent movie set. The whole business of silent acting seemed phony and ridiculous, entailing as it did pulling exaggerated faces while a director shouted at one through a megaphone and an orchestra played unsuitable

music in the background. At Stolls, they were usually building other sets all around, and the hammering, shouting, and
crashing noises that went on were highly distracting. It was
not until the advent of sound forced even the director to be
silent that actors were able to think properly about what
they were doing.

My picture was called *The Squire of Long Hadley,* and
showed me as a young cockney from the East End who inherited a country estate and was snooted by the surrounding
gentry. My rival for the affections of the girl, Sir George
Mulcaster, Bart, was played by a heavy young man, and I
sympathized with the author when he exclaimed on seeing
us that we ought to swap parts.

It was a relief to finish shooting and relax with a bit of
money in my pocket and only eight performances a week to
think about, but a month or two later the picture came out
and achieved a little success, only a little being possible because American pictures completely dominated the English
screen. It didn't exactly put me in Ronald Colman's shoes,
but it secured me another offer, which this time I accepted
without telling Miss Molesworth. Not only did I work all
day on *The King of the Castle,* but on Saturday nights after
filming at Cricklewood in the morning and doing two performances of Langford, I sat up in the train all night to Corn-
wall, where we did shots on a cliff on Sunday. Small wonder that I finally became nervously exhausted, and had to
consult a doctor, who insisted I take a couple of weeks' holiday. I went to Madeira, by sea of course, with my friend
Reggie Reixach (pronounced Ryshak), and for the first time
saw tropical sunshine, and the brilliant colors of bougainvil-
lea. I remember diving into the azure sea and coming up to

find myself face-to-face with Bernard Shaw, splashing along on his back. I returned rested and refreshed, though a little ashamed to find the other members of the cast, all older than myself, still working steadily at their jobs. Horace Hodges told me gravely that my understudy was extremely good, and this startled me a bit. I resolved to do one thing at a time in the future.

At the end of two years, *White Cargo* moved to the Princes Theatre, with another cast and lower prices, and I found myself free at last.

Other times, other customs. In Southern California, I lived on a beach which is frequented by young people. They are beautiful in their abbreviated swimsuits, and their behavior is free and uninhibited in a way which would not have been conceivable to us. They lie on the sand with their arms about each other, kissing as if it were the most natural thing in the world, and then spring up and play volleyball or dive into the sea, apparently untrammeled by the inhibitions and taboos that governed our relations to the opposite sex. We never saw our girls in swimsuits; they were bundled up with tweeds and sweaters against the cold. We rarely dared to put an arm about them, and kisses were reserved for a few stolen moments on the front steps when we brought them home at night. It was not that we didn't think about such things, for contrary to the impression they give to foreigners, Englishmen are deeply passionate. The young Englishman thinks about sex nearly all the time. Nearly? Well, not quite. When he is playing golf, for instance, he is thinking about sex up to the moment he addresses the ball, but then he stops. He swings the club with intense concentration, hits the ball, follows through and watches it closely until it comes to rest. After a cry of pleasure, or more often of despair, he puts the club back in the bag and resumes thinking about sex. This intense preoccupation, to which I was no stranger, is hampered in its expression by the upper class English boy's upbringing which is controlled first by his nurse, then by his governess, his mother, and finally by his wife, all of whom tell him firmly that the thing to do is to wait for the right girl and to love her and nobody else, and that all other ideas are wicked and wrong. Poor English boys! Sometimes, though not in my case, a father will interpose some more sensible advice, but the strict segregation of English schools leaves an adolescent no opportunity for experiment. The 600 boys at Malvern were never given the chance to speak to a woman of any age, except perhaps the housemaster's wife. The editor of the school paper once appealed for letters and suggestions to brighten up his pages; I wrote suggesting that the girls of Malvern Girls College be invited over to a dance in the gym once or twice during term time. On our way into morning chapel he whispered to me furtively, "I had your letter, but of course I couldn't print it!"

In my early twenties I was a product of the system. I was obsessed by the mere idea of femininity and often felt faint if I saw a pretty girl — and it seems to me that I saw many more than I do now. After I became an actor I saw a lot of them and, as the homosexual invasion of the theater was then starting in force, I and a few others really should have had the field to ourselves among the young actresses, but my early training held me firmly and I was steadily faithful to one girl. She was a nice girl, warm, kind and humorous, but I am afraid I didn't bring her happiness. Pride, prejudice,

and poverty prevented that. I couldn't afford to take her out
to nightclubs or entertainments, and I would never have
dreamed of suggesting that she come to my rooms. She lived
with her family, so where could we meet? I used to borrow a
car from a friend and drive her into the country after the
show, returning at two or three in the morning.

We didn't park, or pet in the modern way, we just kept
driving, enjoying each other's company, admiring the moon
and talking about the theater, life and literature, for we were
both ardent if unguided readers. She taught me a sentence
from a book by Hilaire Belloc — "While you are dreaming
of the future or regretting the past, the present, which is all
you have, slips from you and is gone" — and we both agreed
sagely that this was the secret of life. The chains of my upbringing were still heavy upon me, however, and it was
many years before it occurred to me that perhaps she was
seeking to convey to her callow lover the message that there
is no time like the present where a woman is concerned. I
would kiss her good night on the front step for as long as I
dared and go home in frustrated misery, which may explain
the somewhat raffish advice I give to young fellows today.

The strain of this love affair evidently told on my girl as
well as upon me, for she began to speak in general terms of
marriage, and of how nice it must be, and this disquieted me
very much. After all, I had dropped my Leonie in Liverpool
and I feared I might be fickle, a trait which my womenfolk
had all told me was very bad. Also, I wasn't sure that I
wanted to marry this particular girl, and I didn't think marriage was for young actors anyway; I still don't. It was a
serious quandary, complicated by my ignorance and intensified now that I was out of a job; it was solved unexpectedly.

One day Violet Vanbrugh asked me to lunch and introduced me to Dion Boucicault, the famous director, actor, and manager, who was also the husband of her sister Irene. It was he who staged all the first productions of the plays of Barrie and Pinero, and he had guided his wife to a great career. He was one of the greatest names in the theater, but surely one of its smallest men, for he scarcely came up to my elbow. Neat, dignified, and precise, he had a small, cold voice and a tremendous air of authority. During lunch I was tongue-tied as he put a series of searching questions to me and looked at me steadily. Finally, as the coffee was served in Miss Vanbrugh's drawing room, he said coolly, "I am taking a company to Australia for eighteen months, which will play a season of Sir James Barrie's plays. I invite you to come as my leading man. You would play Valentine Brown in *Quality Street,* John Shand in *What Every Woman Knows,* Simon and Harry in *Mary Rose,* and Crichton in *The Admirable Crichton.*" I was dumfounded. These were the greatest parts written in the last thirty years, in plays which had all been triumphant successes, and I was only twenty-three. Miss Vanbrugh, who had been watching me, smiled and patted my hand. I knew that I owed this wonderful offer to her.

"Think it over for a week, and let me know your answer," he said, and left.

I went straight to Golding Bright, the famous play agent, who had been kind to me. He was reading a script as I entered his office, and looked up with a smile.

"Well," he said, "I suppose you have come to ask if you should go to Australia with Boucicault. My answer, of course, is yes."

"Do you think I will be forgotten in London, Mr. Bright?"

"When anybody shows a ray of talent and leaves London," he replied, "I sit down by the waters of the Thames and pray for his return. But don't stay too long; tell him you'll go for a year, and ask him seventy pounds a week."

"*Seventy pounds?*"

"Certainly. If he doesn't take you he will have to take Godfrey Tearle, or some other star, who will cost him a devil of a lot more!"

I often think of the great kindness that I received from everyone during my days in the London theater, so very different from the suspicious and defensive attitude of the average Hollywood producer and agent, and I wonder whether it was the English national character or my own youth and obvious ingenuousness which impelled people to help me. Help me they did, and I shall always be grateful to them and remember their generosity.

Dion Boucicault assembled a wonderful company including Angela Baddeley for the feminine lead, Mary Jerrold, Hubert Harben, and Norman Macowan. All the costumes and most of the furniture and props were carefully made or bought in London, and no expense or trouble was spared over any detail. Each member of the company was called to the office where "the Governor" went over every line of the contract, saying "Now, do you understand that and is it agreeable to you?" before ticking it and passing to the next. Sir James Barrie was introduced to us, and he and Boucicault sat like two little gnomes, wreathed in the pipe smoke, chatting about old days in the theater, until Barrie suddenly turned to me with a twinkle in his eyes. "Now you say something," he said.

Excited as I was at the prospect before me, I doubt if I
fully realized how lucky I was to secure such an engagement.
I had made one West End success, but one success does not
go far in the theater and it is always hard to find good parts
with which to follow it. It is only by acting that a career is
made, and the tragedy of the actor is that there are so few
plays, so few parts, so little opportunity to exercise his craft.
I, who had always been aware of the insecurity of an actor's
life, was now presented with a year of magnificent parts
under a great director, and at a handsome salary. Offered
such an engagement today, I would seize it with both hands.
It was an advantage, not only to my professional but also to
my private life. I saw that this would give me time to reflect
upon the prospect of matrimony. For the whole year that I
was away I reflected on it, and throughout I was strictly
faithful to my girl and carried her picture always with me —
but then, curiously enough, I didn't let her know the date of
my return or make any attempt to see her. I suppose my fear
of long-term contracts prevented me.

The Dion Boucicault company was not due to sail for
Australia until early January 1926, so off I went to Italy with
my friend Reggie Reixach. As those of us who knew Reggie
think of him, we smile and a warm glow floods our hearts; we
all agree he was the best friend we ever had. The son of an
eccentric Spaniard and a Yorkshire woman, he might have
stepped out of the eighteenth century. When he had been
sent to boarding school, his father had carefully selected and
packed for him a large trunk containing fine wines, vintage
port, and Napoleon brandy. Reggie had soon been sent
home, where his education had been unusual, to say the
least, and in the course of time he was sent to Oxford. In
those days, universities made very few demands upon their

students, there being none of the pressure that exists today; Oxford offered the opportunity to study, but if a young man preferred to have a good time there was no objection, especially if his father was willing to pay his bills. Reggie had a wonderful time, and he and his Bohemian friends drank themselves insensible every night, but he claimed it ruined his digestion and when I knew him he rarely touched a drop. He did not care for country life in Yorkshire and as soon as he inherited his father's money he took a lovely house at Richmond in Surrey, built by Christopher Wren on the foundations of Queen Elizabeth's old palace and looking over velvet lawns and walled-in gardens down to the Thames.

Trumpeter's House was the scene of much gracious entertaining in the twenties and thirties, and Reggie particularly loved people connected with the arts. In his drawing room, or on the wide terrace beneath the great Palladian portico, I saw Ellen Terry, Pavlova, Chaliapin, Gladys Cooper, Marie Tempest, Lilian Braithwaite, Gerald du Maurier, Clare and Emma Eames, John Barrymore, Emilio de Gorgorza, Ivor Novello, Alfred Noyes, H. G. Wells, Lord Birkenhead, Yvonne Arnaud, Ronald Squire, Augustus John, and many other great names in the world of art, mixing with obscure ballet dancers, young actors, actresses, and writers, and occasionally with the local bank manager and his wife, or a little Richmond doctor, gazing open-mouthed at the celebrities.

Reggie was sensitive and *simpatico* to an extraordinary degree, concealing a deep knowledge of the world under a gay and frivolous exterior; it only took him a few minutes to evaluate a new acquaintance. "They think I know nothing," he would wink at me, "but they're wrong; I know a lot about human nature. They also suspect I'm a pansy, but they're wrong; I am a neuter." Most of all, I remember him laughing.

We all used to wear white tie and tails with a silk top hat, or possibly a collapsible opera hat, to go to the theater in those days, and it was the Prince of Wales who broke the custom by wearing a white waistcoat with a dinner jacket, and so I see Reggie, in the great hall at Trumpeter's House, leaning on a gold-headed cane and laughing till his shoulders shook at the follies and foibles of his friends. He took a great fancy to my mother, and they did much theater-going and traveling abroad together in later years. He was always dressed with impeccable taste, and attended everywhere by his respectful valet Eastwood, in black jacket and striped trousers, stiff collar and bowler hat. When Reggie traveled on the continent he always stayed at the very best hotels, and Eastwood was always the perfect, imperturbable, and trustworthy English "gentleman's gentleman."

We went, the three of us, across the Channel and by train through the night to Basle. The next morning the beauty of Switzerland burst upon us and I jumped excitedly across the compartment to see the entrancing views on either side below as we dived into and out of the tunnels. I had never been in Europe before — Englishmen don't think of themselves as being in Europe, "Fog in Channel. Continent Isolated" once read the poster — and I was fascinated by the strange look of everything. Toward evening we came down to Como and so to Milan.

We spent a couple of days rattling through the streets in fiacres, hearing *Un Ballo in Maschera* at La Scala, visiting the Duomo, dining in the Galeria, looking at *The Last Supper*, before going on to the enchantment of Venice, to Florence, Rome, Naples, Capri, and the Blue Grotto, and so across the Straits of Messina to the orange groves of Sicily, the Greek Theater of Taormina and the snowy slopes of Mt. Etna. It was November, and cold, but the sun shone brilliantly on us all the way. We picnicked gaily on cold chicken, Bel Paese, and Lacrima Cristi as we drove to visit the estates of the Duca de Brontë, descendant of Nelson, to whom the estates were given by the King of Naples after the Battle of the Nile, and there we saw men in livery working in the fields. A beautiful drive through the mountains to Palermo, the mosaics of Monreale, a sea passage to Naples and the exquisite Greek statuary in its Museum, Pompeii and Herculaneum, and once more we were on the train to Rome and Paris, where we spent a week in theaters and restaurants. With his intimate knowledge of Europe, Reggie planned the whole trip in London, and Eastwood attended to details en route. This first contact with Italy was an experience which was burned into me and started a love affair with that entrancing country which has lasted all my life.

Returning to England, I sailed in January 1926 aboard the P & O liner *Comorin* from Tilbury, waving goodbye to my father and mother, Reggie, and my girl. Down the Thames we wound and out into the North Sea. About midnight, we stopped off Dover to let the pilot disembark. Shortly afterwards, an envelope was brought to my cabin, marked "By favour of the Dover pilot." Inside was a note with the heading of the Carlton Club. It read: "Merci pour un an d'amitié. George Arthur." A graceful gesture from an old courtier, though how he could have enlisted the favor of the Dover pilot was more than I could fathom.

Scene 6

Australia, Down Under

*There she lay, all that day,
On the Ba-ay o-of Bis-cay-o*

S HE LAY on her side, creaking and groaning, until I thought she would never right herself, and then slowly she rolled over and lay on the other side. At the same time, it seemed to me, she lifted her stern in the air and dived downward until, with a sickening heave, she started to climb again. Here I was out on the ocean, bound for foreign parts. Now at last I had crossed the bar and put out to sea, leaving New Brighton Pier, the Mersey Docks, the River Thames, the solid ground, and the smell of the earth behind me. All I smelled was a loathsome combination of oil and steam, all I heard was the creaking of wood and steel, and all I felt was sickness and misery, a tight band round my head, green spots before my eyes — seasickness. I lay, or rather clung to my berth for three days, and like the man in the fable I was at first afraid the ship would go to the bottom, and then afraid that it wouldn't. All my old romantic Masefield dreams of ships and the sea left me, and I prayed only for a piece of dry land. I was to pray many times more in the next twenty years crossing the oceans, and to try many remedies, from Mothersills to brandy stingers; it was not till the invention of Dramamine that I found relief, and even now, I prefer to look down on the romance of the seas from a jet plane at 40,000 feet.

I had much to think about, as I lay in my heaving berth. The last two and a half years had opened windows on life for me and changed my whole existence.

From being a penniless and friendless youth on a street corner, I had become a leading actor. My name was also established in the movie world. I had a bank account, with £200 in it, I had friends, few but loyal, and I had the girl I had left behind me. Now I was starting out on a great adventure, and I was filled with excitement, but, also a little fearful.

In the English theater, we have an innate respect for the older and more distinguished members of our profession, unlike America where, as actors grow older, they seem to become faintly discredited. People like Dion Boucicault, Mary Jerrold, Hubert Harben, and Norman Macowan had long records and eminent names which impressed and frightened me. Members of the Green Room Club, and perhaps even of that holy of holies the Garrick Club, they would surely look down on their young, untried leading man. It was a relief when we passed through the Straits of Gibraltar into the smooth Mediterranean and I came at last on deck to find the sunshine and everybody smiling at me. A day later we put into Algiers, and I went ashore for my first contact with the strange sights, sounds, and smells of the Arab world.

It was an idyllic voyage, six weeks from London to Melbourne, calling at Algiers, Port Said, through the Suez Canal, and down the Red Sea to Port Sudan, and on to Colombo, where we had a weekend to drive through the tea plantations up to Kandy. Two weeks slow steaming across the vast expanse of the Indian Ocean brought us to Fremantle, the port of Perth, West Australia, and thence we crossed the Australian Bight to Adelaide, and so finally to Melbourne. Glorious weather and smooth seas, endless deck games, swims in a canvas bath rigged on the foredeck, siestas in a deck chair, dancing on deck under the brilliant tropical stars, ship's concerts at which we performed — I sang "Tea for Two" and did a dance with one of the girls — and trips ashore in strange ports, combined to pass the halcyon days. In the afternoons we rehearsed on the upper deck, and I was introduced to the autocratic method of Dion Boucicault.

Taking me by the wrist and turning his head sideways to look up at me like a little bird, he would lead me gently from place to place, pausing to read the lines for me. "Now may I hear you say that please? No, no, my boy, not like that, like this," and he would repeat them again. "There, that's better! Now we come over here . . ." and the process would be repeated. Everything, every word and gesture, he taught us by rote, and there was no question of discussion. It was wonderful training for us younger ones, but must have been hard on the more experienced. I wonder what the Method actors would think of it now! Only once, at our dress rehearsal of *Quality Street,* did I venture a suggestion. He had stopped the action because of some difficulty with an actress covering me upstage. "Would it be good if I moved toward the door, Governor?" I asked timidly. There was utter silence in front for a moment, and then that small, cold voice replied, "I think it would be very bad, my boy."

As we passed through the Bight, we were followed by giant albatross, with wingspreads of six feet or more, which hung apparently motionless behind the ship, occasionally using an air current to sweep by us majestically, a wonderful sight to see. The ship's officers regaled us with stories of the days of sail, when they used to drag behind a small triangle of wood, in the center of which hung a bit of salt pork. As the albatross dived to get it, they said, they would give a jerk to the rope and hook him by his curved beak, hauling him onto the deck where he instantly became so seasick that he couldn't rise. We all thought of "The Ancient Mariner" and hoped they didn't incur ill luck by killing one. The modern steamer goes too fast for albatross, and after a couple of days they give up following.

As we lay in Adelaide harbor, the chief officer came to me. "Come up on the bridge," he said, "and I will show you how the cobbers work." We went up and looked down at the tall, lean men taking cargo out of the hold. There seemed to be three to every job and they moved slowly. Every two hours a whistle blew and there was a cry of "Smoke-oh!" All work stopped, and the cobbers sat down to smoke and drink tea out of billy cans. As the hour of noon approached, work grew slower and slower. The mate swore. "Look at the blighters," he said. "Two more cases which they could whip out in ten minutes, but no — they will mess around until the noon whistle blows and then quit." That's exactly what happened. We lay in harbor till Monday morning, incurring dock dues, the cost of feeding the ship, and delay to passengers and mails, until on Monday they came aboard again, whipped the cases out and we sailed. It meant an extra half day's pay to them, and Australian labor was riding high in those days.

Australians are an independent people, with a slight chip on the shoulder where the English are concerned, which is

perhaps not to be wondered at. Fiercely proud of their country, they nevertheless all speak of "going home" for a trip one
day. I had been warned to be on guard against some initial
hostility, and was not disturbed when we arrived at the bar
of Menzies Hotel in Melbourne to have an Australian man
turn to me and say, "English, aren't you? I knew a bloody
Englishman once." "Yes," I said, "some of us are bastards,
aren't we?" He looked at me shrewdly. "Have a drink," he
said. We became the best of friends, and later I visited him
on his sheep station in New South Wales.

Our opening night at the Kings Theatre was unexpectedly
quiet. Laugh after laugh went by, with the audience sitting
silent, and it was only at the interval we learned that they
couldn't hear a word of the play. The intimacy of the top
deck had not warned us to speak up; nor, to our surprise, had
the Governor.

In the next few performances I taught myself, by trial and
error, a system of projecting the voice in a big theater. I discovered that if I produced it only in the throat, the voice was
limited and could soon tire if subjected to strain, but that if I
gave it impetus from the diaphragm, and sustained it on a
column of air against the vocal chords, it gained immeasurably in strength and resonance. I have used this system ever
since, and it was only when I took up singing a few years ago
that I discovered that this is the traditional system that all
singers use.

The Australians were crazy about the theater, and still are
for all I know. It seemed that any dinner party automatically included the theater, and they didn't seem to mind seeing the same play repeatedly. Old musical comedies like
Maid of the Mountains or *The Merry Widow* would run for

years in Melbourne and Sidney. They were pleased and surprised when we changed our bill every six weeks. Soon after we opened, we began to rehearse *What Every Woman Knows.*

Rehearsals under Boucicault were a serious matter. We were all careful to assemble on stage a few minutes before the appointed time. Usually the curtain was down and a small chair and table, on which were a glass of water and a script, stood downstage, flanked by the stage manager, and the assistant stage manager. Promptly the door would open and the Governor would appear, dressed in bowler hat, stiff collar, dark suit, a short dark overcoat with velvet collar, patent leather shoes and spats. With short, precise steps he would walk to the table, hand his hat and cane to the stage manager, and say formally, "Good morning, Mr. Thomas."

"Good morning, Mr. Boucicault."

Turning to the company, he slowly removed his gray gloves. "Good morning, ladies and gentlemen."

"Good morning, Mr. Boucicault."

And then, after a little polite joke to one of the girls, at which we all dutifully smiled, "We will take the beginning of the second act, Mr. Thomas."

"Yes, Mr. Boucicault!"

"Now my boy, give me your arm. That's right. Now you enter here, you pause — that's right — and now you come over here. You turn. You look at her — no, no, my boy, not like that, like this — that's right! And now you say . . ."

Ten years later, I was to play John Shand to Helen Hayes' Maggie in the film of *What Every Woman Knows,* but the procedure was very different. It was directed by a most engaging character named Gregory La Cava, in a sports shirt

and rumpled pair of once-white slacks. Gazing alternately at
the script and the printed edition of the play he would rub
his head in perplexity, heave a sigh and say, "This guy Barrie
beats me!" Then he would throw them both away, call the
script girl and begin to dictate. We would retire to our dressing rooms and wait until typed pages were brought to us.
"This is your dialogue today." Miss Hayes, Donald Crisp,
Dudley Digges, David Torrance, and myself would gaze at it
aghast. The arguments and the bickering would go on until
Irving Thalberg was sent for and he, enigmatic, oriental, and
authoritarian, would render a decision. The picture showed
the effects of this dissension.

I was enthralled by my work in the theater during those
first months in Australia, as I have never been since. No
sooner had we opened one play than we were rehearsing the
next and our lives were spent as actors' lives should be, working at our craft. This is the tragedy of the actor's life, that
under the conditions of the modern theater he cannot practice his craft at all unless someone invites him. He is like a
taxi, standing on a rank, waiting to be hired; he then re-
hearses for three or four weeks and plays one performance on
which all depends. If the press the next morning turns
thumbs down, the play comes off; if it is a hit, he is doomed
to the endless repetition of the same movements eight times
a week; either way he returns to the rank to wait, sometimes
for many heartbreaking, empty months. He cannot, like a
painter, start another picture. He cannot even, like a musi-
cian, practice on his instrument. He can only wait and hope.
In the Boucicault company I came to the theater at night
eager for the performance, refreshed by the hours I had
spent during the day working on another part.

Soon after the opening of *What Every Woman Knows,* we started on *The Admirable Crichton.* I had grave misgivings about this part, which had been created by H. B. Irving, because I was just passing my twenty-fourth birthday and I knew that I was much too young. I felt I didn't carry the guns for it, and I was so worried that I asked for an interview with the Governor at which, plucking up my courage, I falteringly asked him to relieve me of the responsibility. He heard me out, and then said politely, but firmly, "My boy, I should not have asked you to play the part if I had not thought you capable of doing so." He then dismissed the subject. My instinct was right, however, for Crichton was our only flop. I was momentarily startled, as the curtain fell on the first night, to hear the tremendous applause, mixed with cries of my own name, and this was the first time I learned that the success of a play cannot be judged by its opening reception; the cheering audience, the enthusiastic friends, the excited congratulations, and the celebrating party all fade quietly away as the newspapers begin to roll inexorably off the presses. The next morning the rough Melbourne critics blasted the play as outdated, and Boucicault's direction as ponderous and old-fashioned. Of myself, one said, "As Crichton, the only heights to which Brian Aherne rose were physical ones. These were so great that we were surprised not to see snow on his summit"; and another, that in the island scenes I seemed more like an ardent young boy than a responsible man, in which of course he was right.

Mary Rose was our next, and destined to be our greatest success, but before we began rehearsing there was something of a managerial storm.

"Dot" Boucicault had, in his youth, been very successful as

a manager in partnership with Lionel Brough, and the name
of the Brough and Boucicault Company was still one to con-
jure with in Australia. In his middle years he had produced,
under the Charles Frohman banner, many famous plays in
London, principally those of Pinero and Barrie. With his
wife, Irene Vanbrugh, he had returned to Australia and
made a great deal of money on tours preceding ours. It
was the magic of his name, even more than that of Barrie,
which drew the public to the box office, and he knew it. His
contract with the J. C. Williamson Company, which managed nearly everything out there, must have been compre-
hensive and ironclad, for it gave him carte blanche and sole
control of everything, and even included a clause stating that
he did not have to talk business to any of the Tait brothers,
the producers. He was a true snob, and he felt that the
three brothers, known to the profession as Agitate, Cogi-
tate, and Hesitate, were beneath his notice. The only partner with whom he would deal was Sir George Tallis, an
agreeable man who had the advantage, in Boucicault's eyes,
of having a handle to his name, but even Tallis was dealt
with on sufferance, and once, when he and E. J. Tait dared to
hide in the circle at a dress rehearsal, the Governor insisted
on ringing the curtain down until they left.

He was not interested in protecting their money, which he
regarded with the proper scorn of an artist. The theater of
his time was occupied with the presentation of visual reality,
which had been brought to a fine art in the 1890s and early
1900s. He didn't understand or care for the dialectics of
Shaw, the emotional reality of Ibsen and Chekov; in his productions platforms, steps, and rostrums were built, machines
were used to project passing clouds and sea waves on the

backdrop. Long imitation grass was brought from London for me to cut down in the *Crichton* island scene — though grass grows wild in Australia; a large cavern for Mary Rose's disappearance was designed and made by Maskelyne and Devant, the magicians; furniture, costumes, props, fires that lighted, practical gas jets, all the paraphernalia of reality was shipped out and had to be handled by a small army of experts. No sooner were Tallis and Tait ejected from the rehearsal of *Crichton* than the Governor's voice again stopped the show.

"Will you come on stage please, Mr. Thomas?"

The stage manager emerged.

"What is that cloth I see on the tea table? I distinctly remember saying it should be Irish lace."

"Well, that's hard to find here, sir. We thought perhaps no one would notice —"

"*I* notice, Mr. Thomas! Ring the curtain down please and go out and find me an Irish lace tablecloth. I am sorry, ladies and gentlemen. A mistake has been made, and we shall have to wait until we can correct it. Never mind, that is what we are here for."

We retired to our dressing rooms and waited, while the stage manager and the property man desperately scoured Melbourne for an Irish lace tablecloth. When we finally got going again, there was another lecture about the gloves carried by the coachman, which it seemed should have been made of dogskin, though what dogskin was nobody knew except the Governor.

After all this travail and vast expenditure of money, the Taits were shocked by the receipts of *Crichton,* and apprehensive about *Mary Rose,* with its many sets and quick

changes, its organ pipes, harps, incidental voices, and shooting stars, which they feared might cost far more than it could
take in. They decided on a showdown with their autocratic
director. Sir George Tallis was deputed to write and ask for
an interview. In his answering note, Boucicault ignored the
invitation to the office, and gave Tallis instead an appointment at the stage door of the theater at 1:00 P.M. on Tuesday
of the following week. As this was Tallis' customary lunchtime, it was hardly convenient, and he also chafed at the
delay, but he wanted to seem amicable, and so he agreed. At
the appointed time he and the general manager of the company, Mr. Wenman, arrived at the stage door of the Kings
Theatre.

"Mr. Boucicault?"

"Not here yet, sir."

They waited. They waited half an hour. They telephoned
his hotel. Mr. Boucicault had gone out to lunch. They
waited again. Finally Tallis would stand it no longer.
"Come on, Wenman," he said. "We're going to lunch! Let
him make the next move!" And they left.

About 3:15, mellowed by lunch, they decided to forget the
affront and go back.

"Mr. Boucicault?"

"Not here yet, sir."

At this moment, a large hired limousine stopped at the end
of the alley. The chauffeur opened the door and the Governor stepped out. Bowler hat, stiff collar and cuffs, short
black coat with velvet collar, spats, and stick on his arm. In
his right hand he carried a cigar. Tallis and Wenman
watched, burning with anger, as he stepped precisely toward
them. As he reached the stage door, he pointed with the

cigar. "I'll see you in five minutes," he said to Tallis. "I don't want you," to Wenman, and he went in.

Mary Rose in my opinion is a beautiful and deeply moving play, and this production of it was wonderful. In the title role, Angela Baddeley gave the finest performance of her career. Hubert Harben and Mary Jerrold as Mr. and Mrs. Moreland, Norman Macowan as the Scotch ghillie, and myself in the dual role of Simon and Harry were all ideally suited to the parts. The Governor, on his mettle after *Crichton,* revealed an understanding and love of the play which illuminated it. Just before the opening, he said he couldn't bear to hear the sound of clapping hands and to see bowing actors at the final curtain, and he put a note in the program asking the audience to refrain from applause. As Harry, the Australian soldier, I watched Mary Rose pass through the window upstage and vanish; a shooting star swept across the night sky, the harps throbbed, and unseen voices called musically "Mary Rose . . . Mary Rose," as the curtain stole slowly and softly down. Absolute silence would ensue, and I would sneak down to a hole in the curtain and watch the audience as the lights came up. They would sit staring for a minute or two, as if bewitched; a woman would take her handkerchief from her bag and dab her eyes; a man would grope aimlessly for his hat; finally they would rise slowly and stumble up the aisle. It was an astounding sight. The Governor's courageous decision was absolutely right, and the dramatic result was something I have never seen equaled in the theater.

The cable cars ran up Collins Street, Melbourne, when I was there, just as they still do in San Francisco, and I used to enjoy sitting outside on a soft summer night after the show and going to the end of the line. I played golf occasionally with Harben and Macowan, but to tell the truth, after rehearsals were over and the plays running smoothly, I was lonely. I had little in common with Australian people, who frightened me with their rough-and-ready self-assurance, their strong, accented voices, their steaks and chops for breakfast, and their capacity for drinking. It was all so very different from my secluded home life, the stiff regimentation of Malvern, or the cosmopolitan literary and artistic world into which I had peeped in London. I was also learning that it is hard for actors on tour to get to know anyone outside the company, and this is mainly a question of hours. Actors who are working can rarely lunch, and never go to cocktail parties or to dinner, and late supper in Australia was impossible owing to the rules of the labor unions. The cobbers had to be finished with their work and out by eight o'clock, which meant that even the dining room of Sydney's great Australia Hotel was closed at seven, and if we wanted supper after the show, we had to make do with sandwiches put in our rooms at seven, and left to dry and curl at the edges. I made a few real friends in Melbourne, Fred and Elsie Dennett, who have remained dear to me to this day, and Norman, now Sir Norman, Brooks and his charming wife. Brooks had been Wimbledon singles champion for five years running, 1910 to 1914, and early in the 1920s he came over and played again. I had seen the famous match in which, wearing a cloth cap and using the same old flat-ended softly strung racket he had used for years, he defeated the American champion Francis

Hunter. The crowd roared with laughter as Hunter struck the ball with a sharp "ping" one end and Brooks placed it artfully back with a soft "thog" the other. The strangely contrasted match between the new and the old styles of tennis went on for five sets, and the applause was deafening at the end, but Brooks was so tired that he was easily put out the next day.

It was Norman Brooks who told me always to have some sympathy with a champion. Remember he may be a little tired, a little off his game, or have a headache or a muscle strain, he said, and he knows he risks the loss of his championship in every match; the challenger, on the other hand, has all to gain and nothing to lose; he goes all out for every shot, takes risks willingly, and is cheered every time he wins a point. It is much the same for the star of a play: a youngster with no responsibility and a short, showy part can steal the play and the critics will rave, though the whole production hangs upon the star's name and is impelled and sustained by his work.

The Boucicault company was composed of three married couples, two single men, and three girls whose conversation came strictly under the heading of Sir George's first type. While on tour, one rarely has the chance to make friends outside the company, and perhaps this explains the camaraderie of the theater, and the romances which so often develop. "Yes, of course I loved her," said the actor, "but you see the show closed in Atlantic City!" It is the same with the ballet: "I always marry dancers," said Balanchine to me. "It is so much more convenient. We get up and go to bed at the same time, and we wear the same shorts!" I felt I wanted something more and, as always, I withdrew into a world of books and dreams. My father's influence was still strong upon me, and offstage I must have seemed a stiff and starchy young fellow in the girls' eyes, as they were dull in mine.

After Melbourne, the cities of Adelaide and Sydney received us rapturously, and we added Frederick Lonsdale's *Aren't We All?* to our repertoire in order to give Boucicault a chance to show himself as an actor. We were very ill-suited to the play, but he was drily amusing, and by then we had become devoted to this prickly, difficult, but charming old character, whose old world courtesy and care for us was unremitting.

"Mr. Thomas," he would say to the stage manager as we gathered at the railway station, "I hope I shall be satisfied with the accommodations arranged for the ladies and gentlemen of my company. Kindly see that they get a good dinner on the train. I would suggest the fish, which is excellent here. Please speak to the chef about it. Chablis for the gentlemen and Chateau Y'Quem for the ladies — don't forget the cigars, Mr. Thomas. Upman please."

Sydney, with its fabled harbor, is one of the beautiful cities of the world and I would like to revisit it. We would drive to the Blue Mountains on weekends, and have picnic suppers after the show on Sydney Heads, the girls plucking at ukeleles and singing Nick Lucas' songs as we watched the moon over the Pacific. A tour of New Zealand was announced before the Williamson Company realized that my contract alone was about to expire, and great heartburning ensued. Half the company wanted to go, and would regale me with stories of the marvelous New Zealand fishing; the other half implored me to stand firm, so that they could return to London. Remembering Golding Bright's advice, and fearful of being forgotten in England, I refused. They could not replace me, and so at the end of a year the tour closed. I told myself I could always go back to Australia, but I never have, and when I did get home I was over six months out of a job.

The company was shipped home on the cheapest possible boat around the Cape, six weeks at sea with one stop, but I felt I wanted to see something of the world on the way home, so I took my passage money and started out on my own.

It was five o'clock in the morning, and just getting light when I got off the train. An oil lantern still shed a faint pool of light on the wooden platform. The rolling land of New South Wales lost itself in the darkness around. My host Bill, who was about my age, appeared leading another young man, one side of whose head was bandaged. "Kicked in the eye by a sheep," he explained as he was helped aboard. "Just a jackeroo," said Bill, as we turned from the departing train and got into an open two-seater car. A jackeroo? That's a young man, usually English, who has been cut off with a shilling by his family and shipped out to Australia, where he finds a job working on a sheep station in the back blocks in return for a few pounds a month and his keep.

The sun soon blazed over the bare, dry hills, broken here and there by the inevitable rugged gum trees, as we bumped along a dirt road. As often happens, there was a drought. The backbone of Australian trade has always been wool, and some of the stations run to a million acres or more in Queensland. There great fortunes have been made and lost, depending entirely upon the coming of rain. Sometimes it doesn't rain for several years, the feed and the water holes dry up and the sheep die by thousands, all over the range. The owner ships feed and water from railheads progressively farther away, until finally the bank forecloses and he is forced to sell for a song. Next month, perhaps, the rain comes pouring down, the grass springs up, the water holes fill, the new owner puts out his lambs, and his fortune is made. It is a hard, lonely life, particularly hard on the women, many of whom cannot stand it and drift off with the children to the cities, but Australians are hardy people, as they have proved in two world wars, and they love their country. As we drove along, Bill told me of the "White Australia" policy, which has rigidly excluded all but white immigrants and given preference to those of English descent. The result was to avoid the racial problems which have plagued the U.S.A. and South Africa, and now threaten to do the same in England, but the Australian population has been so limited that when I was there in 1926 there were only about 6 million people in the whole continent. However, the Japanese menace in the last war scared them, and immigration is now more liberal.

The house in which Bill lived with his widowed mother and two young sisters was a typical outback frame structure, with the inevitable corrugated iron roof, put there in the hope of catching rain, and surrounding stables and sheep pens. After a huge breakfast of lamb chops and strong tea we all got on horses, Bill, his sisters, a couple of hands, and myself, and started to "ride the fence."

There is no picturesque cowboy costume out there. The men sat slouched in the saddle, wearing dark worn suits with waistcoat and watchchain, and a hat such as you would see in Birmingham, and never roused their horses from a walk all morning. The fence riders go out for two or three days at a time, walking their horses all the way and carrying with them only a bedroll, tea, bread, salt, and a billy can. They make a hole in the ground in which they put a billy can of water, building over it a fire of eucalyptus twigs. As the fire burns they cook lamb chops on a forked stick, timing things expertly so that by the time the meat is cooked the water boils; throwing in tea, they are then ready for their unvarying meal. The scent of the eucalyptus, or gum tree, gives flavor to all, and for those who like a strict diet of mutton, it's fine. My father would have been quite happy with it.

As we rode, we wore nets suspended from the brims of our hats to keep away the flies. The back of the man ahead of me was thick with them, and when I touched my own back they rose in a dark cloud. Returning to the stables, they asked me almost wistfully if I would not care for a better horse the next day, but, scenting danger, I declined. I had heard that the fellows were half-dead of boredom, and that their greatest diversion was to put the visitor on an unbroken horse, especially if he was an Englishman.

Late that night, when the house was quiet, I was tiptoeing along the passage from the bathroom when I heard voices through a half-open door.

"Yes, mother," said one of the girls, "he's very good-looking, but he seems so reserved. I just can't talk to him!"

"Well, dear, perhaps he's shy."

"I don't think he's shy," said the other girl. "I think he's just stuck-up!"

"Now Ruth, don't talk like that! I'm sure he's very nice when you get to know him."

"Maybe, but how do you get to know him? Anyway, I thought actors were supposed to be so charming!"

I tiptoed on to my room, and sat down by the window to think. There it was again. Here in the middle of Australia, in a family with whom I had thought I got on pretty well. I had even thought the girls liked me, though they were very young for me. Why was it that people didn't understand me? I felt like a puppy dog, eager to be loved and anxious to please, and yet I had to admit to myself that sometimes the old de Lacy in me rose, and formed a barrier through which I found it difficult to communicate with others, unless they were exceptionally sensitive and understanding people. Perhaps, I thought, in this case there was the added difficulty of communication between the English and Australian backgrounds, speech, and habits of thought. Perhaps my Irish blood, or the contrasting influences of my father and mother warred within me; my father would have been oblivious to the good opinion of these people, but my mother would have made everybody like her. Since then, of course, I have realized that one can't get along with everybody, but I was young and lonely and confused. Surely, I thought, somewhere in the world there must be a woman who would put her hand in mine and say, "I understand," to whom I need not explain myself, for whom I would be all right the way I was. I sat for a long time, looking out into the starry Australian night and hearing the unfamiliar noise of cicadas beneath my window, and I went to bed finally with a heavy heart. Was I really "stuck-up?"

The next morning I decided to make a real effort to be popular. As a beginning, I asked for a better horse. All eyes brightened. "Not *too* fresh!" I hastened to add.

The stable yard unmistakably contained more people than had been there the previous day. They were idly leaning

over the fence, apparently with time to spare, and I was looking at them anxiously when suddenly a stable door burst
open and a huge horse, with two men hanging on the reins,
came charging out, kicking over some buckets which made a
frightful noise and excited it wildly. A couple of men seized
me, and, crying "Up, you go!" threw me into the saddle; two
more flung open the gate, and after a couple of wild leaps
among the buckets the horse took off across country. Useless to shout "Whoa!" My hat flew off. I dug in with my
knees and hung on to the reins, like John Gilpin. Down a
long hill he galloped, straight into a stream, which unaccountably had water in it that morning. He must have been
as surprised as I was, for he stopped in the middle and exe-
cuted a couple of fast bucks before taking off again, lickety-
split up the hill. It was a very long hill, and after some minutes he began to puff and pant, and show signs of slowing,
but I, by some miracle, was still in the saddle, and I now
seized my chance to kick him in the ribs by way of revenge.
When it seemed to us both that we had covered half New
South Wales, we finally agreed to stop and I fell off and was
sitting on the ground, blowing as hard as the horse, when the
others came up, all laughing delightedly. Tension was eased,
and I was accepted, at least by the men, one of whom gave
me a hat to prove it.

That night I was leaning over a gate, talking to Bill's
mother and looking at the moon, when she suddenly said to
me, "Why don't you stay here and run the place with Bill?"

I stared at her. "But I'm an actor," I said.

She stirred impatiently. "An actor! What's that! I can see
you're a man, and this is a man's life. Stay here and be
happy!"

I stared again. I saw an attractive woman, though any

woman in her thirties seems kind of old to a man of twenty-four. Was she interested in me herself I wondered, or did she think of me for one of her daughters? I didn't have the nerve to try to find out, so I turned away and looked at the moon instead. There was a long silence, and then as if by common consent, we moved slowly back to the house, the crickets rasping loudly around us. Her words had disturbed me, for I still had little faith in the acting business, despite my £70 a week, and I lay awake that night turning the thing over in my mind. This would certainly be a proper job, a life's work in fact, and I have always been more at home in the country than in cities, which depress my spirits, but could I find happiness in such isolation? Could I stand the loneliness, the heat, the flies, the absence of any friends, and the lack of that contact with the intellectual world that had so excited me in London?

I got out of bed to open the windows, and found, for the first time in my experience, that they were screened. We don't have screens in England, and I don't remember seeing them in Australian cities. I threw them open wide and leaned on the windowsill for a long time looking at the Southern Cross, brilliant in the dark night sky. I went back to bed. At dawn I awoke suddenly to find the counterpane crawling with strange insects, and a huge praying mantis genuflecting on the sheet just below my chin. Springing up in horror, I decided that place was not for me.

A month or so later, my friend Bill shot himself in his car on a lonely road. I have never known why. I wrote to his mother, but she did not answer.

Scene 7

Rolling Round the World

BACK IN SYDNEY, I carefully examined a map of the world. I could take a boat north to Thursday Island, Sourabaya, and Singapore, and there transfer to a Dutch liner going home through Suez, or I could cross the Pacific and the U.S.A. and so go around the world. The next day I sailed for Honolulu on the old Oceanic Line's *Sonoma*, a small and ancient tub which wallowed slowly along, her two reciprocating engines beating sometimes together but more often apart, so that the whole ship shuddered abominably. The three-week voyage was broken by a day of glorious tropical beauty in Fiji, and another of rain at the American naval base in Pango Pango. Was the story of Somerset Maugham's *Rain* a true one, I asked the commandant? He didn't know, but assured me that there was no record of a suicide on the island.

I had a raging toothache and the motley passengers were all very bored with each other by the time we sighted Hawaii. The last evening was spent in a frenzy of indignation, caused by a very smart young man who had come aboard in Fiji laden with sporting equipment, guns, fishing tackle, and tents, but who had spoken to nobody. Calmly reading a book, he would pass the salt at meals or draw his legs up on his chair as the games-players managed to trip over them on deck, but never a word to anyone. On the last night, he was cornered in the bar and asked the reason point-blank. "I looked around when I came aboard, and saw nobody worth talking to, so I decided not to bother," he replied. We felt, each one of us, that at least he might have spoken to us!

I spent ten days in Honolulu, grazed my chest and knees on the coral rocks and banged my head with a heavy surfboard while struggling with the surf on Waikiki Beach, took bus trips around the island and enjoyed the rest, but as always I was lonely, and was glad to get aboard the *Maui* and go on.

Early on Christmas morning, as I lay seasick in my berth, smelling the sickly-sweet coconut smell of our cargo of copra, the engines stopped, and after ten minutes started again. I rang the bell. "Man overboard, sir," said the steward. "Drunk maybe. Went down in the wake. Sharks probably got him by now. Merry Christmas, sir!"

In the last day of the old year we came through the Golden Gate and I saw the glory of San Francisco, glittering in the sunlight, smelled its sharp, fresh air, and promptly fell in love with it. It was a magnificent introduction to America, and my spirits rose to meet it, just as they always do when I visit that most enchanting and colorful of all American cities. A letter from Reggie enclosed introductions to people in Los Angeles and New York, and I felt once more back in civilization. That night, as I was going to bed, I heard a tremendous cacophony of sound and I hastily dressed again and went out. It was New Year's Eve, the American New Year's Eve so very different from our own. Every ship in the harbor was blowing its siren, and every car its horn, the streets were ankle-deep in confetti and streamers, and the gay, laughing crowds blew paper trumpets in my face. I was struck for the first time, as so often since, by the simple, childlike American capacity for enjoyment. It is one of the American people's most charming traits, and one misses it in Europe. Old nations are a little like old people, sensible and experienced and rather tired; they don't understand, and are often irritated, by the enthusiasms of the young who, in their turn, easily become impatient with the old. We are often dazzled by the American theater, which seems to skate with such brilliance and dexterity over the thin ice of comedy, but can break through and fall into a sticky mass of sentimentality. This is due, it seems to me, to the exuberance of youth. The comedy of the older nations seems more cynical, and their sentiment more reserved, as is the case with older people. The laughter of the old is rooted in disillusion, but that of the young is based on the pratfall.

A few days after my arrival I received my first elementary lesson on the extraordinary position of women in the American scheme of things. Mrs. Norman Brooks had given me a letter of introduction to the president of the Matson Line, who kindly invited me over to Berkeley, and drove me around the University campus, showing me the lovely lighted Christmas trees and displays that American people put out before their houses, a charming custom made impossible in Europe by the climate. As I sat having a drink with my host and hostess and their friends, a young girl of about fifteen came into the room, whereupon every man in the room got to his feet. Hastily I did likewise, and we remained standing until she remembered to tell us, quite graciously, to please be seated.

Since then, I have taken the advanced course, and have learned that America is indeed the country of woman, the country where everything is designed for women's comfort, cars, chairs, and even bathrooms, the country where household linen is marked with the woman's initials, where 70 percent of invested capital is held in women's names, and where the marriage contract, though signed by both parties, contains an unwritten but nevertheless ironclad proviso that if those parties should agree to dissolution, it is the woman who brings the action and dictates the terms, and the man who pays. One sometimes wonders how a Spaniard or a Frenchman can ever be contented with the American woman who, for all her lively charm and beauty, is so often spoiled and unhappy.

Los Angeles, in my mind, was the same town as Hollywood and I knew no better than to accept the advice of a traveling salesman whom I met on the train and go to a downtown hotel. There was only one room available, and for that night we shared it. "Have some Sal Hepatica?" he asked hospitably as we turned in. I declined. "Oh, always take Sal Hepatica!" he said reprovingly, and snored happily all night. Next day I sent off letters of introduction to Douglas Fairbanks and Mary Pickford, the actor George Fawcett, and to Elinor Glyn. They must have been puzzled to see my curious address, but all replied with invitations. Directed by the hotel manager, I set off on a series of interminable journeys by streetcar, the first to Venice which, being on the sea, sounded charming, but turned out to be a dessicated slum hardly worth a day's bumping along back streets.

Douglas Fairbanks was one of the most delightful men I ever met, filled with joie de vivre and with kindness to those younger than himself. He gave me lunch at his studio, together with Mary Pickford, Syd Grauman, Maurice Gest, and the famous mind-reading couple, the Zanzigs. Talk was gay and lively, the Zanzigs gave an astonishing exhibition of their powers, and Doug took me all over the studio. Mary Pickford, the idol of my youth, had a heavy cold and seemed unhappy. She asked Zanzig, who was a clairvoyant, to tell her about her future. He asked for her ring to hold and they went into another room. She returned looking even unhappier. Fawcett asked me to dinner with two beautiful Mexican actresses who evidently found me rather foreign and strange, as I did them.

The great experience was to meet Elinor Glyn, whose book *Three Weeks* we had read secretly in the shrubbery in our youth, declaiming to each other:

> *"Would you care to sin*
> *With Elinor Glyn*
> *On a tiger skin?*
> *Or would you prefer*
> *To err with her*
> *On some other fur?"*

She received me in a great apartment on top of the Ambassador Hotel. I waited ten minutes before her entrance, and I had leisure to look out over the city through the high dormer windows and to admire the pale green walls, white furniture, and tiger-skin rug upon the floor. "Would I prefer — ?" But no, what was I thinking of!

The door opened and she moved toward me, dressed in diaphanous white, her red hair coiled on top of her head, her piercing green eyes fixed upon me and her hand held out to

be kissed. "Good afternoon," she said, "I am Madame Glyn."
My knees buckled a little, but I took her hand and shook it
firmly; she seemed a little taken aback by this, but immediately led me to a deep sofa and poured tea. "We English,"
she said, "must have our tea."

I had come with an introduction from Lord Stonehaven,
the Governor General of Australia, who had said to me
kindly, "Going to Hollywood? Girl I know there — Elinor
Glyn — give you an introduction if you like," and Madame
was evidently impressed by the coronet on the envelope. She
told me stories of her years at the Russian court in St. Peters-
burg, of driving across the snow in a drosky, covered in furs,
with the bells on the horses tinkling and Prince Yousupoff by
her side. She spoke of directing John Gilbert in some Russian epic. "I sat by the camera and looked into his eyes and
poured the spirit of Andreyevitch into his soul," she said.
Why is it, I wondered, that every time a Russian is mentioned in book or play, it is always by a different, unpro-
nounceable name?

I soon realized that it would be best to stick to the aristocracy in this conversation, for she had a fine scorn for the
lower classes; fortunately life with my parents had prepared
me for this.

"The world is going to the dogs," I said. "It will soon be
run solely for the masses. As Lord Curzon once said to
me — " I got no further, for it seemed I had pressed the right
button. I did not know then, and indeed only learned a short
time ago, that there had been a great and famous love affair
between Madame and his Lordship. The knowledge that I
had met him established me once and for all in her favor.

She took me to the MGM studios and introduced me to

Norma Shearer, Marion Davies, John Gilbert, Edmund Goulding, H. B. Warner, and other movie greats. She arranged a silent screen test for me for Irving Thalberg to see. She took me, as her escort for dinner, to Marion Davies' house, where I sat with Charlie Chaplin, the Duncan sisters, Ralph Forbes and Renée Adorée, Myrna Loy, Theda Bara, and Richard Barthelmess. She took me dancing at the Coconut Grove, just the two of us, and I still in my Liverpool dinner jacket. She took my hand across the dinner table and commanded me to feel her pulse. "I shall now make it go faster," she said. She did. "I shall now make it go slower," she said. She did. My eyes bulged. She gave me advice: "Don't marry till you are at least thirty. Have many love affairs, but never get serious. Say to the girl in the morning, 'Get up, and make my coffee!' Be rough with them, be brutal, be a man! If you marry and settle down, you will be ruined as a romantic actor. Your eye will lose its restless, hungry look. The audience does not pay to see a fat contented man, they want to feel that he lives dangerously, as they cannot." She pointed to actors whose careers, in her opinion, had been ruined by contentment. We danced. I thought myself a good dancer, better than she, but we evidently didn't have the same ideas about it, for she suddenly clamped my arm tighter about her waist and said, "Oh, don't be a clergyman!" On returning to our table she fixed me again with eyes which, I swear, were green. "I have discovered the secret of eternal life," she said. "Every year I grow younger and more beautiful! You will remember me, because you will never forget my eyes." I shivered a little. I have not forgotten them.

She was, like Cleopatra, a wonderful piece of work, but to

tell the truth Madame Glyn frightened me, more than some-what, as Damon Runyon says. When I left Hollywood she held her hand high again. "I hope you no longer believe in the legend of the tiger skin," she said. I put my hand beneath hers and dropped a gallant kiss upon it.

A few years later, she came to London and was persuaded to invest her money in a couple of motion pictures. The English producers, poverty-stricken themselves, were adept at getting money out of people by flattery, and Madame was rich and vain; they ruined her. Worse than that, her feelings were wounded. She was telling an actor on her set at Elstre about getting younger and more beautiful every year, when she overheard a stagehand behind the lights say to another, "Young? 'Er? Wy, she wos old w'en 'Yde Park was a potted plant!"

I telephoned to MGM to ask if Mr. Thalberg had seen my test. Yes, said his secretary, but Mr. T. did not think it necessary to delay my departure for England just then. I was rather relieved, because I was holding a cable in my hand asking me to return to London for a picture, but if only he had known it, Thalberg was to regret that message in future years.

In these days, when we fly from Los Angeles to New York in four and a half hours, it is astonishing to think that I was on a train which took four and a half days, and stopped three times a day for the passengers to get off and eat their meals in a station restaurant. All the way to Chicago I sat out on the observation platform amid the cinders and dust, wrapped in my thin overcoat and a rug, watching America go by, freezing rather than face the fetid atmosphere inside.

The combination of steam heat, stale cigars, and unwashed humanity was hard to take in those days, some years before the chills and drafts of air conditioning made railroad travel miserable in another way. I added a fifth day to stop off at the Grand Canyon, about which the adjectives impressive, awe-inspiring, and majestic have been worked to death without conveying a tithe of its impact on the mind. I stopped another day at Niagara Falls, framed in ice and snow, and spent the night with a charming old doctor who possessed a bust of Voltaire, before which he fell on his knees after dinner, crying, "He is my God!" And so I came, on the hard coach seat of a day train, to New York City.

The Algonquin Hotel was, and still is, a great theatrical hangout, but it is not a good point from which to start an exploratory ramble of the city. Turn right as you leave the door, and walk over to the Hudson River and back, as I did, and you will feel dirty and miserably depressed by lunchtime; try again in the afternoon, this time turning left and going to the East River and back, and you will decide it is better to stay indoors, especially if the streets are deep in slushy snow and ice, as they were. Next morning I tried exploring Broadway and its environs, about which I had read and heard so much. I ate my lunch in one of those dreadful places in the West Forties that have a lot of glazed hams in the window. By the time I got back to the Algonquin, I was ready to leave New York and never see it again. I think those first two days left an impression on me which I have never got over. London, Paris, Rome, Boston, San Francisco, Washington, and even Philadelphia are exciting and often beautiful cities, but New York still seems squalid, dirty, and ugly to me. When others speak of it as being stimulating and beautiful, I find myself staring at them in disbelief, for all I can see in my mind's eye is the tenements, the garbage cans, the blowing dust, dirt, and fragments of newspapers, and the sullen, unhappy-looking people on the pavements of the East and West Forties.

Wandering along West 43rd Street one dark afternoon, I heard a cry. "Why, Jack O'Hara! What are you doing here?" And there was Peggy O'Neill, with her radiant smile and her mocking twinkling eyes. I was so pleased to see her that I could have hugged her, but she was still the big star in my mind and I was still a little in awe of her. It was not till I got to the corner of Broadway that realization of my utter loneliness came upon me, and I plucked up my courage and ran back down the street. Perhaps she was alone too, perhaps she would lunch with me, dine with me, go to a theater with me, or just talk to me. It was too late, she had vanished in the crowd. I never saw her again. She was a delightful creature.

Suddenly the magic mantle of American hospitality was cast over me once more, as my letters of introduction brought response. I lunched with Mrs. "Neely" Vanderbilt on Fifth Avenue, and saw the largest paving stone in the world in the pavement outside her house. I lunched with the Kermit Roosevelts, kind and friendly. I met Gilbert Miller in his office, and he was unforgettably charming to an unknown young actor. I saw Ethel Barrymore give a brilliant performance in Maugham's *The Constant Wife,* and she asked me to supper afterwards, in her apartment high above Central Park South, with Harry Kendall and her stage manager George Cukor, whose sharp American wit delighted me. "I wish I knew of a part for you, my dear," she said. "You should stay here." I saw Helen Menken, Basil Rathbone, and Arthur Wontner in a gripping, chilling play, *The Captive*, for which they were all shortly to be arrested. I saw Lenore Ulric in *Lulu Belle*, which I didn't like, attended a lecture by Sacha Guitry, visited Wall Street, and sat in Mrs. Vanderbilt's box at the Met to hear *Das Rheingold*, and from there went straight to a second-class cabin on the *Majestic*, which rolled me home to England. My mother and Reggie stood on the dock, waiting for me. And so it was the theater that fulfilled my ambition and took me around the world.

Scene 8

The Magic Chain

A Woman Redeemed was the name of the picture awaiting me, and you can guess what it was like from the title. Once more I was on the bus to Cricklewood, but this time feeling it was a breeze because I had no show to do at night. At least it helped to swell my bank account, which was lucky, because when it finished I was six months out of work. I thought regretfully of New Zealand and began again the old search for a proper job. Perhaps, I thought, I could work with my father on some speculative building scheme in Birmingham. I talked to him about this, and persuaded him to incorporate some American improvements in a small house that he was building for sale. Two years later, he hadn't sold it because Birmingham people would not accept central heating — unhealthy, they said. He tore it out at great expense, and blamed me ever afterwards, so that idea was no good. I began to remember du Maurier's words to me: "Have you a private income?" Alas, no!

At last the telephone rang. The little Everyman Theatre at Hampstead was to do a play, starring Gertrude Elliot, for a couple of weeks. There was a small part in the last act; would I read it? The salary was only £5 a week, but I would read anything, play anything! I was at rehearsal that afternoon, arriving just in time to hear the actor playing Miss Elliott's husband explain that he couldn't do it since he had secured a job in the West End. The director looked at me; would I have a go at it? I looked at Miss Elliott, who was old enough to be my mother. Indeed I played opposite her daughter, Jean Forbes-Robertson, four years later. I liked my bit in the last act, and thought the leading man dull and humorless, but I was willing to oblige, and after all, what did it matter up in Hampstead, where nobody would see me? I gummed on pieces of gray hair, a mustache, and a middle-aged manner, and had a go at it.

The Divine William tells us that the opinion of one must, in our estimation, outweigh a whole theaterful of others, and he's right as usual. We didn't have a whole theaterful at the Everyman, we only had a few locals and such as Miss Elliott could draw, but by one of those extraordinary chances which can indirectly influence our whole lives, the one was there. I don't know when he was there, and I don't even know his name, but I do know that he was a Frenchman and a dramatic critic. He was in London, reviewing the theaters for his paper, and having completed his task he spent a couple of nights with friends in Hampstead. They took him to the Everyman. His article concluded by saying:

> One of the best performances in London is given by a very young actor named Brian Aherne at the little Everyman Theatre up in Hampstead, and I saw it quite by chance. Where the majority of English actors are content to play themselves, to project their own personalities on the stage, this one takes the trouble to "compose" his part, as we say in France. Clothes, voice, gesture and attitude of mind are all parts of the character he plays, whom we see whole, unique, a distinct and living person. This is what we admire and strive to achieve in our French Theatre, and which seems so lacking in the West End of London.

I don't quote this merely because it is a good notice; the years have taught me the folly of listening to newspaper critics, good or bad; I would never have seen, or known, or cared about this one had not Sir George Arthur happened to be in Paris that day. He bought two copies of the paper, one of which he sent to me, and the other to Mr. Angus McLeod, head of the Daniel Mayer Corporation, theatrical producers. He enclosed a note to Mr. McLeod, suggesting that he take a look at my performance, and on the last night of our little run McLeod was in front, though of course unknown to me.

I have often pondered over this curious chain of circumstances, each link of which seemed mysteriously and almost magically riveted to the next, and I have wondered what would have happened to my life had one link failed, or been missing. I might well have refused the offer of £5 a week for two weeks, with two weeks unpaid rehearsal. The leading man might not have got a better job, and I might have stayed with my bit in the last act. The French critic might not have dropped in unexpectedly, and might not have liked my work when he did, or at least might not have taken the trouble to say so. Sir George might not have been in Paris when the article appeared, or might not have happened to read it. He might not have had the thought, or taken the trouble, to send it to McLeod, and McLeod might not have dropped in on that last night at the Everyman.

I say all these things might not have happened, but I don't believe it. I believe, and I can only speak for myself, that the main events of my life were written at my birth and have remained immutable, like the pages of a play, to be acted out slowly, scene by scene, until I shall reach the final curtain; a foolish belief you may think, but one which I have held since childhood, indeed it was very strong in me as a little boy, and from my earliest consciousness I seemed to be aware of the long journey before me on which I set out like a reluctant traveler. When major events occur, I find I greet them with a shock of recognition, a certain knowledge that they are bound to happen.

Sometimes, lacking any true indication, I wait and listen. When I stood in a Liverpool office and heard the roar of the ship's siren, when I was alone in Leicester Square with four and tenpence in my pocket, when I gazed at the night sky from the window of an Australian sheep station, I seemed each time to wait for a still, small voice to speak, for a small push in the direction of my destiny.

I did not anticipate, I did not plan any link in this particular chain of circumstances which led me inexorably to the greatest event in my life.

It was a cold crisp morning in October 1927, when I went to an appointment at the office of Angus McLeod. He would like to introduce me, he said, to Sidney Howard, author of the Broadway success *The Silver Cord,* which McLeod was shortly to produce at the St. Martin's Theater. Mr. Howard would direct the play, in which his wife Clare Eames and Lilian Braithwaite would star. Marjorie Mars, a promising young actress, would play the girl, and there were two parts for young men, for one of which he was considering me, and he would like Mr. Howard to see me. "This part would suit you," said Mr. McLeod "and you shouldn't play parts of older men, as I saw you do in Hampstead." I agreed humbly. If only I could get the chance, I was more than willing to play a suitable part or indeed any part!

I walked into the office and I saw Queen Elizabeth in a red coat, sitting in a chair with a cigarette in her hand, looking at me quizzically. There was no doubt about it, for I was very familiar with the portrait of the young Queen Elizabeth in the National Gallery, the lean proud face, the high forehead, the enigmatic steady eyes, the aquiline nose just slightly off center, and the air of high breeding, intelligence, and wit. I sat down and stared at her. Surprisingly, her hair was brown, instead of red. One of the men spoke to me, and I stammered some reply. My experience and ability were discussed and there was some talk about the play and the part, but I couldn't pay attention to it; I was waiting for her to speak. When she did, she asked me if I believed in God.

I forget what I answered, but it seemed to amuse her, for she laughed gaily and sat back, watching me through the smoke of her cigarette, her hazel eyes twinkling. I told her of standing outside the Guild Theater in New York, looking at the pictures of herself and Alfred Lunt in *Juarez and Maximilian,* and of my regret that I had not gone in. So I had once stood outside the New Oxford Theatre in London and looked at pictures of Duse in *The Lady from the Sea.* We spoke of New York, and she laughed at my description of my walking tours of the West Forties in the snow. We exchanged quick, lively opinions of the Broadway theater. Finally McLeod rose to signify my interview was over. I stood up, still looking at her.

"Well," Howard said to her, "how do you think you would like to act with him?"

She regarded me steadily for a moment, then she held out her hand and gave me an enchanting smile. "I don't think," she said slowly, "that I could object to acting with the Hermes of Praxiteles."

I came out into Golden Square and saw the sunlight on the trees. A barrel organ was tinkling gaily across the street. I walked on air along Piccadilly and into St. James's Park, where I sat down on the grass. It was a lovely, tranquil autumn day and the trees were turning to gold. As I looked up, I could see fleecy white clouds sailing slowly over the Palace. I felt excited, and strangely happy. Who was Praxiteles, I wondered?

Rehearsals for *The Silver Cord* were intensive, stimulating, and professional. Sidney Howard was a brilliant director who knew his play thoroughly and had a gift for infecting the actors with his own enthusiasm. Denys Blakelock and I worked hard on our difficult parts and watched with fascination the technical brilliance of Clare Eames and Lilian Braithwaite. Miss Eames had one long speech in the first act which Denys and I had agreed was superfluous and almost unplayable; we confidently expected it to be cut, but when she attacked it with easy confidence, lighted by variety of pace and tone and informed by genuine feeling and flashes of humor, we stared at each other in amazement. Neither of us had ever seen such acting, such precise and perfect technical accomplishment. It was like listening to a great violinist performing a brilliant cadenza.

The opening was a triumph, but the notices were stolen, as we guessed they might be, by Marjorie Mars with a short and tremendously effective hysterical scene. Poor girl, she never had such success again. I knew about hysterical scenes; I had had one in *White Cargo*.

My old friend Horace Hodges came to see the play, and wrote some helpful advice. Closing his letter, he said, "Miss Eames is a greatly talented actress. Her personal distinction and her mastery of her craft entitle her in my opinion to be ranked with Irving Booth, Kean, or any of the great ones of the past." Two weeks later, Sidney Howard returned to America, and we settled down to a run.

It wasn't long, perhaps a few weeks, to the evening when she looked at me and said unsteadily, as if she feared the answer. "Brian, you do love me, don't you?"

I fell on my knees beside her. "Oh Clare," I said, "I adore you!" I forgot she was a married woman with a child. I forgot she was six years older than myself. I forgot my Puritan upbringing. I forgot that I was nothing but a penniless young actor. I heard the angels sing. I was lonely no more. My heart was suddenly flooded with comfort and happiness, my spirit lifted to undreamed-of heights of vitality and joy. I was awake! I was alive at last.

"How do I love thee? Let me count the ways," wrote Elizabeth to her Robert Browning, and the ensuing lines of the verse which she gave him on a birthday morning are, to sensitive minds, among the most beautiful written in our language. Sometimes, in the years that followed, I would ask Clare, as Robert may have asked his Elizabeth, how it was possible that she should love me. Shaking her head a little and smiling tenderly, she would reply with four simple words which, to my ears, were as beautiful as those of Elizabeth Barrett: "You're just my idea," she would say. She had a brilliant and cultivated mind, entrancing humor, extraordinary sensibility, and a gentle, loving heart. She was intolerant of fools, but because she loved me my follies and inadequacies seemed only to touch and amuse her.

Few people care about poetry today. Perhaps the pace of life is too fast, our activities too many, or the competition of television, movies, newspapers, magazines, and radio leaves us no time for it. A few years ago, I was in a large bookshop in California where I complained that their stock of it was very small.

"What's the use of carrying more?" said the man, "Only you and Katharine Hepburn buy it!"

I had always been fond of it, in a stupid, uninstructed sort of way, and *The Oxford Book of English Verse* lay with Palgrave's *Treasury* on my bedside table, but none of my family or friends read it or even spoke of it, and I had come to believe that it was a small, secret foolishness of my own. Now I had found Clare Eames who said "Yes!" to this, as she did to my other dreams. To her, the poets were a part of life; Browning, Keats, Shelley, Wordsworth, Henley, Gray, Noyes, Masefield, Brooke, and many of the moderns, were all her dear and familiar friends, and she was constantly finding new ones. Once, when she was in the hospital, her temperature shot up and she became unaccountably worse. Her doctor was alarmed until I discovered that the crisis was the result of her reading Stephen Vincent Benét's *John Brown's Body*, which I had given to her.

One of the first books she gave me was Tolstoy's *Anna Karenina*, which made a deep impression on me because I seemed to see a parallel between her story and that of the tragic, romantic Anna, and I feared that I might become her Vronsky. After that, she gave me *War and Peace* (which is a great experience for anyone), Lawrence's *Sons and Lovers*, Maugham's *Of Human Bondage*, Bennett's *Old Wives' Tale*, E. M. Forster, and Evelyn Waugh, the great biographies which were then coming out by Strachey, Feuchtwanger, Zweig and others, and the philosophers, the Greeks, the Victorians, Hume, Kant, and Winwood Reade, with the moderns, Huxley and Bertrand Russell. She explained to me the basic theories of Freud and Jung, and for a few days even had me struggling with Karl Marx. Together, we explored the wonderland of Shakespeare, excitedly planning the parts which we would play in the future.

All this was heady wine for me. For the next three years my heart was flooded with glorious sunshine, such warmth and comfort as I had never known, while intellectually I was conscious of wide horizons expanding, almost exploding, before me. Clare's coming was to my silent, dreamy life, like a sudden peal of bells in an empty house.

Our happiness was not without its difficulties. My mother was deeply distressed by what she naturally regarded as a most unfortunate liaison for her son. My father said nothing, but Clare's father wrote me from America a stiff, cold note of disapproval. Sir George and Lady Arthur, discreet and formal as ever, invited us both to dine with a few aristocratic old friends but said nothing; nor did Miss Vanbrugh, though I fancied sadness and regret in her manner. Reggie, kind and loyal but ever worldly wise, spoke his fears seriously. Some of my lady friends were downright nasty to me. I suppose we must have been a minor sensation in the theatrical world of New York, where Clare was famous not only as a distinguished actress and the wife of Sidney Howard, but also as a director of the Theatre Guild. All the talk there upset her husband very much. He did not care for Clare, but he cared deeply about what people said, and he felt he was placed in a humiliating position. He cut off financial support, refused a divorce, and insisted upon the return of the baby and her nurse.

I had to leave *The Silver Cord* because I fell ill with a mysterious malady which was diagnosed as a combination of flu and toothache, both of which seemed to get steadily worse despite the doctor's drugs. Seated at my bedside one day, Clare suddenly leaned forward and pressed my cheekbone. On my resultant howl she announced, "You've got sinus!" I had never heard the word before, but I was to know it only too well for many years to come. I was rushed to hospital and underwent a peculiarly painful operation to cut a window into the cavity from inside my nose, through which the poison was supposed to drain, but for many years I suffered recurrence of sinus infection, until I believe it became psychosomatic with me, for it would always happen on an opening night, or at any moment of crisis when I needed to feel at my best. I saw many doctors and took many treatments in vain. I was rejected for service in the Second World War on this account. It was only when I discovered the benefit of dry desert air in California that I found the ultimate cure.

I had a long convalescence from this illness, during which *The Silver Cord* closed and Clare's difficult situation was brought sharply home to her. Without her baby, without a job, without money, and with no established position or connections in the English theater, it must have taken very great courage to entrust her life, against the advice of all who were near or dear to her, to a young actor who was hardly equipped to undertake such a responsibility. Few women, and certainly few American women of her background, would even have considered it. Her father was a retired cap-

tain of the U. S. Navy, a proud man and a strict one; her aunt
was Emma Eames, the great prima donna of the Metropolitan Opera, a majestic and imposing figure living in retirement in Paris. Like others of her family and friends, they
were stunned and shocked by her conduct. But Clare Eames
was no ordinary woman. "Be true to the God within you,"
she would say. "Listen to your own secret heart, and you can
do no wrong." She faced the great crisis of her life with
courage and integrity, though not without deep distress.

Young as I was, I doubt if I fully realized the tragedy of
her position. I started work soon on two pictures for Anthony Asquith, *Shooting Stars* and *Underground*, which
achieved some limited success in England, and I was naturally much occupied with my work, while Clare could only
sit alone in her small rented flat and wait for my return.
When she told me of her decision to return to America, I
had no doubt at all that she would come back to me. She felt
she owed it to her baby, to her family, and to her marriage
vows to make one more effort to reconstruct her life there,
but I think we both knew she would come back; and so she
did, in three months, with a contract in her pocket to make a
picture for Rex Ingram at his studio in Nice. I joined her
there, and together we drove home through Northern Italy,
the Tyrol, the Black Forest and down the Rhine. The die
was cast for us, and our happiness together was supreme.

Scene 9

Plays, Personalities, and Politics

FATE NOW sent me a number of parts in a variety of
plays, none very successful but all contributing to my
experience, which is what a young actor needs. It is
much better, in the early years, to be in a series of flops than
in one obstinate success, not only because of the experience
but also because critics, managers, and directors are constantly seeing one's work. It was in this period that I, quite
unwittingly, helped Laurence Olivier to become the great
actor that he is.

I was approached by Basil Dean to play the lead in *Beau
Geste,* his stage adaptation of the highly successful book and
movie, in which Ronald Colman had played the part. "This
will put you where Colman is today!" said Mr. Dean, echoing
the promise of Joe Grossman some years before, and under
his powerful persuasion, I agreed to do it, though I did not
like the script. No sooner had we shaken hands and parted
than I read the play again and found I liked it still less. I ran
to Miss Vanbrugh in despair and she drafted a polite and
tactful letter for me to send him, explaining that I had been
so overcome by his charm that I had agreed to do something
that was not actually within my capacity. Poor Mr. Dean,
though an outstanding director, was so singularly and notori-
ously lacking in charm that he must have been taken aback

by this excuse. His manager telephoned me in a fury, saying, "You have set your career back ten years by this piece of folly!"

That Sunday there was a performance of a play called *Journey's End* by the Stage Society, in which young Laurence Olivier played Stanhope, the lead. Nobody thought at that time that war plays would draw a penny, for there had been several such that had flopped badly, but Basil Dean, who was in front, so admired Olivier that he went around and offered him the part I had rejected in *Beau Geste*. Olivier was delighted to accept what appeared to be a great chance for him.

Now, it so happened that an American actor named Maurice Browne had recently closed a failure in London. Having no money and no job, he was glad to accept an invitation to stay for a few days with some rich English friends down in Devonshire. The story current at the time was that after dinner on Saturday night his host and some local gentry who were present asked Browne how they could get the chance to invest money in a theatrical production. Browne replied that he would keep his ears open, but when they rather shyly mentioned the sum they had in mind he nearly fell off his chair. He said at once that something had occurred to him, but that he would have to leave immediately if he were to secure it for them. He caught the milk train up to London, arriving in that deserted city early on Sunday morning. On the way up, he noticed in his paper that the Stage Society was giving one of their Sunday performances that evening and, having nothing else to do, he went to see it.

And so it was that while Basil Dean was in Olivier's dressing room, getting his signature on a contract for *Beau Geste*,

Browne was making an agreement with R. C. Sheriff for the production of *Journey's End*.

Beau Geste was a dire failure which ran only for a week; *Journey's End* ran for four years in London, another four on Broadway, played all over the English-speaking world, and was made into a successful movie. Colin Clive, who played Stanhope superbly in London and in the picture, failed to convince managers that he could play anything else, while Olivier proceeded through *Beau Geste* and a long series of other short runs, to build a great and successful career.

The sequel to this story was that Maurice Browne's Devonshire backers were delighted with the success of their investment and saw no reason why they should not repeat it. They took imposing offices in the Haymarket, with "MB" embroidered on the carpets and on the cap of the doorman, and proceeded to lose all the money they had made. One hopes that Browne managed to put a bit away, for it is good to see an actor strike lucky once in a while.

I played Young Marlowe in *She Stoops to Conquer* out at the Lyric, Hammersmith, under Nigel Playfair's famous management. Twenty years later, when I played him at the City Center, New York, I went to Barris, the old Cockney wigmaker who has supplied the Broadway theater through all living memory.

"Alfred," I said, "I'll tell you a secret. I played this part in London twenty years ago!"

"Ah," said he, "you looked it then; you've got to act it now!"

I played Archer to Edith Evans' Mrs. Sullen, in Farquhar's enchanting eighteenth-century comedy *The Beaux' Stratagem*. Later, in America, I sent the play to Ina Claire, always a theatrical idol of mine. She never answered, but I heard from a mutual friend that she was indignant that some impertinent young actor had sent her a play in which he had the lead, while she would have had only a "bit part." Great actresses cannot necessarily read, but had she had the opportunity to see Edith Evans' performance she would have been in no doubt that Mrs. Sullen was an entrancing, exciting starring part.

I played, with an all-male cast, in another flop play about the war, *Tunnel Trench,* which barely lasted the week, but we, the young men of the company, had such a good time with boxing matches in the dressing rooms, football down the corridors, and laughter and practical jokes on stage, that we all volunteered to go on another week for no salary. We did less business than we had the first, but nobody cared.

A dark, sensitive Welsh boy was fired during rehearsals of this play by Reginald Denham, the director. I remember saying to him, "Don't worry. You have talent. I am sure you will do well." He did; his name was Emlyn Williams.

I played Brandon in *Rope,* which was brilliantly directed and produced by Reginald Denham. This play was known for some reason as *Rope's End* in New York. Anthony Ireland and myself were young homosexual murderers who planned the perfect crime, and the author denied that he was thinking of Leopold and Loeb when he wrote it. Sir Gerald du Maurier came to see it. At a party at Ben Webster and May Whitty's flat afterwards, he said to me, "Saw the play. Disgusting! Not theater. Might as well come out and be sick on the stage. It's easy to shock an audience if you want to." When I look at modern plays I sometimes think of that remark. It's easy to shock an audience; it's not so easy to entertain it.

One night, as I sat in my dressing room, after what I thought had been a particularly thrilling performance of *Rope*, with which we had stunned the audience, I heard some English society people getting into their car outside. There was much lively talk about nightclubs and supper places, and then, as the men got in, I heard one say to the other, as if by afterthought: "I say, funny sort of play, what?"

"Yes. Sort of — er — murder thing."

"Ah, that's what I thought. It was — er — a sort of — er — murder thing." The door banged and they drove away.

Rope was taken to New York and Lee Shubert begged me to go with it, telling me that I would never find a better part in which to make my first appearance before an American audience, but I would not go. I also turned down Stanhope in *Journey's End*, for New York, and several Hollywood offers. Clare and I both felt that we must stay in London at that time, partly because she loved England, partly because she shrank from facing the malicious tongues of Broadway, but mainly because we did not want to embarrass Howard.

I made two more pictures, with Elissa Landi and Madeleine Carroll, and though I did not make much money I seemed to be always active. It was otherwise with Clare, and, apart from an unforgettable Sunday night performance of Jean Jacques Bernard's *L'Ame en Peine*, she found no work. This was a heartbreaking situation for a great actress, but she bore it bravely.

Together we explored England. She, the American, showed me Westminster Abbey, the Tower of London, and Kew Gardens in springtime. I took her to the great cathedrals, Canterbury, Salisbury, Ely, Norwich, Gloucester, Wells, and Exeter, and from her wide knowledge of history she brought them alive for me so that I came to know the people who built them and the generations that had passed through them.

Indeed, she opened many windows for me, not the least of which was music. She was shocked to learn that I had never heard a great orchestra play symphonic music, and took me at once to the Albert Hall, where we spent the first of many ecstatic Sunday afternoons listening to Beethoven's Fifth and Tschaikowsky's Fourth.

At last she received an offer from Gilbert Miller to play in Somerset Maugham's *The Sacred Flame* in New York, which her financial straits, her longing to see her child, and her hopes of one more appeal to her husband impelled her to accept. Once more we were faced with separation, though we agreed that, come what may, this must be the last.

About this time, I became interested in theatrical politics. A remarkable young man named Coulson Gilmer had formed an organization called the Film Artistes Guild, which hoped to improve working conditions for actors in the studios, and I accepted his invitation to become vice-president. At the same time I began to attend meetings of the old Stage Guild, which had been formed by well-meaning idealists in the theater, and at one of these I found myself making a speech against Sunday opening, in consequence of which I was invited to be on the Council. I dutifully attended Council meetings, until one day we considered the case of a manager who had stranded his company in some remote English provincial town. In response to a request that he appear before the Council, he wrote us a derisive refusal. The Council heard it read in silence, and then regretfully turned to other business.

"Wait a minute!" I cried to the chairman. "What can we do about this rascal?"

"Well," he replied slowly, "I suppose we can ask him to resign."

"Nothing more?"

"We have no power to do more."

I left the Council meeting and went straight to Coulson Gilmer.

"These organizations are useless without power," I told him. "What can we do to get it?"

"Become a registered trades union," he replied. "Only so can we take action against an employer in defense of our members. Without the protection of the Trades Union Act we cannot strike a manager without rendering ourselves liable to legal action and possibly heavy damages."

"Come!" said I. "Let us go at once to the London Trades Council and find out about these things."

We went and we met an interesting man, Alfred Wall. We explained that the whole acting profession feared trades unionism and, being extreme and often eccentric individualists, actors would never be brought to agree to sympathetic strikes, picket lines, and all the bitter strife that seemed to be engendered by industrial organization.

"If the boilermakers of Sunderland come out on strike," we said, "it would be unthinkable to ask the actors to close their theaters or to join in a quarrel that was not theirs."

Gravely he assured us that this was not required, that an association of actors could be formed under the protection of the Trades Union Act which could act for itself, without ties to any other kind of labor.

As a result of this talk, Gilmer and myself registered the

Film Artistes Guild as a trades union. We then went to see
Godfrey Tearle, a great actor, great gentleman, and president of the dying Stage Guild. To our surprise we found he
was quite familiar with all aspects of the problem and agreed
heartily with us. However, he could not very well preside at
the destruction of his own organization, so he suggested that
we form a committee and give him evidence of progress before he could think of joining us. And so, from there we went
to Ben Webster and May Whitty, old and beloved members
of the profession who had ever been in the forefront of the
liberal movement. After much talk they agreed to join us, as
did Edith Evans, Walter Hudd, Denys Blakelock, Margaret
Webster, Sybil Thorndike, and Lewis Casson. Sitting round
the dining table in the Webster flat, we declared ourselves
the Provisional Committee of the British Actors' Equity Association, a registered trades union. Our next act was to
elect ourselves life members of the Association.

That table now stands in the office of British Equity, as it
is popularly known, but few of our many members can know
what it signifies. I worked as a counselor of British Equity
for four years, until my career took me more or less permanently to America, and helped it from birth in 1928 through
all the vicissitudes of childhood. Twenty-eight years later, in
1956, I received an offer to play in a short television film in
England. To my dressing room came a young man with
printed forms in his hand.

"I represent British Equity," he said. "Please sign here.
Your entrance fee will be so much and your dues so much."

I felt like a ghost as I looked at him, and perhaps there was
a moment's silence, because he said uneasily, "What's the
matter?"

I returned to the present. "I don't pay," I said. "I am a life member."

He stared at me in astonishment. "A life member? I've never heard of such a thing."

"Look it up," I suggested.

Two days later he was back. "By God, you're right!" he said.

If I don't take much interest in theatrical politics nowadays, it is because I am by no means sure that all this organization, all these offices and employees and committees and meetings and rules and dues and fees, all the fights and strikes and dissension have been worth the ultimate result. Parkinson's Law applies to trades unions as much as to government departments: once established, they are not only self-perpetuating, but must steadily increase in cost and complication, ever expanding, taking larger offices, hiring more employees, casting about for fresh causes and projects to justify their expansion. But acting is not a business. Talent is rare, and he who has it can make his own terms. Perhaps those who have no talent should not be actors. I don't know. However this may be, neither the opportunities for employment nor the dignity of the actor's position are comparable to what they were in my youth.

The weary months dragged by for us, sustained only by letters which took a week to cross the Atlantic. Clare had to close her play in New York to undergo an operation. I was in the middle of rehearsals for *Craig's Wife* with Phyllis Nielson-Terry, directed by the author, George Kelly, when I too had to have an operation for appendicitis. My own misfortune was not unwelcome to the company, because rehearsals had been very difficult. Kelly, uncle of our own Grace, Princess of Monaco, was a brilliant but eccentric character who insisted on reading all his lines with the actors as they rehearsed.

"Don't let me worry you," he would cry. "You will catch my tune!"

Phyllis Neilson-Terry was more than worried. She was so upset that she couldn't learn a word. Finally, he wrote a letter to the management saying that it was impossible to direct the play unless he had Miss Nielson-Terry's co-operation.

"Who is this author who thinks he is Shakespeare?" she replied indignantly. "He should be only too thankful to have a Terry to speak his miserable lines!"

Everybody was glad to stop and wait six weeks for my operation.

Suddenly, the sun broke through again. Clare was back to play her part in *The Sacred Flame*, with Gladys Cooper at the Playhouse. I recovered and *Craig's Wife* went on, to fold in a fortnight. It was a clever play, but unsuited to London. "What a horrible woman," said the critics. "How those American men must suffer!" And doubtless they thanked their stars that their wives were not like that.

While his daughter, Phyllis, was flopping, old Fred Terry revived *The Scarlet Pimpernel* at the Strand Theatre, and we went to see him. He was then in his late sixties and must have played the famous part, off and on, for forty years, but his performance was wonderful — fresh, vigorous, and romantic.

"That," said Clare, "is my idea of a matinee idol de luxe!"

I agreed, and said so to Horace Hodges.

"When Terry made an entrance," I said, "it was as if the whole stage grew lighter!"

Hodges regarded me indulgently.

"My boy," he replied, "it *did* grow lighter! Fred's lighting plots provide that all lights shall be raised one point on his entrance."

After all, this is theater, and who shall say he was wrong? I dare swear that Laurence Olivier does the same today.

My mother used to say that when she died she hoped she would go to Heaven, if only because she had a vitally important question to ask Saint Peter on her arrival.

"Peter, dear," she would ask, "tell me, who wrote Shakespeare's plays?"

And well she might, for Shakespeare not only knew every secret of the human heart, not only wrote incomparable acting parts and exquisite poetry, but understood and wrote about the motives of his characters. After him the eighteenth-century dramatists depicted brilliantly the manners and modes of their time, while those of the nineteenth were content simply to present action on the stage; it was not until Ibsen looked deep into his characters that the drama became interested again in motives. In our own time Tennessee Williams and others explore the reasons for human conduct and sometimes find very nasty reasons, too, but when Sidney Howard wrote *The Silver Cord* he was years ahead of his contemporaries.

The play deals with the relationship of a mother to her two sons and the women in their lives. Victim of an unhappy marriage, the mother turns to her sons for comfort, smother-

ing them with possessive love. When her boys become engaged she subtly undermines them. Christina, the elder
boy's fiancée, perceives what is happening and fights back,
forcing the mother into the open, where she fights like a ti-
gress to hold her sons.

Howard derived the play from his own experience, and
from a subsequent course of psychotherapy which he under-
took, but soon abandoned, with the great psychiatrist, Dr.
Jung, in Zurich. In later years Moss Hart was to make similar capital out of his experience with psychiatry in his brilliant musical *Lady in the Dark*.

This was my first introduction to a subject which is now a
familiar topic of conversation to us all, and it was Clare who
explained to me the basic theories of Freud, the existence
and power of the subconscious mind, and the unsuspected
motives that underly human conduct. I began to think that
my own mother was unduly distressed about my romance,
and I decided to go home and talk it out with her with reason
and affection.

I found her lying on her bed, weeping uncontrollably. I
tried gently to explain that I was a boy no longer, but a
grown man who was able to take responsibility for his actions. I said that my relationship with her must inevitably
change with the passing years, but that always we should be
great and good friends.

She gave a cry of despair. "I'm not your friend," she
wailed. "I'm your little Mum!"

I was deeply shaken by this encounter, for she was very
dear to me. I gave her a copy of D. H. Lawrence's *Sons and
Lovers* and tried to make her understand that I must live my
own life as it seemed right to me, and that nothing could

affect my love for her, but I knew that a gap had widened
between us which, indeed, was not healed for years.

I went downstairs and joined my father, sitting quietly at
his usual supper of cold mutton and Cheddar cheese. We ate
in silence, and after we had finished he lit his pipe and took
up the evening paper.

"Mum is going through a difficult time in her life," he said.
"We must be patient with her."

I agreed, and we discussed it no further. I looked at him
over my book and thought how little I really knew him. At
that time I knew nothing of his relationship with my mother,
imagining always that they were perfectly happy and contented with each other; it was not until nine years later that
he stood on the lawn of my house in Beverly Hills and told
me of the misery of his life. Yet I did suspect that all was not
well with him, for while I was in Australia he had suddenly
sent me a cable which read, "Come home at once. Can't go
on like this." In those days, however, it took six weeks to get
a letter to England, three months for an answer, and I never
had an explanation. I now thought of this, but our English
reticence prevented discussion of it. Nevertheless, we
seemed to come silently a little closer to each other that evening, and after I was back in London he began to send me
occasional little notes on one pretext or another and even
came once or twice up to town for the day, on a cheap "excursion" train, to see me. I did not ask if my mother knew of
these visits. We would lunch together, and he would terrify
the waiter by placing a monocle in his eye and scrutinizing
the menu carefully, after which he would put it down and
ask severely, "Have you any decent mutton?"

On occasion he would accept beef, but no other foods

seemed to interest him. Roast mutton, hot or cold, was his staple fare. Having eaten it, he would again place the monocle in his eye, glare at the waiter, and ask, "Have you any eatable cheese?" By this, he meant a sharp Cheddar cheese, but he said it as if there were some marked difference between eatable and uneatable cheese. My mother, who loved good food, suffered all their married life together from this singular restriction of his appetite, which made their endless succession of meals together impossibly boring.

After accepting a Havana cigar, and after a little monosyllabic conversation about nothing in particular, he would say, "Well, old chap, nice to see you. I must be off to catch my train now."

My newfound interest in psychiatry brought me to the realization that in some obscure way he was reaching out to me, that he needed help in some inner distress, and on Clare's advice I took him one day to see a doctor, though I did not dare to tell him that the doctor was a psychiatrist. I waited nervously in the waiting room for an hour. Finally, the psychiatrist came in. "There's nothing wrong with that fellow," he said. "All he needs is a job."

We walked down Harley Street together in silence. Suddenly he spoke. "That chap tried to hypnotize me!"

"Oh? I am very sorry, Dad. That's not what I wanted for you."

"Nonsense!" he said, gruffly. "I believe in it. Only wish I could have helped him by going off, but I couldn't!"

He went off, instead, on the bus to Paddington Station.

Scene 10

The Raging Storm

I DID NOT CARE FOR *The Sacred Flame,* and thought it not one of Maugham's best plays, but it did for Clare just what she wished. It took her to New York for a few months only and brought her back to London in a success. Her stay in America was difficult, for she had constantly to evade the press. She was only able to see her child by slipping into the house secretly, like Anna Karenina, when her husband was out. We both suffered from the agony of separation and from illness and operations while apart, so that her return to play with Gladys Cooper and Mary Jerrold at the Playhouse Theatre was like a sudden gift from Heaven. Again we decided never to be parted. The play opened to much acclaim and soon was an established success, thanks to the magic of Gladys Cooper's name and the general brilliance of the performance. Clare was again hailed by the London critics and it seemed that the only thing we had left to wish for was a change of heart on Sidney Howard's part, and this was more than a wish, it was a deep longing, for throughout our love we never lived in the same place together. I continued to live in my Bayswater flat, attended by my faithful housekeeper, Miss Mead, while Clare lived in a series of dismal upstairs flats in Kensington or down the Cromwell Road. I suppose we were too proud, we had too much respect for each other and for our families, and above all for Clare's child, to do otherwise. We were not light or irresponsible people, and the great emotion which overpowered and possessed us both was not without an element of sadness.

One night, when I went to the Playhouse stage door to pick her up for supper after the show, I found she was not there. Her understudy had gone on for her. I rushed to the phone. She was alone in her flat with severe abdominal pains. The taxi seemed to crawl along the Cromwell Road, but at last I reached her. I telephoned to Reggie Reixach, who sent his doctor up from Richmond. Together we carried her into Reggie's car and drove her to the doctor's "nursing home" on Richmond Hill. A few days later she underwent there a major abdominal operation. It took her six long months to recover.

In the year 1929, the silent movie vanished, blown off the screens of the world by a single cry from Al Jolson in *The Singing Fool.* I found myself shortly in the Elstree Studios making a war picture called *The W Plan,* for Victor Savile, with the beautiful Madeleine Carroll. It was an "all-talking picture," and the wonderful thing we now discovered was that we, the actors, did the talking just as we had been trained in the theater; the director, the cameraman, and their technical retinues were all deprived of their megaphones and huddled into small glass-fronted, unventilated booths in which they crouched miserably with the cameras, able only to make signs to us, when we bothered to look at them. This was not often, as we were fascinated by the new breed of sound experts — studious, worried young men who crouched round the set, endlessly hanging, laying, and changing cables and listening through earphones. It seemed they had to change a cable several times before they could record a single line. Gone were the sound of hammers, the shouts of the construction workers, and the wail of the orchestras, which used to play "mood music" for us in silent films. Only delicious silence reigned, in which we could think at last about our lines and pay attention to our acting.

Until the advent of sound, the cameraman and his court had been the great temperamental wizards of the set, controlling everybody and everything, even the director, by their requirements, but now the soundmen swept them aside and nobody allowed them time or paid them any attention. Suffocating in their booths, they made no demands for extra angles or additional takes; indeed, they set up three or four cameras on a scene and took several angles at the same time. They were forgotten and embittered men.

The sound experts conferred gravely in their control room, usually down a passage away from the set, struck tuning forks and listened, changed cables, tightened and loosened microphones, and impressed us all with the knowledge that they were expert participants in a great mystery. Their head man had even been to Hollywood to confer with his fellow wizards there, and this gave him a special aura. His importance, at that time, seemed even greater than that of the director, traditionally king of the set.

It was hardly likely that the caged lions in the booths would submit without a battle and a couple of years later the booths were gone, the cameras soundproofed with coverings called "blimps," and the crew and director once more liberated on the set, while the soundman had been relegated with his equipment to a room off the set, from the windows of which he, in turn, had to look out like a caged lion. Now a compromise has been effected whereby the director, camera crew, and soundmen are all on the set, while the actual recording machines are remotely placed, and everybody can talk, shout, push about and be important. The noise and confusion do not stop until the cameras are actually rolling, so that the poor actors have about fifteen seconds in which to compose themselves and think about the scene. It's not much, but at least there is silence while we speak, and silent pictures never gave us that.

I enjoyed *The W Plan*, in which I played a spy and spoke some German. I made £400 out of it, the largest sum I had ever earned in pictures. I never made any money in London.

Very few English actors have made money in their own country. It seems that only those who have been successful in America, or have gone abroad for seasons in Australia, South Africa, and Canada, have been able to save money or build any estate to protect them in old age. Forbes Robertson, Martin Harvey, Dion Boucicault, Irene Vanbrugh, Marie Tempest, Fred Terry, and others of the old school did it in the theater; Ronald Colman, Aubrey Smith, Cary Grant, David Niven, Madeleine Carroll, Greer Garson, Merle Oberon and others did it in motion pictures — well, come to that, in a small way, so did I! A few years ago Ronald Squire, one of the most distinguished actors of my youth, was out in California for a picture and came to lunch with me at my house on the beach in Santa Monica. Lying back in a deck chair, after a swim in the ocean and an excellent lunch, he looked out from under a wide-brimmed straw hat at the blue Pacific, took a draw on his cigar, sighed contentedly, and said, "Oh, my boy, how wise you were!"

I looked at him with surprise. "I envy you," I said. "Distinguished career, fascinating London life, member of the best clubs, a great theatrical name . . . "

"Nuts to all that!" he grunted. "I haven't any *money!*"

Alec Guinness and Laurence Olivier have both astonished me by saying the same thing.

I was used to being short of money and my wants were small, but Clare's situation was now grave indeed, and had it not been for Reggie's kindness and hospitality I don't know what she would have done. Sitting on the terrace of his lovely Christopher Wren house and walking through his walled-in garden that bordered the Thames, she slowly regained her health. Finally, she received an offer to play the part of the maiden aunt in a revival of Edward Knoblock's play *Milestones,* at the Criterion Theatre. It is a fascinating part to which her talent was peculiarly suited. Without any apparent change of make-up except a wig, she slowly aged from a young, vibrant, romantic girl to a tired old woman. Being a revival, the play was only put on for a limited run, but it gave her the chance for what was possibly her greatest performance, and one which held me spellbound.

Following this, she was offered the part of Beatrice to Baliol Holloway's Benedick in *Much Ado About Nothing,* and she was very excited by the idea, but now the gods, in whom she so believed, struck her again, successive and crushing blows.

Until this time, nobody had ever questioned the right of actors of any nationality to accept work in a country other than their own. Language had been the only barrier against a free interchange of artists. English and American theater people were constantly crossing the Atlantic, and English actors were especially popular in the 1920s, not only in New York but also in Hollywood, where the advent of the talkies made their speech and their training much in demand. I myself had turned down a number of important engagements on Broadway and was now under pressure from the Hollywood studios, which held out lures of contracts and parts and money which would have been hard to refuse if my heart had not been elsewhere engaged. We discussed the idea of going to Hollywood earnestly, but it did not seem likely that Clare would find a place on the screen, and I would not agree that she, who had sacrificed so much for me, should also sacrifice her career in the theater. Then I must admit that we were both theater-trained, and were inclined to look down on motion-picture work as being a betrayal of art in the pursuit of money — a foolish notion that I have since outgrown. Finally, Clare shrank from seeing Sidney Howard, who had embraced a successful career as a Hollywood writer.

And so, instead of going to Hollywood, where we might both have been greatly successful, we put our pennies together, took the Little Arts Theatre and put on Clare's translation of the French play *S. S. Tenacity,* which she directed and in which I played. Patrick Hamilton, author of *Rope* and later of *Gaslight,* adapted Anatole France's *The Procurator of Judea* as our short curtain-raiser, and we enjoyed ourselves and felt we were doing something worthwhile. We worked very hard and surmounted many difficulties, and in the end we lost £40.

A small pebble fell into the still, calm waters of international theatrical relations. It was almost unnoticed at first, but soon its widening ripples reached either side of the Atlantic, growing in their passage until they became great waves of controversy and ill-feeling which still beat, senselessly it seems to me, upon our profession.

This pebble took the form of a letter from the Ministry of Labour to the manager of a little outlying stock theater at Kew, informing him that an obscure American actress, who was to play a very small part in his new production, could not be employed. The letter cited the Alien's Restriction Act of 1921, the purpose of which had been to prevent a flood of cheap labor from coming into England from the Continent after World War I. The manager, astonished, as well he might be, by this communication, brought it to the infant British Equity Association for advice. We perceived at once the dangerous implications of this new policy, and we arranged for the Minister to be questioned in the House of Commons.

Yes, he said, he had decided that the provisions of the Act must apply to all foreign labor, including actors.

Would this mean that all American actors were in future to be excluded from the English stage?

Rather frostily he replied that in certain cases, where exceptional talent was involved, permission might be granted.

Who was to be the judge of exceptional talent?

"I am, sir!" snapped the Minister, and sat down.

Sitting round the table in the Webster flat, we of the Provisional Committee faced this situation with consternation. As actors we all believed in a free interchange between the theaters of all nations. There are not really so many parts that Americans can play in England, or vice versa; still fewer that can be played by Frenchmen, Italians, or Germans, and the artistic lifeblood of the theater can only be enriched by competition and emulation; we had no fear that we might suffer by a comparison with mediocre performances, and we welcomed those from whom we could learn. We feared reprisals in the States and restrictions which, once imposed, would never be lifted. Most of all we feared the power of exclusion resting in the hands of a government department. Now, many years later, the Minister of Labour still exercises this power, but usually only after receiving the advice of the British Actors Equity Association on each individual case.

It was Clare's birthday, and we lunched gaily at the Ivy restaurant. Theatricals always went to the Ivy. M. Abel, the proprietor, and Mario, his smiling lieutenant, greeted us as friends, escorting us to chosen tables; big stars and important managers, directors, and writers in the front room, lesser lights in the back room, unknowns upstairs; one's standing was indicated by one's seating at the Ivy. The food was delicious, the service impeccable, the prices reasonable, and the atmosphere a combination of elegance and coziness.

Why is there no Ivy in New York or Hollywood? Agents would be almost unnecessary if there were, for many a play was cast over the coffee cups at the Ivy.

With an air of excitement and mystery, Clare produced an envelope containing, as she said, a great treat. In it were two tickets for the matinee of *Caprice* at the St. James's Theatre, starring the legendary New York players Alfred Lunt and Lynn Fontanne. We spent the afternoon in a state of euphoria, watching these two great artists play high comedy as I have never seen it played before or since. They were then at the height of their powers and the speed, vitality, and attack, the variety of pace and tone, and the technical dexterity with which they interrupted and spoke through each other's lines were a revelation to me. It was one of the great and exciting experiences of my theatrical life.

We were tingling with pleasure as we came out and strolled along Piccadilly. George Alltree, Clare's manager, came toward us.

"Why George," she cried, "don't look so serious! What's the matter?"

He stopped and looked at her like a loving but unhappy spaniel. "Clare, dear," he said, "I have bad news. The Ministry of Labour has refused permission for you to play Beatrice in *Much Ado!*"

I played at the Arts Theatre again with Keneth Kent in A. A. Milne's *The Lucky One,* and made a ridiculous French Revolution film with Madeleine Carroll, called *Madame Guillotine.* We worked in a converted house down at Walton-on-Thames and were driven there daily at breakneck speed by a pimply faced young assistant named Amery. After some hair-raising escapes, we refused to ride with him. He was a very foolish and unpleasant young man and it did not surprise me when he turned up as an assistant announcer with "Lord Haw Haw" in the Second World War and was finally hanged. There was no script to this picture, which the director made up as he went along. We spent several days doing long shots, riding in and out in great excitement, and driving tumbrils through screaming mobs of extras. I noticed the director looked very tired. What was the matter, I asked him.

"Haven't slept for nights," he groaned.

"Why?"

"I sit up all night trying to figure out some close-up action
to match all these long shots!"

Working late one evening at the studio, I received a telephone call from Margalo Gillmore, who was dining with
Clare at the Robert Sherwoods' house in Regents Park. Clare
had been taken suddenly ill and a doctor had been called
who said she had eaten something that had poisoned her.
She had been put to bed and given a sedative and sent a
message that I was not to worry. Haunted by thoughts of
her previous operations, I spent a sleepless night, but she
seemed better the next day and I could only accept the doctor's diagnosis.

A letter arrived from a California lawyer informing her
that Sidney Howard had divorced her for desertion. There
was no financial or property settlement and no custody or
visitation rights of her daughter, but within a year the decree
would be absolute.

I started to rehearse a play, a translation of the old French
classic *Le Genre de M. Poirier*, with Jean Forbes-Robertson,
Horace Hodges, C. V. France, and George Curzon.

Suddenly Clare was ill again, with severe abdominal pains,
and once more back in the old nursing home in Richmond.
On the Monday of my opening she underwent a major operation for an intestinal stoppage. Next morning I told her my
first and only lie, that the play was a great success, and she
smiled happily. In point of fact, it was a dismal failure, and
destined to last only one week, the most terrible week of my
life.

My part in this play was long and very taxing, calling for
much bravura acting in the classic French comedy style. My

days were spent at the nursing home and my nights at Reggie's house. On Friday, they told me they had operated yet again during the night. When they told her they must do so she said only, "Very well, but don't tell Brian."

Friday's night's performance, to a tiny audience, was a nightmare for me. The costumes, the wigs, the make-up, the lights, the elaborate stylized dialogue were all links in a heavy chain which seemed to shackle me in unreality, suffocating and weighing me down. At last the curtain fell and I staggered to my dressing room. The stage manager awaited me, his face grave and solicitous.

"A car is waiting for you," he said. "You must go at once to Richmond."

For an instant my heart stood still. He put his hand on my arm.

"Yes, she is alive," he said, "but you must hurry."

With his help I tore off my costume and dragged on some clothes. As I sprang into Reggie's car the chauffeur slammed the door without a word and swung the car across the Strand and down onto the Embankment. It was raining in torrents. Skidding and swerving, taking impossible chances, we tore along by the river, down the Kings Road, over Putney Bridge, and across Roehampton Common. At last we roared up Richmond Hill and stopped.

The old doctor was waiting at the door and took me by the arm.

Nurses were round the bed. Her eyes, wide and terrified, were fixed on me and she fought for breath. I held her hand.

"If she can sleep," the doctor whispered, "she may have a chance."

And then, as if the gods spoke to announce their will, there was a sudden tremendous clap of thunder. For an hour the storm raged, lighting the room with brilliant flashes and filling the air with deafening explosions of sound. And so, holding my hand and looking desperately into my eyes, while the storm was still at its height, she passed away.

Someone at last helped me to my feet, laid me on a bed, and gave me an injection. When I awoke the day was clear and peaceful. Against a cloudless sky the trees stood dressed in golden autumn glory and through them I saw the Thames, flowing slowly down to Twickenham. Reggie came and took me home to Trumpeters House. Gently he helped me to a chair on the terrace and brought a coat to cover my knees. I sat, stunned, staring at the lovely garden.

"What about the shows today?" he said, at last.

Shows. What shows? Slowly my brain cleared and I remembered that it was now Saturday, that the play was closing but there were still a matinee and evening performance to give. I knew there would be almost nobody in the house, that, in the theatrical phrase, one would be able to shoot deer in the balcony. I asked him to phone the manager and explain that I would be unable to appear.

Reggie came back and we sat for a few minutes in silence. I felt his loyalty and friendship surrounding me. Finally he looked up.

"The manager sends you his sympathy," he said. "He was deeply shocked by the news about Clare. He asked me to tell you that he understands how you feel. He also said there is no understudy and he will have to close the theater."

Again we were silent. I looked at the English chrysanthemums in the border, burnished by the autumn sunshine. A flight of rooks swung slowly above the elms beyond the river.

I looked at my watch; it was noon. Unsteadily, I stood up. "Tell him not to close his theater," I said. "I will be there."

Four days later I stood before an open grave in Richmond Cemetery. Reggie was beside me. Finally the clergyman finished and in the silence that followed I heard a distant boom and the wail of a siren. It was exactly eleven o'clock on Armistice Day, the 11th of November, 1930, and the whole Western world came to rest for two minutes in memory of those who had died in the Great War. Kate North pressed a bunch of violets in my hand. It was dark, damp and cold, and I shivered as I watched the wooden box being lowered into an oblong hole newly dug in the wet earth. As it came to rest, there was a pause. I stepped forward and threw in the violets, then I turned and stumbled down the path. I tripped and fell. Reggie's arm helped me up and tried to hold me but I wrenched myself loose and began running, desperately, blindly seeking a way out of that terrible place.

I went on stumbling, tripping and falling; I went on blindly running, for the next twenty years.

CURTAIN

ACT II

Scene 1

America

IT WAS the last day of 1930, New Year's Eve, and faint sounds of revelry came to me as I lay in my berth aboard the old *Mauritania*. Built for speed, long and narrow, top-heavy with four funnels to give her a racy appearance, she pitched and rolled like a cork as she battled the storm which had struck as she cleared Cherbourg and headed west into the wintry Atlantic. Now and again the skylight of my cabin on the top deck was darkened by a gigantic wave which blew right over the ship. A knock on the door and in came a boy with a wireless message. Shakily, I opened it.

BON VOYAGE. KATHARINE CORNELL

How nice, I thought, how courteous Americans are compared to ourselves. Bracing myself against the roll of the ship, and trying to focus my eyes, I scrawled a reply:

MAL DE MER. BRIAN AHERNE

This was our first contact.

The events of the previous weeks crowded through my mind. At first, stunned by grief, I had shut myself up in my furnished rooms in Bayswater, guarded and gently cared for by my housekeeper, Miss Mead, and then one day I had re-

ceived an unexpected caller. Leon M. Lion, an eccentric
actor-manager whom I knew only slightly, had come to see
me and insisted that I should work. Under the influence of
his kindness, I had accepted a part in his production of a
trifling comedy called *A Marriage Has Been Disarranged,*
with Mary Newcombe and Lady Tree. I was very bad in it
and the play flopped in a week. Suddenly I had decided to
leave London and to accept one of the Hollywood offers
which at that time seemed always open to me. I made a test
for Winfield Sheehan of Twentieth Century Fox and was immediately offered the lead in the film of *Cavalcade,* to be
followed by a standard seven-year contract. I went home to
tell my parents that I was going to California. They accepted the news sadly. Nothing was said about my personal
sorrow, but both kissed me tenderly when I left and my father came to the station to see me off. "Take care of yourself,
old chap," he said. I can see him now, alone on the platform,
tall and distinguished in his shabby blue suit, and somehow
touchingly forlorn, as the London train carried me away.

Lilian Braithwaite invited herself to tea. A "Grande
Dame" of the theater, she could seem formidable to the
younger generation, as is the way with older English actresses — unlike the American stars, who tend to be formidable in youth and to diminish with age. Lilian could be kind
and gentle, as she now was to me, but she could be catlike if
she wished; her sharp witticisms were known as "Lils," and
widely quoted by actors.

"Eva Moore is to play in New York," said a friend. "Has
she a large part?"

"I shouldn't think so," murmured Lilian. "She went on a
very small boat."

Ivor Novello gave Fay Compton a large and expensive brooch.

"Dear Ivor," said Lilian. And then, after a pause, "He gave me one too. I'm wearing it. Can you see it?"

That dark, November afternoon, as we sat drinking tea before my coal fire, she was quietly sympathetic and kind. As she left, she said, "By the way, Guthrie McClintic, the husband of Katharine Cornell, is at the Ritz and would like to talk to you about playing Browning with her, in *The Barretts of Wimpole Street* in New York."

I had not seen the play, but I went to the matinee next day and thought it a fine, though rather flowery piece of writing. I much admired the performances of Gwen Ffrangçon — Davies and Cedric Hardwicke, and I thought the part of Browning short, difficult, and unrewarding. I felt the play as a whole needed cutting. I didn't stay in my seat for the last scene, but paused to watch it from the back of the house. Going into my rooms, I met actor Anthony Ireland, who lived above me, and told him of the Browning suggestion.

"Oh, why don't you do it, Brian," he said. "It's a nice bit — and you'll like New York. Heated rooms and good plumbing!" I made an appointment with McClintic for the following morning; my appointment with 20th Century-Fox was set for the afternoon.

A few years ago, after his death, I wrote a piece about Guthrie McClintic and our first meeting. Here is an extract from it:

Some of the old actor-managers, and some of the new ones for all I know, used to have all the stage lights raised one point on their entrance and lowered a point on their exit, so that their presence on stage made everything seem a bit brighter. Guthrie

McClintic's presence, whether on stage or in a room, had the same effect. One could laugh with him, cry with him, sometimes be angry with him, but one never failed to feel that in his presence life was warmer, brighter and more exciting. It is over thirty years since I myself first felt this. He and his wife, Katharine Cornell, had decided to go into management with *The Barretts of Wimpole Street*, a play which had been turned down by every manager on Broadway. They discussed the casting in Hollywood, where he was working and she was resting, and for some reason they thought of me for the part of Robert Browning. Neither of them had seen me so Guthrie set out for London, and a rough trip he had of it. It was the early days of the airliner and it was November, but he reached Kansas City the first day and spent the night in a hotel. The second day he had a wild ride through weather so bad that the pilot gave up and made a forced landing in a field where the plane tipped up on its nose. The passengers were told to jump out quickly because of the danger of fire and Guthrie, jumping from the tail, sprained his ankle and had to be carried to the train which took him on to New York. One might think that anyone of Guthrie's superstitious nature would have taken this as an omen and have given up the idea of hiring Brian Aherne, whoever he was, at that moment, but he was not deterred. Boarding a ship, he crossed the Atlantic in frightful, stormy weather and when he landed was stricken with some internal ailment which necessitated his going straight to bed in the Ritz Hotel. And that is where I first saw him, in bed.

I think that neither of us can have approached this meeting with enthusiasm. Disregarding doctor's orders, he had struggled to the Royalty Theatre to see my bad performance on the last night of our dismal week's run, and must surely have wondered how he could politely dismiss me without making the offer. For my part, as I went up to his room I was wondering how I could politely decline it. I was in for a big surprise. Instead of a high-powered American executive, such as had frightened me before from time to time, I met a quiet, sensitive gentleman, with smiling eyes, who put me instantly at my ease and gave me for the first time the sensation that both the theater and life in general were somehow warmer and more exciting than I had supposed. I asked him how he could consider me after seeing *A Marriage Has Been Disarranged,* but with a laughing gesture he waved it away, saying that anyone could have the misfortune to get into a bad play, and that anyway he had felt so ill he had only stayed for half an hour. I began to realize that I was talking to a very exceptional man and a genuine artist.

As we talked about the theater and mutual friends, I began to consider seriously in the back of my mind the part of Browning. "It *is* a nice bit," I thought, "and I don't think I could actually fall down in it." And I began to think how much happier I could be with this man than with those Hollywood characters who frightened me so much. Frankly I told him of the Hollywood contract awaiting my signature that afternoon. I also confessed that I was suffering from the effects of deep personal grief so that I hardly knew if I was equal to an important engagement, whether in the theater or in motion pictures. He heard me with quiet sympathy, and then he said, "I quite understand, and I only want to say that we would like you to come with us and we will do everything we can to help," and then his charming smile came again and he said impulsively, "Oh, why don't you chuck the movie contract and come and have a shot at it? If you're not happy we won't hold you. Just tell us and I promise we'll let you go home whenever you like!" And so it was agreed. A couple of years later, when he telephoned me from New York to invite me to play Tarquin in *Lucrèce*, he said gaily, "Same deal, you know! If you're not happy we won't hold you!"

And so for the second time I approached the U.S.A., this time the classic westerly way, coming in slowly past Sandy Hook to stop off Staten Island for the officials to come aboard, and also a telegram from Guthrie McClintic: "Please make yourself available to the Press." The New York press! I shuddered at the thought and kept an apprehensive eye open as we passed the Statue of Liberty, Ellis Island, the fantastic skyscrapers of the downtown block, and finally, with much fussing of powerful little tugs, swung around and inched into the dock at 43rd Street, but the only person waiting for me was a tall, gentle man who introduced himself as Alan Atwater, the Cornell-McClintic company manager. A hotel room was reserved for me, he said, and I should rest until eleven when the McClintics would pick me up and take me to their house up the Hudson for the weekend. Courteously he steered me through customs, explained the value of American money, and took me to the New Weston Hotel, and for the first time I felt around me the warm protecting arm of these wonderful people, a comforting feeling I was to know many times in the years that followed. In this, their first venture into management, they set a standard of care for the welfare of their company which they always maintained, and which I have only seen equaled by Dion Boucicault.

Late that night I met Katharine Cornell. We picked up Eugenie Leontovitch after her performance of *Grand Hotel* and drove to the small, comfortable house in Sneden's Landing which has always remained for me a haven and a place of enchantment.

(William) Brian de Lacy Aherne at the age of four

The author's parents. The probability is that Mother was out of earshot (*see page 1*) when Father uttered the un-Victorian word "Damn!" which set this book, as well as the author's career, in motion

Lacy and Lulu's impressive wedding tableau includes "The Pater" and "The Mater" (*extreme left but one*) and "Gag" (*far right*)

Set piece at five

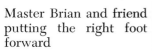

Master Brian and friend putting the right foot forward

On tour in Australia in 1926: in Barrie's *Mary Rose*, Act I

Mary Rose, Act III

Valentine Brown in *Quality Street*

As John Shand in *What Every Woman Knows*

Clare Eames, whose tragic early death cut short a brilliant career in the theater

Katharine Cornell, superb actress and longtime friend

American film debut with Marlene Dietrich in *The Song of Songs*, 1933

With Helen Hayes in movie of *What Every Woman Knows*, 1934

Sylvia Scarlett with Katharine Hepburn, 1935

I Live My Life with Joan Crawford, 1935

With Merle Oberon in *Beloved Enemy*, 1936

With Olivia de Havilland in *The Great Garrick,* 1937

Captain Fury with Victor McLaglen, 1939

Maximilian to Bette Davis' Carlotta in *Juarez,* 1939

Lady in Question with Rita Hayworth and Glenn Ford, **1940**

My Son, My Son with Madeleine Carroll, 1940

With Jeanette Macdonald in *Smilin' Through*, 1942

Once again with Joan Crawford, in *The Best of Everything*, 1959, and in a scene written by the author himself

Overseas during World War II with *The Barretts of Wimpole Street* (Katharine Cornell, McKay Morris and Margalo Gillmore), in which, as Robert Browning, the author had made his successful New York stage debut in 1931

Robert Browning and fans

The Constant Wife with Katharine Cornell and Grace George, 1952

Quadrille with Edna Best, Lynn Fontanne and Alfred Lunt, 1954

My Fair Lady with Anne Rogers, 1957–1958

Shades of Mrs. Rice's dancing class

Brian Aherne and his former wife, Joan Fontaine, at the home of Dale Warren on the South Shore of Massachusetts in 1941

With José Iturbi and Ruth Chatterton who introduced the author to the pleasures of flying in the the early 1930's

The author's first and favorite plane, a red and black Waco F3 biplane with a checkerboard tail, in which he made several solo transcontinental flights

With Greer Garson in *Ways And Means* for British War
Relief

Check for proceeds from the movie *Forever and a Day* — made by
Hollywood actors, writers and directors of English nationality —
is given to President Roosevelt (participants include Basil O'Connor,
Joan Fontaine, Roland Young and Lady Hardwicke)

On two of the many U. S. camp tours made during the war years;
"Just talk to the boys and girls," the author was told. "They like
to see you"

Actor turned farmer

View of the author's ranch (*lower right*) and surrounding land
in Thermal, California

Mr. and Mrs. Brian Aherne

Rehearsals, with Charles Waldron as Mr. Barrett, Joyce Carey and Margaret Barker as the sisters, and Brenda Forbes as Wilson, took place in the McClintic house on Beekman Place, overlooking the river, and later on the stage of the Empire Theater, now torn down to make way for a modern office building. Jo Mielziner designed a beautiful production, the only flaw in which — though neither I nor anybody else ever seemed to notice it — was that my clothes as Browning belonged to a period years before that of the play; like the unsuitable backdrop of *White Cargo*, they were accepted by the audience without comment. Even Helene Pons, who made them, was heard to exclaim "Oh! I am in lov! Wiz Mr. Browning's trousers!" They were indeed beautiful, but quite inappropriate. Incidentally, so well were they made that when we last did the play in New York, after our return from our long tour overseas with the Army in 1944–45, we all wore the original costumes, slightly let out perhaps, but still serviceable. Gertrude Macy, a wonderful girl who became my loyal and lifelong friend, acted as general manager, stage manager, and Miss Cornell's personal secretary, a combination of duties which she has been expertly juggling ever since.

McClintic's enthusiasm, invention, and romantic fervor swept us all along, and under his direction Robert Browning became suddenly and excitingly clear to me. I believe this play was more important to him than any other in his long career. As I heard his fervent voice read some passages it suddenly came to me that I had heard such words before from another voice which had brought me love and assurance, as Robert did to Elizabeth, like a burst of spring sunshine. Suddenly I experienced that blessed moment that all actors pray for, the moment when the character springs to life. I knew how Robert Browning spoke and moved and felt, and I was happy.

On February 15th, 1931, we opened to rapturous applause at the Hanna Theater, Cleveland, a city which, by an extraordinary coincidence, was the birthplace and home of Clare Eames. Her parents still lived there, but I did not meet them. The wound on both sides was too deep and too recent. I stood in the pale winter sunshine outside the house in Euclid Heights which had known her so well and looked at it until the tears blinded me and I moved away. The next week we played Buffalo, Katharine Cornell's hometown, and there the electric sign on the marquee read:

KATHARINE CORNELL
BUFFALO'S OWN

I have often been told, and have read, that the opening of *The Barretts of Wimpole Street* at the Empire Theater, New York City, was a memorable night in the theater. I was strangely unmoved. I knew nobody out front. The play obviously went well and I was pleased with my performance. Afterwards, I walked alone up Fifth Avenue and went into Childs for something to eat before going to my room at the Gotham Hotel. Next morning, I looked at the notice in the *New York Times.* After a glowing approval of the play, the critic spoke rapturously and at length about Miss Cornell's beautiful performance and finally passed to mention of other members of the cast. Of myself, he said, "As Robert Browning, Brian Aherne fills the theater every time he steps on the stage." Well, I thought, it's not much, but it's all right. I didn't read any others. Why should I? I didn't care.

During the following months it might be supposed that I who, it seemed, had become overnight the new romantic sensation of Broadway, should have had a wonderful time, but I was not capable of that. I have sometimes wondered why I did not seek psychiatric help at this time. Grief can become a sickness which needs trained help, but although I knew about it, I did nothing. My upbringing, my education, and my whole English background had instilled into me the necessity for self-reliance. "How can you hope to govern others," they had said to us at Malvern, "unless you learn to govern yourself?" The others they spoke of were presumably the Wogs, the Fuzzie-Wuzzies, and the Hottentots they expected us to be governing in the far-flung reaches of the British Empire, where the jungles and deserts held no psychiatrists and a man must solve his problems alone.

For a few hours each day, it was well that I was occupied with my performance of Browning, but though superbly placed in the action of the play, it is a very short part, a mere seventeen "sides" in the script, with more time spent in the dressing room than on the stage, and I never found him truly satisfying. Furthermore, he is difficult to play correctly; he does not "play himself," as some parts do, and needs exactly the right touch, tempo, and attack to make his proper effect; on many of the thousand or so performances of him which I subsequently gave, I felt that I failed. One such that I remember was the opening night of the last revival we did, at the Barrymore Theater in 1945. Coming direct from the huge, cavernous Opera House in Boston, I failed to judge the pitch of the Barrymore, overplayed, and got a deservedly bad press for it next day. Perhaps it is not generally wise for an actor to challenge critical opinion a second time in a part

in which he has been successful. Laurence Olivier once said
to me, "If you have made a hit, don't try to repeat it. Put it in
a bag, lock it away, and do something else!"

This was the moment, shortly after the talking picture had
conquered the screen, when the Hollywood studios were
combing the world for new talent, and now I began to receive a flood of offers from studios, agents, directors, and talent scouts; they haunted the stage door, called me at all
hours, dogged me in the streets with suggestions, arguments,
and temptations. When we took *The Barretts* on the road,
they turned up in strange cities. Paramount even sent a senior executive to Kansas City who, failing to contact me,
boarded the company train and rode to Los Angeles with us,
sitting across from me at meals and constantly waylaying me
for a friendly chat. The pressure on Miss Cornell was even
greater, of course. Irving Thalberg, the young genius who,
under L. B. Mayer, ruled Metro-Goldwyn-Mayer, had turned
down my test five years before, pursued us both with gentle
insistence, and went so far as to offer to make a major picture
with Miss Cornell, to show it to her and then, if she did not
like herself in it, to destroy it! She would not agree even to
this extraordinary contract, which would surely have been
unique in the annals of the motion-picture industry. My own
offers seemed to be standard, so that any choice lay between
the people who made them. Financially, they offered a
seven-year exclusive contract, with one year guaranteed
and the others a series of six options to the studio, but none
to the actor. Starting salary was usually $500 a week for
forty weeks in the year, rising $250 each time an option was
taken up.

I did a lot of thinking about the movies during the years 1931 and 1932, and it did not seem to me that the game was worth the candle. The average professional life of a successful star, then as now, seemed to be roughly seven years; if at the end of that time he was very hot at the box office, of course he was free to sign a more lucrative contract either with his own studio or some other, but if, as seemed more usual, the public had begun to tire of him, the studio would be quite ready to wave him goodbye and start a new young sensation at $500 a week. What was the star to do then? "Option time" was a time of terror for many. Furthermore, the amount of money that could be saved on a seven-year contract, while living at the high Hollywood rate and paying commissions and taxes, was certainly not enough to support one for long after the salary stopped coming in. Many a young performer bought a house, a car, and maybe a yacht on the strength of some good notices in the press, the admiration of the fans, and the flattery of his own publicity department. Many a pretty girl and many a handsome boy, coming from poor circumstances in some little midwesten town, had their heads turned, drank of the Hollywood champagne, and awoke a few years later to an empty bottle and a hangover. Even if they were lucky enough to combine talent and brains with their beauty, it seemed to me that only a very few could hope to stay at the top, and even those had no control over the material they were given to work with. Some of the great stars could feel sufficiently secure to refuse a script, but the studios had a neat way of dealing with them; they were simply "put on suspension," which meant that their salary was stopped while the picture they had refused was made, and the lost time was added to the period of their contract. Eventually, it was Olivia de Havilland who, with great courage, broke this bond in the courts. Martin Gang, a then comparatively unknown lawyer, argued that the provisions of the California Statute of Limitations must apply to workers in the motion-picture industry as in others. The statute says that no employment contract in the State of California may be enforced for more than a period of seven years. Olivia, having taken several suspensions at Warner Brothers, reached the end of a seven-year contract to find that Warners still claimed a further three years of her services. In a long and costly action she won a court decision in her favor, which was bitterly resented by the producers, but earned her the gratitude of the profession.

Glittering, therefore, as the promises were, neither Miss Cornell nor I felt that we should abandon the theater in which it seemed we might have a so much longer and more satisfying life. Were we right or wrong? I cannot answer that question, even now. We could not foresee the decay of the theater, the collapse and change of the movie industry, or the emergence of television. Miss Cornell was on firmer ground than myself, because she was a great American star who now had her own management and all kinds of plans for the future. I was simply a talented young actor who happened to have made a success in a good part. The risk was greater for me, so I let it be known that I would be willing to make single-picture deals; but no studio was likely to invest money and time on an actor who might make a success and then go off to another studio for treble the salary, and at that time there were no takers.

At our opening in Los Angeles in April 1932, Douglas Fairbanks, Sr., brought a large party of movie greats for whom, as the house was completely sold, we had to put a line of small chairs right across in front of the orchestra, so that their brightly lighted faces stood up before us. It was an unnerving sight to see so closely the heads of Douglas and Mary, Douglas, Jr., and Joan Crawford, Irving Thalberg, and Norma Shearer, Norma Talmadge and Joe Schenk, Constance Bennett and Gilbert Roland, Charlie Chaplin, Ruth Chatterton and Ralph Forbes, John Gilbert and Ina Claire, and a dozen others, but that night I played my brilliant, baffling part well. Afterwards, Ruth Chatterton gave a smart party for Miss Cornell at her beautiful house in Beverly Hills. Stepping back from the buffet with a plate in my hand, I bumped into someone who stood, hard and unyielding, behind me. I turned in surprise; it was Sidney Howard, looking straight in my eyes, a few inches away. He said, "I seem always to be in your way, Brian!" For an instant we looked at each other, and then I said, "I am sorry, Sidney," and moved away. I never saw him again. He remarried and died tragically, crushed by a tractor against the wall of his barn in Massachusetts.

Douglas Fairbanks called me, full of friendly good humor. "Come and see me this afternoon," he said. "I'll send a car for you." I found him again at the United Artists studio, as vital and enthusiastic as ever. He showed me his steam room, his new machine for golf practice, and the pictures he had shot on a cruise of the Pacific and then, in a burst of boyish confidence, came to his great idea.

"Look here," he said. "I saw you act last night, and I think you are the just the fellow I have been looking for! Between you and me, they don't want me any more on the screen.

Fashions change in actors. I am old now and the American public only wants to look at youth. Besides, the talkies have come and I guess maybe my voice is not so good. Anyway, I don't sell like I used to. Now here's the thing: I don't want to retire — I want to direct! You see, I own all the properties I made in the past and my idea is to remake them as talkies — *if* I can find the right fellow to play the parts. Well, I have been looking them all over, and there are some good actors on the screen today, but they none of them have any vitality. That's what I must have for those parts — vitality! Now I saw you on the stage last night, and boy, you've *got* it! How would you like to play the parts and let me direct you?"

I listened in amazement. Douglas Fairbanks was my idol, the idol of every young man in the world. Who could ever replace him?

"I thought we would start with *The Mark of Zorro*," he went on excitedly. "How would you like that? Say the word and we can get going as soon as you finish with this play!"

Falteringly, humbly, I explained to him that the vitality which he saw on the stage in Browning was nervous, not physical. I was no athlete. I could not jump over haystacks or fight ten men at once, nor could I ever hope to follow Douglas Fairbanks in those glorious parts which he had made his own. To tell the truth, I was shocked by the very idea. After a moment's disappointment, he took it like the true gentleman he was; picking up a book, he wrote something on the flyleaf and gave it to me with a charming smile.

"Now," he said, "what would you like to do, go over the lot, or come up to Pickfair for a bite of early dinner before your show?" He had taken me over the lot in 1927, when he was making *The Black Pirate*. I wondered if he remembered that, but I didn't mention it, saying only that I would be grateful to see Pickfair. Chatting amiably about his travels in the Far East, he drove me through Beverly Hills, which he and Mary had helped to lay out in the early days, and up the winding Summit Drive to his famous house on the hill. Mary Pickford and her brother Jack joined us for a drink and Mary asked me directly if I was going into pictures. "No, darling," said Doug before I could answer, "I'm afraid he doesn't want to accept my suggestion. I am very sorry." Mary looked at me somberly. "I think he is quite right," she said. Doug laughed uneasily, and I watched her as she went to the window and looked out at the neat Pickfair garden. Then she spoke almost tragically of the futility of ambition and the evanescence of fame. It was my first encounter with the misery that attacks the great stars as their careers begin to fade. They are the gods and goddesses of the modern world and to ordinary mortals they seem to dwell on Olympus, so that we expect them always to be happily smiling, as they are in their photos. I felt as if I should not be listening, and this encounter with grim reality disturbed me very much.

After she left the room, Doug turned to me with a charming, reassuring smile. "I am sorry," he said. "Mary is a little depressed today. You see, motion pictures have been her whole life and she really has no other interest, whereas I am very lucky. I enjoy sports and traveling and all kinds of things, and I think my life will always be full of interest. Yes, I guess I am lucky." In later years I was to come to know a different Mary. Her religion became a great comfort to her and she wrote a touching little book called *Why Not Try God?* After her split with Douglas she found serenity and happiness in her marriage with Buddy Rogers.

As the chauffeur drove me down to the Biltmore Theater I opened the book Douglas had given me, and read what he had written in it. It said, "I am sorry — I thought you were Zorro! Douglas Fairbanks."

My encounters with the stars continued. Ramon Novarro, great silent-screen hero, gave a party at his hilltop house. "I suppose they are after you for pictures?" he asked. I agreed that they were. "They will promise you everything," he said bitterly. "You will get nothing!"

John Gilbert, the dashing debonair, surely the ideal screen male, was sweating out the balance of a lucrative contract signed just before the explosion of the talkies. With the imperfect, experimental sound of the day his voice seemed high and squeaky and he was instantly dubbed a flop. Metro-Goldwyn-Mayer were using every device to mortify and humiliate him so that he would be willing to tear up the contract or accept a settlement. The story ran that the studio called him down one night to do a scene in a picture, telling him to wear full evening dress. It was winter and the set was an outdoor pool, round which shivered a group of "dress extras."

"Now, Mr. Gilbert," they said cheerfully, "you come out of the house, see, with this girl on your arm, and then for a lark these drunks grab you and throw you in the pool, see?"

Jack could refuse and break his contract or do as he was told and continue to draw the money. He did as he was told. Something of course went wrong and he was told to do it again; he did. He was thrown into the icy pool many times that night, with the aid of a lot of whisky, and he continued to draw the money. It was not money such as a Burton or a Sinatra may draw today; his contract was only for three years. As a single man he paid high taxes, even then, and as a big star he had big expenses, so you may ask why he would suffer such treatment, why did he not walk out and do something else. Jack knew this was the end of his career in pictures. Still in his thirties, still occupying in the eyes of the public the position of a great star, he sat idly in his beautiful house on the hill, and while he held out his money would come to him every week for the duration of the contract, but like many other great stars, both then and now, he knew he faced professional extinction, personal nonentity, and complete inactivity. If motion pictures don't want him, where can a great screen star go? What can he do? How can a Gilbert or a Garbo live? The gods and goddesses cannot jostle with the crowd, cannot take a job in an office, go to a restaurant or to a shop, make a journey, stay in a hotel, or even walk the streets like ordinary mortals, without exciting amazement and attention. Jack bore his misery with outward grace, but the reason for his life was taken from him and I could see that inwardly he suffered cruelly.

Success usually comes to the business or professional man in the latter part of his life, but to the actor it comes, if at all, when he is too young to appreciate or evaluate it, and all too often he lacks the maturity and judgment to make the most of it. It would please me very much today to be in demand in Hollywood but at that time, having just passed my thirtieth birthday, I was confused and frightened by all that I saw and heard and I was relieved when *The Barretts* company moved to San Francisco, closed there, and disbanded in New York. I sailed for England feeling that I had escaped the grip of a monster which could destroy me.

Scene 2

Actor's Nightmare

UPPER PORCHESTER STREET seemed at first to be just as I left it, though perhaps rather smaller and more drab than I remembered. My dear, gentle Miss Mead smiled a welcome at the door, there was a good coal fire burning cheerfully in the grate and a nice English tea laid out on the table. I was glad to be home.

I think I expected to be bombarded with theatrical offers in the next few days, but as the weeks passed without any sign of interest from the world of the London theater or from my old contacts in the British film industry I began to feel uneasy. The proceeds of my American engagement, after expenses and taxes, would not support me indefinitely. Perhaps I was mistaken, but it seemed to me that an American reputation was regarded in London with suspicion, tinged possibly with envy, and this was the first time that I had some inkling of what foreigners mean when they accuse us of lacking warmth and generosity of spirit. I had been in America long enough to have become accustomed to the outgoing and easygoing American attitude; I now felt in England, as I certainly never had before, the curious, chilling effect of British inhibition and reserve, and although I understood it perfectly and was indeed myself by birth, upbringing, and education, an outstanding example of the British character, I nevertheless felt uneasy about it. Time has not, even now, eradicated this feeling, but I am better able to adjust myself to it. One just does not behave in England quite the same as one does in America and Australia, and the Australian girl on the sheep station who thought I was a stuffed shirt has had her counterpart, I fear, only too often in America. We British know ourselves — or think ourselves — to be warm, generous, and rather cozy, but unfortunately this is not the picture that we present to the world. Our manners have been formed by centuries of life on our cold, damp, and misty island and we are apt, when dealing with foreigners, to seem cold, damp, and misty to them. They don't understand because they live in bright, clear air and they are used to wide horizons where they must move fast to cover great distances and shout to make each other hear; they don't have time or necessity for all the complicated subtleties and reticences of English life.

My own parents, I found on my return, seemed curiously narrow, prejudiced, and almost exasperatingly dull. London, so filled with interest and excitement during my youth, so thrillingly romantic during my three golden years with Clare, seemed somehow stale and empty. I would walk the streets and squares as we used to do together and, as time passed, I began to be obsessed with the idea that her death had been only a nightmare, or that perhaps she had wanted to leave me and had tricked me in some way, that she was alive somewhere and if I looked hard enough I might find her — down that street perhaps, in that bus, round the next corner. Often I saw some chance resemblance from behind and I would run to catch a look at a startled stranger. I walked many familiar miles alone, always looking, looking. I sat on park

benches, at café tables where we had sat together. My
search became more and more desperate as I became con-
vinced she was hiding from me. There came a point where I
knew I must leave London if I were to preserve my sanity.
I went to Paris, but there again memories surrounded me. I
fled to Holland, Salzburg, Munich, and Bavaria. One day, on
a mountainside near Garmisch-Partenkirchen, it came to me
that there was a thing I had to do, a thing that would clear
this terrible obsession from my mind: I must go at once to
Richmond. Hurrying back to my room to pack, I found a
cable from Irving Thalberg, again offering me a film contract. I cabled my thanks and regrets and set out for England.

A couple of days later I walked slowly up the hill to the
grave — and there I stood, paralyzed with amazement and
horror. For there, on a new white tombstone, I read the
name of a man who had died only a few weeks before!

I ran down through the town, across Richmond Common
till I came, panting, to Trumpeters House. It seemed an age
before Eastwood in his black coat and striped trousers, def-
erential and impeturbable as ever, opened the door.

"Mr. Reggie is in the garden, sir," he said. "Oh, he will be
pleased to see you!"

I found Reggie limping along a sunny garden path lined
with English hollyhocks, delphiniums, and peonies.

"Oh Bri!" he cried delightedly. "Here you are at last!
How wonderful!"

I stammered out my appalling discovery. Yes, he said, the
Eames family had moved her back to America and buried
her again in Hagerstown, Maryland. He thought I knew
about it. Leaning on his cane and moving with difficulty

because of his arthritis, he led me to the terrace under the great Christopher Wren portico, where Eastwood served us tea. Soothed by the remembered peace and beauty of the place which in former years had meant so much to us, I accepted his invitation to stay with him until I felt able to return to my rooms. The trees in Porchester Square were bare, and hardly visible through the damp, London fog, when one evening Guthrie McClintic's cheerful, friendly voice came over the phone from New York. They had decided to do a translation, adapted by Thornton Wilder, of *Le Viol de Lucrèce* by the French writer André Obey. Would I come over and play Tarquin for them?

Lucrèce had, I knew, been specially written for Jacques Copeau's young company, which he had meticulously trained in a special, stylized school of acting. I had seen this company and had been impressed by the extraordinary combination of ballet movement and vocal orchestration which Copeau used. I could not think that any company of actors, however talented, could reproduce the same effect under normal conditions of rehearsal, an effect which was only suggested by the script and which must have taken months of painstaking work and complete dedication. Tarquin, the seducer, had only a dozen lines and had mostly to be pantomimed. I was dubious about the whole idea. McClintic's enthusiasm, however, was as compelling as ever, his kindness as warm. After all, it would get me out of London. Despite my misgivings, I packed at once and embarked aboard the *Berengaria* on another stormy winter crossing.

I shall never forget the opening night of *Lucrèce* in New York. The play, with gorgeous settings and costumes by that old master Robert Edmond Jones, choreography by Martha

Graham, a gently radiant performance by Miss Cornell, and with several members of *The Barretts* company, Joyce Cary, Brenda Forbes, Charles Waldron, John Emery, and myself in the cast, was a costly beautiful bore and a monumental flop. But I have another, special reason to remember that first night, for a terrible thing happened to me.

The curtain was announced for 8:30 P.M., and since I had an elaborate make-up and rich, Renaissance costume to put on, I decided to be in my dressing room by 7:00. Following my usual custom, I ordered a light meal to be sent to my hotel room at 6:00 and at 5:30 I lay down for a rest. When I awoke, the room was very quiet and I had a strange feeling that something was wrong. I lay for a minute before it struck me that it seemed unusually dark outside. I put on the light and looked at the clock: it read five minutes to eight! No, I thought, it's not possible — this is the actor's nightmare, the dream that has awakened me, shuddering with horror, so many times in my life — the dream that I am too late, that I haven't learned the lines, can't find the clothes . . . Suddenly I was galvanized into action. Grabbing the phone, I confirmed it — six minutes to eight!

My tie, my shoes, my jacket, coat, and hat, a rush to the elevator. I ring for it and I wait, and I wait, a year, ten years — oh God! why won't he come? Downstairs the lobby is filled with people, theatergoers through whom I push my way. Outside they fill the pavement, looking for taxis. A taxi! I *must* have a taxi! I run down the street and suddenly I see a woman getting out of one. Pushing a man and two women aside, I jump in and slam the door in their faces. Thick, heavy traffic — a sudden break down Sixth Ave. — jammed again at 44th St. I jump out and run, panting, to the Belasco, where the audience is already going in. There is

the usual anticipatory hush backstage. Apparently nobody
has missed me and I meet nobody as I rush up to my room,
tearing off my clothes as I go.

The tights first — oh Christ! they're on backwards! Tear
them off and start again — keep calm — think, think — get
the costume on, so that at least you can go on stage — now a
quick slap of make-up, only a smear of color, no more —
spirit gum on the face, find the scissors, cut the crepe hair
for the beard, stick it on and trim it with shaking fingers.
"Beginners please!" The sound of everybody going down to
the stage. "Good luck old man!" A head in the door — "Oh!
Got your wig off? Better hurry, hadn't you?" "O.K. I'm
coming!"

Shall I send a message, telling Gert Macy to hold the curtain? I can't! I don't dare! Everybody is out front who matters, the critics, society, the whole theatrical world. Great
reputations and a big investment are at stake and this is the
starting gate, the moment of truth, the climax of months of
work and planning.

My hands shake so that I drop the scissors, my wig slips
sideways and I drag it straight — there is no time to glue it
down. The stairs are silent now. I fumble with the laces of
my high Renaissance shoes. A voice calls; "Mr. Aherne on
stage please!" "Thank you, I'm coming!" Breastplate, cloak,
belt and sword — down the stairs, three at a time, and
then quietly onto the stage. Nobody must suspect, become
alarmed, least of all Miss Cornell. The voice of the audience
stills as the houselights dim. As I take my place the stage
goes dark. Gert whispers from the prompt corner, "Everybody ready? Attention please! Curtain going up!" There is
the sibilant sound of the curtain as it rises. Ted Emery
speaks the opening line and the audience gives us the usual

welcoming round of applause. I am here! Zippers and buttons may not be fastened, the seams of my tights are probably crooked, my make-up sketchy, my wig-join showing and my beard sprouting in tufts and patches, but I am here and nobody knows it might have been otherwise. I am here, that's all that matters; now I must keep steady, speak firmly, move with authority — I am here, I am an actor, and the curtain is up. But suppose I had not been there; suppose I had not wakened when I did?

The next morning I learned that the waiter with my tray had knocked long and loud at the wrong door and, failing to get an answer, had gone away.

The telephone jerked me from a sleep of exhaustion. "Mr. Rubin would like to speak to you." J. Robert Rubin, head of the Metro-Goldwyn-Mayer office in New York, one of the great powers of the motion-picture industry, a smooth, polished man, a man of steady gaze and highly trained legal mind who ranked beside Nicholas Schenk, Louis B. Mayer, and Irving Thalberg at the summit of MGM in later years to become my friend, but now a rather frightening figure.

"Good morning, Brian," he said pleasantly. "How would you like to go out to the coast pretty soon at our expense and have another discussion with Irving about a contract?"

"What?" I said. "I can't do that, Mr. Rubin. I opened last night in *Lucrèce* with Miss Cornell."

"Oh yes, I know, but I shouldn't think that will hold you long, will it?"

"Good Heavens!" I cried. "Are the notices as bad as that?"

"Oh yes, I'm afraid so."

There is nothing so unnerving and wounding to an actor as a theatrical failure; the failure of a film is shared by so many others, and mainly by the producer and director, that the actor just feels unlucky, and he gets his money anyway, but in the theater he seems to be directly responsible. He loses not only money but reputation which, as Iago says, "is oft got without merit and lost without deserving." Few critics can perceive bad writing and nobody who is not familiar with a manuscript can judge the direction of a play, but everybody can see what the actor is doing — or thinks he can see it — and can blame him if the thing doesn't come off. Worst of all, failure undermines the actor's faith in his own judgment, and this can be a painful wound. We were all very depressed while the play lasted.

The day after we closed was cold, dark, and wet, reminding me that I would soon be back in London looking for a job. I decided to distract myself by going to the movies. The film was *Shanghai Express,* in which I saw for the second time the new and ravishingly beautiful star Marlene Dietrich, whose beauty seemed even greater than it had in *The Blue Angel.* I floated back to my hotel room like any moonstruck movie fan. Next morning I received a call from Jesse Lasky of Paramount Pictures asking me if I would play the lead in their forthcoming picture of *Peter Ibbetson,* and before I could draw breath to refuse, he added, "As this is a great starring part and as you are of course unknown to the American motion-picture public, we would like to ask you to agree to play first opposite Marlene Dietrich in her new picture which is just about to start, *The Song of Songs.* We feel this would be an excellent introduction for you."

Well, I have to admit that I forgot about Irving Thalberg and J. Robert Rubin and Metro-Goldwyn-Mayer. The London theater and the London fog suddenly didn't seem very attractive when success, money, sunshine, and Miss Dietrich beckoned me to California. Within a few hours, Paramount officials were shepherding me into a drawing room on the Twentieth-Century Limited, though I hadn't read the script, I had no agent, and I had no contract; one of them rode as far as Harmon with me to draw up a letter of agreement for my signature. I had no idea what money to ask and accepted his suggestion of $10,000 per picture, which seemed a fortune to me. The next morning I walked into the dining car of the Sante Fe Chief, out of Chicago, sat down, picked up the menu, and heard a familiar voice saying in astonishment, "Well! And where are you going?"

I looked up and my blood ran cold for there, facing me, his cool gray eyes wide with suspicion, was Mr. J. Robert Rubin.

The next three days were very hard for both of us. I knew nobody on the train but Mr. Rubin; he knew nobody but me. After the first shattering explanations, which he seemed hardly able to comprehend, we did our best, and I stayed in my room as much as possible, but as we rode across the farmlands, the badlands, the mountains, and the deserts of America, we met repeatedly in the dining car and club car and struggled to make polite conversation.

So here I was, in Hollywood at last! Warm sunshine, flowers in the garden outside my window, attentive voices from Paramount Studio on the telephone, a limousine and chauffeur awaiting me; why, I wondered, had I any hesitation about coming before? It all seemed too good to be true — and it was.

I lunched at the Paramount Studio commissary with my director, Ruben Mamoulian, and afterwards he gave me a script of *The Song of Songs* to read. I sat alone in a small studio office and turned the pages with my heart slowly sinking; it was no more than a rough outline of a thin little story about a German peasant girl who falls in love with a young sculptor and is betrayed by him. It was no good, I had no doubt of that, and my part was a thankless one. I wondered how Marlene Dietrich could have been induced to accept it. Nowadays, pictures can succeed without stars, but at that time it was a name like hers that drew the public into the theaters; two bad pictures and they would not be drawn; three, and the studio would regard her as an unprofitable investment and fail to take up her option. Small wonder the stars were anxious, for they were in the Big Game and playing with loaded dice which they had not chosen. On the other hand, the front-office executives often regarded the stars with angry impatience; a big studio, after all, was a factory which employed hundreds of people continually and thousands intermittently; production could not stop because of the whim of some spoiled young beauty who might be replaced the following year by another, and the Hollywood moguls felt, with some reason, that the man who pays the piper calls the tune.

I put down the script of *The Song of Songs* in blank despair. I got up and paced the floor. What should I do? Should I go back to the hotel, pack my bags, get on a train, take passage on a boat, and make the long journey back to London? In other words, should I run away? I opened the door and looked out into the silent corridor, half inclined to do so. Somewhere in the distance, a typewriter clicked. On the door opposite I saw the name Louis D. Lighton. He was, I knew, a very distinguished producer, the man who made

Wings, Skippy, Lives of a Bengal Lancer, Captains Coura-geous, Anna and the King of Siam, and many other wonder-ful pictures, and was a close friend of the McClintics. On an impulse, I went in and introduced myself to him, placed my problem squarely before him, and asked his advice.

"No," he said, "you cannot walk out like that. If you do so, the studio can sue you for heavy damages, but even if they should decide not to do so, you can be sure that no Holly-wood studio would ever employ you again." I thanked him and from that moment we established a friendship which re-mained close and strong until his tragic death in Mallorca, twenty years later. He was right. I, who had a choice, had chosen wrong, but I had signed this contract and must abide by it, relying on *Peter Ibbetson* to rescue me. Meanwhile, there was nothing for it but to do the best I could with the part. Daily, I expected Miss Dietrich to float in on her cloud of mysterious beauty; finally she arrived. The beauty was there, all right, but instead of mystery I encountered a very practical woman.

"Why have you come to do this silly picture?" she asked at once. "I have to do it because of my contract, and because Mr. von Sternberg has walked out and I am left without any protection, but you are the great actor from New York and can do what you like. Are you crazy?"

I was too embarrassed to tell her the foolish truth, that I had come to meet her, but she was soon laughing and she baked me a fabulous Viennese cake; she is a great cake-maker.

There are two kinds of actors. There are those who, like Ronald Colman, Gary Cooper, Clark Gable, James Stewart,

John Wayne, and Cary Grant, play themselves and continue to do so in every part, to the great delight of the producers, the stockholders, their fans, and their bank managers. There are also those, like Paul Muni, Laurence Olivier, Alec Guiness, and Rex Harrison, who are not interested in projecting their own personalities but in trying to look and sound like the characters they have to play, and these are known in the profession as "actors' actors." They seem to do their best when they hide their own personalities behind a make-up or a prop, like the actor in the old theatrical story who was unable to feel at home in his part until the director gave him a green umbrella to carry, when everything suddenly came right for him. A few, like Charles Laughton, Spencer Tracy, and Frederic March, looked for cover but had personalities so strong that they came through anyway. The green umbrella lot, to which I belonged, can be a sore trial to directors, and especially to movie directors, who have to work fast, because such actors have to evolve their creations slowly, and it is not immediately apparent what they are going to do. I thought that, as *The Song of Songs* was a period piece, I might make an offbeat character of my part, but I was unable to explain this to Reuben Mamoulian, who insisted that I play the character as a straight romantic lead. Conflict developed and he took a firm stand.

"Somebody has to be captain of this ship," he said, "and it is going to be me! You will do what I say, and I will take full responsibility."

I knew very well that, in the final result, responsibility is always borne by the actor, and I had no reason to feel any extraordinary confidence in Mamoulian, but neither my interest nor my conviction was too strong, so I gave in. I was unhappy about it, as I fear was all too apparent on the screen, for lack of conviction does not produce a good performance, but I doubt if it would have made any difference to the fate of the picture, and Ruben and I have remained very good friends.

The last day of shooting on *The Song of Songs* was one for the book. About sixty people were gathered on a set which represented my studio. By ten o'clock we had finished what was called the "establishing shot," in which Miss Dietrich entered and began to reproach me for my dastardly conduct. Mamoulian sat down, picked up the script, turned the page, and found nothing. "Where is the last scene?" he asked the script girl. "I don't know, Mr. Mamoulian. We have never received it." Miss Dietrich and I knew it wasn't there, but we had tired of asking useless questions. Mamoulian burned.

"Call the production office!" he roared. "Tell them to send the writer here at once!"

There was a pause. The assistant returned to say that there had apparently been seventeen writers on the script at various times, and the production office was not too sure who was on it now, but they promised to find out and let us know. After another and prolonged pause, word came that the writer had been identified and called, but his wife said he was out; on his return, she would send him down to the studio.

There being nothing else to do, Mamoulian called, "Lunch, everybody!" and we all left the set. Miss Dietrich went to her dressing room to bake a cake, while I went to mine to consider, once more, how I could manage to bake Miss Dietrich.

Late that afternoon, we were called back to the set, where we found Mamoulian arguing with a rumpled character named Sam Hoffenstein. He had published a slim volume of verse, which had had some success, entitled *Poems in Praise of Practically Nothing*, which, I suppose, had led Paramount to believe that he was the right man for *The Song of Songs*. He was now indignantly defending himself.

"This is really too much!" he was saying. "I've been off this damned thing for weeks! I'm busy on something else!"

"Oh, now Sam," pleaded Mamoulian, "come on — help me! Just give me some words — a page will do. We've got to finish the picture today."

Sam scratched his head and grumbled about a bit, and then delivered himself of a line which will always endear him to me.

"Goddamn it!" he cried. "I don't see how I can write any words for this scene. It seems to me that it is up to the actors to convey it!" With that, he left the set.

We all took pencil and paper, and sat around writing suggested endings. Mine, of course, finished with a long, strong speech for myself, and we actually shot it, but next day the front office said it wouldn't do at all, so we were called back another day to shoot a scene written by Mamoulian himself.

Accustomed as I was to the rapid shooting on an English set, where every penny counted, I was astonished at the slowness of the work on a major Hollywood picture. Often we made no more than two or three shots a day at that time. When we were about to start the picture, I had received an offer from the great London manager, C. B. Cochran, to play Branwell Brontë in Clemence Dane's play *Wild Decembers*, with Diana Wynyard, who had made a name for herself in the film of *Cavalcade*. I had accepted a rehearsal date in London which seemed quite reasonable, but to my dismay *The Song of Songs* ran on so long that I was nearly three weeks late leaving Hollywood. To gain time, I ventured on the primitive airline of those days and was airsick all the way to Kansas City, where the flight stopped for the night; next morning, I had to beg off and go on by train to New York. I missed my boat and arrived in London in time for only a few days' rehearsal. Naturally, everybody in the company hated me. At the dress rehearsal I was all at sea and miserably unhappy.

The following day, a surprising and heartwarming thing happened. It was Sunday morning and the sun was shining. As I sat gloomily at my breakfast, the phone rang; it was Mr. Cochran, whom in fact I had never met, inviting me down to lunch at his house in the country. Gratefully, I accepted. In the afternoon he took me for a stroll in the garden and asked me kindly if I was happy in the part. I replied rather violently that I was not.

"In that case," he said, "why do it? If you wish, I could postpone the opening for a few days and get someone else, but you must tell me now. Do just as you wish, of course."

I knew this meant a loss of money and a great deal of work and worry for him, but he spoke so kindly and so directly to me that I had no hesitation in accepting his offer on the spot. Cochran was not only a great showman; he was also, to use a word that is little understood these days, a gentleman.

My next blow, not altogether unexpected, was a check from Paramount in payment for *Peter Ibbetson*, the second picture I was supposed to make under our contract, together with the polite intimation that they did not feel the public

response to my initial appearance on the screen was sufficiently warm to warrant continuance of our association.
This was the first and last time I was ever paid for doing
nothing and it was not an enjoyable experience. As I sur-
veyed the past year, with the failures of *Lucrèce* and *The
Song of Songs* and the debacle of *Wild Decembers*, it was
apparent to me that I had really come to the end of my acting career. The time had come, I thought, to abandon this
foolish, precarious profession and to look seriously for another job, a proper job which would fill my life with occupation and interest. An old idea surfaced in my mind: why
should I not study law and become a barrister? My grandfa-
ther Thomas had been a very successful lawyer in Birmingham and perhaps I had inherited an interest from him. The
drama of an English court appealed to me, and in my early
years I had spent many fascinating hours listening to the
great barristers trying cases both in Birmingham and London, but then I had had no money to study; now, I thought, I
might have enough, with care, to see me through. It seemed
to me that my theatrical experience should prove very useful
at the Bar and later, if I were sufficiently successful, in politics. I had already bought some lawbooks and made prelim-
inary enquiries when, one day, a little London theatrical
agent came unannounced to my door and asked me hesitantly if I would accept the part of Lewis Dodd in a British
film of *The Constant Nymph* to be directed by Basil Dean.
Six weeks in the Austrian Tyrol and a month in London,
with a fine English cast.

"What made you think of me?" I asked him.

"Oh well," he said admiringly, "everybody knows of your
success in America. You have a big name now, and we are all

waiting to see your picture with Marlene Dietrich!" He suggested a figure 50 percent higher than Paramount had paid
me for *The Song of Songs*.

Nothing succeeds like success, said Oscar Wilde, and he
might have added, real or imaginary. I realized this was a
miracle of timing and for once I seized my opportunity.

"Thank you," I said. "I'll do it!"

The picture was a great success and I won the annual British Press Award for the best performance of the year by any
actor. I was up again! It was hard to believe.

I saw *The Song of Songs,* which was rubbish but perhaps
not quite as bad as I feared, and I cannot remember it with
entire regret, because through it I made a lifelong friend who
is very dear to me, Marlene Dietrich. Those of us who know
her well must always regard her as one of the most extraordinary women of our time. She was and still is a great and
glamorous beauty who has created from her own intelligence
and cultivation a unique position in the estimation of people
everywhere. A curious mixture of sophistication, complication, and simple domestic virtues, she is exceptionally well
educated for a woman, well-read in several languages, in-
nately musical, wayward, humorous, autocratic, self-reliant,
and fiercely loyal to those whom she admits to her friendship. Her little book of wisdoms, *Marlene Dietrich's A.B.C.,*
is unusual and revealing.

Time went by as I waited for news of *The Constant
Nymph* to reach Hollywood. Katharine Cornell asked me to
go on a very long coast-to-coast tour with her, playing Browning, Romeo, and Morell in *Candida*. This was a very hard
decision to make, especially as I had nothing to put against

her offer, but in the end I felt I could not again face the loneliness of American hotel rooms, the desolate streets of strange
cities in winter, the uncomfortable train journeys and the
limited society of a touring company. Risking injury to our
friendship, I declined, and she took Basil Rathbone instead.
I plowed along with my lawbooks and I waited as the winter
slowly passed, like a fisherman who sits watching his line,
waiting for a tug, hoping for a bite.

Basil Dean, who had directed *The Constant Nymph*, persuaded me to play with Jessica Tandy, Leonora Corbet, and
Marie Lohr — dear Marie Lohr, an idol of my youth — in a
comedy called *Birthday*, written by the current young pansy
sensation of the day, which opened at the new Cambridge
Theatre and deservedly closed in a week, giving me another
failure to add to my string. On the seesaw of my life, this
was a very low moment. I felt I was finished in the London
theater, I had refused the Cornell-McClintic offer, *The Song
of Songs* had closed the doors of Hollywood to me, and the
British film industry was completely stagnant. To add to my
troubles, a lawyer friend poured cold water on my legal am-
bitions because of my age and lack of university education.

One night, as I sat alone and desolate before the coal fire
in my room, the soft voice of Irving Thalberg came over
the phone from Hollywood.

"Well, Brian," he said, "have you had enough? Are you
ready to sign with me and come out here to work?"

I had fled him down the arches of the years, and he had
pursued me gently and persistently. Now there he was, on
the line. But I didn't feel I had him hooked; on the contrary,
I felt he was the fisherman and I the helpless fish. I tempo-
rized, haggled for some days, and gave in to the extent of an

agreement to work six months annually in Hollywood, leaving six months for the theater.

"Breaking the habit of a lifetime," he cabled me. "I agree reluctantly to your terms."

"Aha!" I thought. "He has seen *The Constant Nymph!*" And once more I took ship across the Atlantic.

Scene 3

Tight Squeeze

O NCE MORE I faced the cool, gray eyes of J. Robert Rubin across his desk in the impressive MGM offices, high over Broadway. I handed him a sheet of paper on which, as I had no agent, I had written suggested clauses for the contract, and he examined it quizzically.

"I see you have a legal turn of mind," he said.

He added that he didn't believe that such an arrangement, so different from the straight term contracts at the studio, could be made to work successfully. However, since Thalberg was willing to try, he would embody it in a contract, and he notified me that my first assignment would be in J. M. Barrie's *What Every Woman Knows*, co-starring with Helen Hayes. This was good news because I had played the part of John Shand under Boucicault's direction in Australia and I knew that now, with my experience, I could give a better performance than I had given in the theater. Actors who recreate theatrical performances on the screen always have a great advantage, for they know the values of the part and are at home in it. Miss Hayes too had played Maggie with great success on Broadway, before she had triumphed in *Farewell to Arms* and *The Sin of Madeleine Claudet* on the screen. We would be supported by the wonderful actress Lucile Watson, together with Dudley Digges, Donald Crisp, and David Torrance, and directed by Gregory La Cava.

After the winter of my discontent, it seemed natural that it should be a bright spring morning when, a few days later, I signed the contract on Mr. Rubin's desk. I walked back along Fifth Avenue to the Gotham Hotel, feeling very happy. I had believed myself finished in Hollywood and now this wonderful engagement had fallen into my hands; but the day was not yet over, and my guardian angel, who had so suddenly awakened, had more good fortune in store for me. I found a message from John C. Wilson, a nice, amiable man who managed the theatrical affairs of Noël Coward and the Lunts, asking me to contact him immediately. After lunch I went round to see him. Would I care, he asked, to play the Barrymore part in *The Royal Family* in London, co-starring with the great English comedienne Marie Tempest and directed by Noël Coward?

Would I care? I was stunned. I had turned my back on the English theater, believing I was not wanted there, and here was this brilliant, flattering offer! When did they propose to do it, I asked? Well, he said, they had not decided, and much depended upon my availability. I told him of my MGM contract which would tie me up for six months, and told him too that I was leaving the next day for Hollywood. Perhaps, he said, they could wait that long; he would talk to Coward and wire me to the train. Two days later, a Western Union boy tapped on the door of my drawing room — paid for by MGM — with a telegram which agreed to my reporting in London for rehearsals in six months' time. The Santa Fe Chief seemed to ride on air all the way out to Los Angeles. How right I had been, I thought, to stand up to Thalberg, how wise, how clever! *What Every Woman Knows* would establish me in Hollywood and *The Royal*

Family could not fail to do the same in London. Perhaps, after all, acting was my proper job.

There is something in the electric atmosphere of New York that generates excitement and activity: plans are made, decisions taken, and business life moves in top gear. In the California sunshine, and even now in the California smog, things move slower, as many a top eastern executive discovers when he makes that flying trip out to pep up the lazy guys in the West Coast office. One has to change down, as it were. Within two days of my arrival I had signed a six-months' lease on a small house in Beverly Hills, bought an open Ford runabout, and hired a Filippino servant. I also called the MGM studio to report for work. A polite voice asked for my phone number and how to spell my name, welcomed me to California, promised to inform the production department and told me to take it easy.

After a week or so, a minor publicity man called to invite me to lunch at the studio. He seemed quite ignorant of my work but he was nice, asked me the stereotyped questions and made notes. When, I asked him, would *What Every Woman Knows* start shooting? He replied that he didn't know, but rather thought it might not be for some time. At these words, a faint feeling of uneasiness came over me, but I soon put it aside because, after all, six months is a long time and motion pictures were, in my experience, shot in six or seven weeks. After lunch, he walked me politely around the lot, and I thought how strangely silent a great studio can seem during working hours; the streets were almost empty of traffic and the back lot looked like a deserted Disneyland. We looked in on a couple of stages where pictures were shooting. They were filled with people, all of whom seemed

to be waiting. I saw no recognizable stars. Finally we came
to a small white building surrounded by a discreet little
lawn. The publicity man lowered his voice respectfully.
"Mr. Irving Thalberg's office," he said.

A thought struck me. "I think I'll go and see him," I said,
and in I went. I gave my name, took a seat as requested, and
waited patiently for a long time. Just as I was about to get up
and leave, a buzzer sounded, and I was ushered in. The
slight, boyish figure of Thalberg rose from behind a desk that
almost hid him and came to greet me, his soft, oriental brown
eyes smiling gently as he took my hand.

"Well," he said, "it's about time you came to see your new
boss." He indicated a chair.

I stiffened slightly. Did I detect a faint note of triumph in
his voice, in the implication that he was the boss and I the
employee? When I finished this picture, I would be off to a
triumph on the London stage, which seemed to me of greater
importance than any film, but I thought with secret satisfaction that I would not tell him about that yet. Why should
I?

"When do we start shooting, Irving?" I asked.

He took a coin from his pocket and tossed it slowly up and
down.

"Shooting?" he murmured.

"Yes — *What Every Woman Knows* — I'd like to talk to
you about it."

"Oh, that." He sat on the edge of his desk. "Not yet, I'm
afraid. We are working on the script, but I am not yet satisfied."

I stared at him. "Irving," I said, "you know I am here only
for six months."

The coin stopped for a moment and he looked at me directly. "I am well aware of the terms of your contract Brian," he said, "and as you are well aware, I don't like them. If all the stars on this lot were only available for a few months in each year, it would be impossible for us to produce motion pictures!"

I said nothing. The coin started again. "I have decided," he continued, "to start you in a comedy with Joan Crawford called *I Live My Life*. It will be very good for you to be presented to the American public with a very great star who draws heavily at the box office."

I saw the justice of this, but I could not conceal my disappointment. "You will let me do *What Every Woman Knows?*" I asked.

"Oh yes — later," he replied easily. He put the coin in his pocket and stood up, holding out his hand. "Well," he said, "it was nice of you to stop by. I hope we shall see something of you socially as well as professionally while you are here. Goodbye."

I found myself in the outer office.

It is not my intention to describe every picture and play in which I worked through the years, nor to comment on all the stars and directors with whom I have been associated, but of some who stand out in my memory I shall speak. *I Live My Life* was gay and often amusing, rather better than the average comedy of its time. Miss Crawford was friendly and extremely professional, and dear Frank Morgan gave one of his inimitable comic performances. I remember the picture chiefly for the pleasure I got from watching the director, W. S. Van Dyke. An ex-captain in the U.S. Marines, he was a tall, thin, wiry man with a twinkle in his eye and usually a full tumbler of neat gin in his hand. He addressed all men as "kid" and all women as "honey."

"All I ask, kid," he said to me before starting, "is that you know your lines and that you are on the set at ten to nine in the morning, ready to shoot at nine. I shall never keep you after six. You will enjoy the picture." I did.

Shooting a motion picture with Van was much like shooting a television show today. One take was enough for him. He liked experienced actors because they were more likely to give him the scene on the first take. It was said that Garbo, starting her first day's work with him and unaware that the camera was rolling, came through a door and walked down a flight of stairs. As she reached the bottom, Van cried, "Cut! Print it! Now we move to stage eight!" He turned to go.

"Mr. Van Dyke," she said. He stopped. "Shall we not do it again?"

He looked surprised. "Honey," he said, "there's only one way to walk downstairs."

Garbo considered this for a moment and then she gave him a tiny smile. "I like it," she said.

Most of the great directors of that day made many takes — indeed, it seemed the more important they were, the more they made, finally printing three or four and perhaps holding a couple of others so that they could make a choice in the projection room. Van never went in a projection room. I expressed my astonishment.

"Kid," he said, his blue eyes twinkling, "those big shots in the front office have to find something to do to justify their big salaries. They like to cut. I let 'em do it. I direct and then I go home. That's why they love me!"

But suppose they chose the wrong takes or angles? I asked. He winked at me. "I know what I'm doin' kid," he said, "I don't give 'em any choice. All they gotta do is join my stuff together!"

Somehow, he turned out box-office winners. He shot *The Thin Man* in seventeen days, *I Live My Life* in less than a month. I liked Van very much. He died too soon.

After the picture finished I began cautiously to make a few friends, Marlene Dietrich of course, the Louis D. Lightons, Ronald Colman, Ruth Chatterton, Leslie Howard, all of them loyal and lifelong. I played a little golf and tennis, stayed away from Hollywood parties and waited, waited for a call from the studio. The weeks passed until, when *What Every Woman Knows* finally got under way, only two months of my contractual time were left. Anxiously I looked at the calendar. Could it be possible that I would again find myself in the awful situation that had produced the debacle of *Wild Decembers?* The thought of my heavy responsibility to Jack Wilson, Noël Coward, and Marie Tempest frightened me. After a couple of weeks of work it became evident that, contract or no contract, there was indeed a danger that I would be crushed between the slowly revolving millstones of my two engagements. Anxiously I sought an interview with Irving Thalberg and poured out my story to him. After the initial shock, he took it coolly. There was no question of my release, he said, until the shooting of the picture, and of all necessary retakes, was completed — absolutely no question. He suggested that I cable Wilson and ask for a postponement. After some hours of agonizing thought, I did so. It was several days before the reply came.

"Your request for postponement is hereby refused. Theaters contracted, company engaged, all production plans completed. Shall hold you fully responsible for any financial loss occasioned by your failure to report on contracted date and for such damages as we see fit to claim." It was signed by Noël Coward. I showed it to Thalberg who shrugged his shoulders.

The picture dragged on. I lived in a nightmare. I understood perfectly how they felt in London and it cut me to the heart, for these people were among my idols in the theater. To make matters worse, the atmosphere on the set was not happy. Miss Hayes, whom I knew only slightly, was plainly worried by the direction, and to me she seemed difficult, touchy, and remote. I myself must have seemed intolerable, with my constant wish to get it over with and to get away. If it had not been for Lucile Watson, whose kindness and salty humor endeared her to me and formed the basis of a lifelong friendship, I don't know what I would have done.

About two weeks before I had been due to leave Hollywood, we seemed barely halfway through shooting. I cabled a groveling appeal to Coward. Again there were several days silence before he replied that he had been able to prevail upon Laurence Olivier to rehearse in my stead and to play the two weeks out of town in Glasgow and Edinburgh. This was the limit, as Olivier had other plans, so I must report in Glasgow without fail. I breathed again. I would have nearly a month in Hollywood and ten days to get to Glasgow.

It would be unjust to say that Thalberg was glad to see me suffer, but I suspect he was not sorry to see pressure brought to bear upon his pigheaded young actor. It must be remembered that he bore a great responsibility to his company and to his reputation. It was his custom to give a picture several sneak previews, bringing it back for alterations at leisure. Now, reluctantly, he scheduled immediate retakes of the more obvious faults and finally released me. It seemed that everybody, on both sides the Atlantic, was unhappy and I was to blame. I have sometimes felt that the picture did indeed suffer because, although it received a good press and the leading critic of the day called my performance "A grand and glorious surprise," it did not do well at the box office.

On the first possible day, I boarded the train in Los Angeles and started my long journey to Glasgow, where I found a rather frigid reception. Having rehearsed together for a month before opening, the company naturally resented my arrival, since it meant that they had to rehearse all over again. Miss Tempest, then approaching eighty, could barely conceal her dislike of the young upstart from Hollywood. She rehearsed with me perfunctorily for an hour or so, and then sent her understudy. I really couldn't blame her. Olivier, realizing that he had got hold of a terrific part was, I suspected, willing to change any plans to keep it. One night, toward the end of the week in Edinburgh, Coward called me and asked me to come to his suite. In a friendly but painful interview, he asked me if I would release them from the contract, offering me £500 if I would do so.

I need hardly say this was a staggering blow to me. I asked for a few hours to think it over and returned to my room, where I sat alone in despair. All my hopes, all the glittering promise of this year had collapsed like a pack of cards.

The telephone rang. In my agitation, I had forgotten that I had placed a call to my mother and father. I had written, telling them of my plans, and they had been excited to think that they would shortly be able to see their wandering son

playing a great starring part in a London theater. Of course
they were eager to hear how it was going.

"Are you ready to take your call to Birmingham?" inquired
a cool English voice. Yes, ready but not happy about it.
There ensued the struggle to get a call through which still
seems endemic to the English telephone system — long si-
lences, punctuated by strange clickings and buzzings and an
encouraging voice which says cheerfully, from time to time,
"I'm trying to get it for you!" The struggle was intensified
that week by the government which, prompted by some so-
cialistic brain wave, had decreed that long distance calls —
"trunk calls" in England — should be made available to the
masses. All calls made after eight o'clock were to cost one
shilling and to last no more than three minutes. All over the
British Isles, Tom, Dick, and Harry were calling Mum and
Dad and, when the three minutes were up the axe fell and
one had to go to the back of the queue, as it were. The experiment, I may say, didn't last long.

"They're on the line!" cried the voice triumphantly, "but
it's not very clear, sir, so speak up! You have three minutes
only!"

To say the line was not clear was an understatement, and
my mother was getting deaf, so it was some time before I was
able to give her a rough idea of my predicament. I don't
know what I expected her to do about it, but I had to tell
somebody.

"Oh, darling," she said, "what a blow! But I'm not surprised, from what I've heard of Miss Tempest — they say she
is a very difficult lady — and of course I would never trust
that Noël Coward! What a pity dear Miss Cornell has nothing for you."

I heard her trying to explain things to my father, to whom the doings of his theatrical family were always incomprehensible anyway. He took the receiver. "Mum says you are in trouble," he said. "Sorry to hear it old chap. You know I always told you to go into a bank — security, regular salary, and a pension on retirement — nothing like that in the theater, I'm afraid."

The cool voice intervened. "Sorry," it said. "Three minutes!" Click — the line was cut. I jiggled the phone.

"Operator!" I cried, "Is there no way I can extend this call? It is very important to me!"

"Sorry, sir," the voice answered. "You may place another call and await your turn."

"How long will it take?"

"I really couldn't say, sir. There are many calls waiting."

Oh, to hell with socialism, I thought, and hung up. Call New York and I would probably get through right away. New York — my mother's words came back to me — "If only that dear Miss Cornell"; well, maybe she *did* have something for me. I knew that Cornell and McClintic had finished their long road tour and were about to open a Broadway season with *Romeo and Juliet*. I picked up the phone and called New York. Almost at once I heard the surprised and friendly voice of Guthrie McClintic. Would he, I asked bluntly, let me play Mercutio? He was taken aback. All plans had been made, rehearsals were about to begin, and Orson Welles, who had played Mercutio on tour, was cast for the part. However, he asked for a few hours to think it over and promised a quick answer. The next morning, after a sleepless night, I received a cable telling me that if I would take Orson's small salary it could be arranged and I should sail at once. The same day I released *The Royal Family* management from our contract and left Edinburgh. It was to be thirty years before I received another offer to play in the London theater.

I believe that those who saw it will never forget the Cornell-McClintic production of *Romeo and Juliet*. Sumptuously staged at the Martin Beck Theater, directed with enthusiasm by McClintic, and designed by Jo Mielziner at his brilliant best, it had a cast which could not be matched on Broadway today. Basil Rathbone played Romeo to Miss Cornell's Juliet, Edith Evans the Nurse, John Emery, Brenda Forbes, Charles Waldron, the young Tyrone Power, myself, and Orson Welles, relegated to the part of Tybalt. Orson seemed friendly and good-natured about losing Mercutio but secretly, I am sure, the actor in him could never forgive me. In the famous duel scene I often had the impression that he slashed at me with unnecessary venom and twice he broke my property sword off at the hilt, leaving me defenseless. The memory of his loss evidently continued to rankle because, about fifteen years later, I received to my astonishment a nice Christmas card from Orson, postmarked from Spain. He is a genuine man of the theater whom I have always admired, but in all that time we had met only momentarily and I was mystified by this gesture. Several more years passed before I happened, in Lausanne, to buy a book on his life, in which I ran across the explanation. What was his opinion, the author asked, of a rival actor's Othello? Nothing of any interest, shrugged Orson, and then, as an afterthought, he added that it was just Brian Aherne in blackface! The Christmas card had evidently been a sort of *amende honorable,* and I love him for it. Actors are funny people.

Romeo and Juliet was a great and glittering success, with the Martin Beck Theater packed to the ceiling at every performance, but it soon became the cause of distress in the Cornell-McClintic management.

Miss Cornell had, like most great stars who have to carry the main responsibility for a play, suffered under the Broadway commercial system whereby one is either in an instant flop, with its attendant misery, or one is condemned to the stultifying treadmill of eight performances a week, the year round. To an artist of her sensitivity and with a deep respect for her public, this was a grievous dilemma. A brilliant young public relations man, Ray Henderson, had joined the management and had devised a wonderful plan to overcome this difficulty: Miss Cornell, he said, like Bernhardt, Duse, and other great stars of the past, must establish a repertory of four plays which she could put on, take off, and play when and where she wished. By playing each play for a week, she could "force the business" and draw full houses in any city of moderate size, or for a whole season in New York or London. The long coast-to-coast tour which I had refused had been the first step in this grand design, and Henderson was even then in the Far East, preparing the ground for a future world tour. The season at the Martin Beck was announced as being six weeks of *Romeo and Juliet,* six of *The Barretts of Wimpole Street,* six of *Candida,* and six of *The Flowers of the Forest,* a new play by John van Druten. Everybody in the entourage was very enthusiastic — everybody, that is, except Guthrie McClintic who, while he loyally supported his wife and did his best to make her dream come true, was too much a man of Broadway to believe in it. When *Romeo and Juliet* was revealed as a tremendous smash hit and the hottest ticket in town, he was aghast at the prospect of taking it off in six weeks. What? Throw away success? Reject the gift of fortune? Stamp on this triumph as if it were an old cigarette butt rather than a glorious flame? His excitable nature erupted like Vesuvius, and the Martin Beck Theater was shaken to its foundations. We who were not part of the management could feel the walls tremble while the earthquake lasted and then, as the dust slowly settled, it was announced that *Romeo and Juliet* would play an extra two weeks, and was to be followed by *The Barretts*. Basil, who had played Browning throughout the long tour, departed for a Hollywood film, and I found myself once more in my old part.

Our opening night, the house packed with friends and admirers, was heartwarming. A mutual admiration society gathered at the McClintics' lovely house on Beekman Place for supper afterwards and the press, while not as incandescent as it had been at the first opening, was warm and affectionate. Serenity was restored. Within a few days, however, it became only too apparent that the public did not share our confidence. To our dismay, business fell off sharply. Hastily, *The Flowers of the Forest* was put into rehearsal and after four weeks was substituted for *The Barretts*, only to fail ignominiously. At this moment the news arrived that Ray Henderson had been killed in an airliner crash in Greece. So ended his great design. So died the dream of poor Kit Cornell. So, once more, show business demonstrated that it is not a business at all, but simply a crap game in which talent, experience, and careful planning may shorten the odds against you a little, but any chance roll may beat you out. As for Guthrie McClintic, I don't think he was ever consoled.

"Don't put your daughter on the stage, Mrs. Worthington. Don't put your daughter on the stage!" sang Noël Coward, with that combination of wit and common sense that gives such sparkle to his lyrics. And what about your son? Knock him down and tie him up if he suggests such a thing. I thought of my father's words about life in a bank in the weeks that followed the closing of *The Barretts,* and yet my own situation was far better than that of the rest of the Cornell company, who found themselves unexpectedly thrown out of work, in that month of February, 1935, too late to hope for another engagement until casting for the autumn season would begin. At least I could look forward to my six months at MGM, which were due to start on June 1. After some indecision, I decided it would be best to go out to Hollywood, in the hope that the studio could use me sooner.

Again I arrived in Beverly Hills, rented a house, got my car out of storage, and reported my presence to the production department. Again, a polite voice asked my telephone number and how to spell my name, welcomed me to California, and told me to take it easy. Again I waited in vain for the phone to ring while the weeks slipped by in idleness.

Scene 4

Ups and Downs

IT WAS Sunday morning. I sat alone, having my breakfast in the garden, on one of those warm, tranquil mornings that filled the heart with delight in the years before the smog came. I watched a brilliantly colored hummingbird darting among the flowers and thought that, after all, California had much to offer an Englishman from Birmingham. Frank, the faithful Filippino who was to see me through two marriages and to give me twelve years' absolute devotion, came quietly down the path. Miss Ruth Chatterton was on the phone.

"Get ready, Brian," she said. "I'm picking you up in half an hour and I'm going to fly you up to Santa Barbara in my new Stinson Reliant for lunch!"

I shuddered. "Oh, no thank you, Ruth," I said. "I can't stand airplanes — I am always airsick!"

"Not if I let you hold the stick, you won't be," she said. "Like the steersman on a ship — you know — the only man on board who can never be sick!"

I must say it was glorious, steady as a rock. I saw the limitless blue Pacific stretching away to our left, the rolling hills of California to our right, Malibu, Oxnard, Ventura, Montecito, and Santa Barbara sliding very slowly beneath our wings. I held the stick gingerly for a few minutes as we purred up the coast.

"Well done!" cried Ruth. "You have an instinct for flying, Brian!" And she took over as we approached the airport, made a circle around the field, and landed smoothly. I was very impressed by her coolness and efficiency, easily succumbed to her flattery, and then and there agreed to take ten hours' lessons from Bob Blair, her instructor; after all, I thought, if anything should happen to the pilot of a plane in which I was a passenger, it might be as well to know how to land it.

And so I was launched into another world, a world of guys named Al, Gus, and Tex — dressed in overalls, or windbreakers and leather helmets — pilots, mechanics, grease monkeys and line boys, all devotees of the craft of flying, whose talk was not of motion pictures but of horsepower, rigging, and conformation, of gas consumption and aerobatics, chandelles, lazy eights, slow and snap rolls, vertical turns and spins, of the problems of cross-country flight, checkpoints, ETAs (estimated times of arrival), cruising speeds, ground speeds, true and magnetic courses, compass variation and deviation, of winds and clouds, and of the exciting new possibilities of monoplanes, radio, tricycle landing gears, flaps, constant-speed propellers, and other inventions that we were beginning to hear about.

My lessons, of half an hour each, were at Mines Field, now known as Los Angeles Municipal. The grassy little runway has long since been replaced by acres of concrete and tarmac, the stucco hangars by huge complexes of buildings, and a North American Aviation Company factory stands where we used to sit on a bench watching each other practice takeoffs and landings, but as I sit today in my comfortable seat on a gigantic jet preparing for takeoff from Los Angeles Airport to some distant part of the world, my mind always goes back

to the morning when Bob hoisted himself out of the front
cockpit of the little Fleet biplane and said casually, "Well,
I've got work to do in the office. Go on around again."

My heart stopped as I watched his retreating back, but
such is the authority of a flight instructor that I meekly
obeyed; looking along the runway I slowly moved the throttle forward to the full open position. Do everything just the
same, I thought, just the same as if Bob's head were still
there in front of me. The beat of the Kinner five-cylinder
radial motor quickened and the little plane picked up speed.
Gently I moved the stick forward to bring up the tail and
held a little right rudder to correct for engine torque, which
has a tendency to turn the plane to the left. As the tail came
up I moved the stick, always gently, to center and then, as I
felt her reach flying speed, back to bring her off the ground.
When the top cylinder was level with the ocean horizon I
eased off a bit on the stick, as I had been taught, and took a
quick look at the altimeter.

Three hundred feet . . . 400 feet . . . 500 feet . . .
Carefully I lowered the nose until the plane was flying level,
took my foot off the rudder and eased back on the throttle,
until the level was opposite the red mark that Bob had
painted to indicate cruising position. We had no rev counters
in those old planes, no rate-of-climb or other instruments, no
flaps or brakes, only an altimeter and a bank-and-turn on the
dashboard. "Fly by the seat of your pants," Bob said, and
that is what we learned to do.

Now came the moment to make a 90-degree left turn. Gentle pressure leftwards on the stick, with a little left rudder —
that's right — now straighten her out — good — now once
again a 90-degree turn, and when I straighten out I am on

the downwind leg, over the hangars and parallel to the runway. I sneak a quick look down and see the tiny figure of Bob standing where I left him, the little white blob of his face turned toward me. I am momentarily surprised he is not in the office, but quickly resuming my concentration I initiate my third left turn into the crosswind leg of my flight pattern, just over the big oil tank as I had been taught. Now my eyes are glued to the runway because in a moment I shall make my last turn onto final approach and it is this vital moment, when the descent starts, that governs the landing spot. Start the glide too soon and I will undershoot, too late and I will overshoot the runway; two white marks on the ground indicate exactly the area in which I am required to touch down if I am to satisfy my instructor. So close the throttle now — forward on the stick a little to attain gliding position; the ground lifts toward me as the sound of the motor dies — wait — now slowly back on the stick, holding up the nose as she loses flying speed and sinks toward the runway. The ground is flying by as I feel my wings stall and in a second I shall hear the rattle of the tail skid to tell me I am on, then remember to hold a little right rudder — but what's that?

Bump! I hit the ground with my wheels and bounce into the air; I have mistimed it! Out of the corner of my left eye I see Bob running toward me and vaguely I hear him shouting. The plane is still moving forward as I wave him away, push the throttle forward and take off again, grimly determined now to show him I can do it right. This time, I do; a perfect three-point landing between the white marks and the little Fleet rolls to a stop exactly where she should. I have soloed! With seven and a half hours' instruction I have soloed! I think it was the proudest moment of my life.

"Okay," says Bob gruffly. "First one a bit high, but your go-around was okay. That's enough for today. Taxi her in."

As I climb out of the cockpit and remove my helmet and goggles I look at him with the kind of admiration that a small boy feels for the captain of the football team. Private flying was a shoestring operation in those days and it was hard for an operator to make a living. I heard later that Bob went broke and became a farmer. I don't forget him. No pilot forgets his first instructor.

Was he the first? Well, strictly speaking it was Ruth Chatterton who first gave me the controls. It was Ruth to whom I telephoned from the hangar with the great news of my solo. It was she who introduced me to the miracle of flying, whose enthusiasm never faltered when I was tempted to despair, who gloried in my little successes, my first cross-country, the winning of my license, the purchase of my plane — she was my first passenger.

Ruth had been a great star of the theater before she moved into pictures where, for a few years, she was also a great star. Her career followed the pattern of most other stars, but Ruth herself did not. Like other stars, she lived high; she had a beautiful house where she entertained royally; she liked men and married several times, always actors, unfortunately. She had, like all the stars, a big entourage — secretary, domestics, business manager, public-relations man, hairdresser — the lot. She rode her own thoroughbred horse and owned her own plane. She sponsored the Ruth Chatterton Derby for private flyers in which she flew across the country making appearances and attending receptions en route. But she had two things that the other stars did not, brains and character. When the crash came for her, as it inevitably did for most, she knew how to face it. Younger and prettier — and cheaper — girls began to get the parts she had always played. The day came when she received no more offers. Finally Sam Goldwyn offered her the vixenish part of the wife in *Dodsworth*, with Walter Huston. She hesitated.

"Take it Ruth," I said. "Why you would be wonderful in it."

"Yes," she replied, "so wonderful that I would never get another Hollywood offer."

Ruth knew that a woman star must always appear young and beautiful, for this is a great American myth which the screen, like the dress advertisements, must always support. The fairy stories that we see unreeled are never about middle-aged women who, if the screen is to be believed, disappear from life until they reappear in old age as bit parts, dear old silver-haired Moms or hatchet-faced character women. Ruth knew that success as Mrs. Dodsworth would type her as a vixenish middle-aged woman. However, she took the part. She was wonderful in it, and she never received another Hollywood offer. She was too proud to hang around as a washed-up star and, as soon as she felt sure this would be her fate, she sold everything she had there, her house, her plane, her horse, her cars, and went to live in Connecticut where she wrote several successful novels. Occasionally she played in the summer theaters, but for the most part she stayed happily in the country with her last husband, and when he died in 1956, she was alone. I am happy to remember that my wife and I visited her shortly before her death. The walls of her bar were hung with photos of friends whom she had entertained lavishly at her home on Palm Drive in earlier days. I asked her if she ever heard from any of them. No, she said, and when she had played Los Angeles some years before not one of them had even sent her a word. She was alone with her four dogs when she died, and her body lay for three days on the floor, watched by her dogs and surrounded by the mute faces of her former friends. I don't forget her, because she brought aviation into my life and this was to prove a great blessing to me.

When my ten hours of primary instruction were finished, I could make reasonable takeoffs and landings and had been introduced to "eights around pylons," a rather scary maneuver which is not required of students today and which, I must confess, I never learned to do very well. It seemed foolish to stop there; after all, by taking my full fifty hours I could get my private license, and, to tell the truth, I had become fascinated. "Flying is good for the mind," said Ruth, and it is. It rewards self-reliance and the swift exercise of judgment. One never stops learning the various branches of the art, and each step forward brings a glow of pride in one's accomplishment. It brings an exaltation to the spirit and a revelation of the beauties of the sky and the earth.

As the months slipped by, I worried more and more about my career. Financially, I was all right after June came, but time passed and I was assigned no picture, and nobody sent me a play. I began to suspect that Thalberg was bringing pressure to bear on me in the hope that I would give in and sign a long-term contract. I decided to have it out with him. Either our contract had been signed in good faith or it had not; I wanted to know the truth. I asked for an interview which, after some delay, was granted.

"I don't understand you," he said. His soft, brown eyes regarded me steadily, as he stood behind a desk which seemed to dwarf his small, slight figure. His right hand slowly tossed his coin up and down, up and down, and through the window behind him I could see the great doors of stage 8 reflecting the brilliant California sunshine; out there the vast motion-picture factory of Metro-Goldwyn-Mayer was humming with the activity of hundreds of people, but in this quiet, carpeted room there was a silence which seemed interminable. He shook his head sadly.

"I don't understand you," he said again.

I watched the coin as it rose and fell. What could I say to him? How could I explain to Irving Thalberg, the head of the studio, the inspiration of artists, the legendary genius of the motion-picture industry, that I was incapable of doing what he asked? I stirred uneasily in my chair and wished I could escape from those soft, compelling eyes.

"Irving," I said at last, "I don't want to be a movie star."

He walked round the desk and sat in a chair facing me, still regarding me steadily. "Oh," he said. "And what else would you do?"

I sighed. What else indeed. I said something about preferring to work in the theater.

"The theater?" He got up with a touch of impatience. "There is no theater," he said. "At least, no theater that counts any more. Oh, I know that you have had some success from time to time, but the years are passing and where is your career? I think I know about you, and what you can do; that is why I have pursued you these past years. Do you suppose that I have to pursue young actors? Believe me, I don't! I don't have to cable and telephone them to London, to New

York, Paris, Salzburg, and Mexico City — what are you doing in all those places, by the way? — I don't send important men chasing them round the world; I don't have to; I can pick up this phone and get any actor I want, and for the few that I want I am willing to pay high. I am willing to pay high for you." As he stopped in front of me his voice was suddenly quiet. "Beyond that Brian," he said, "I am willing to be your friend. If you will trust me, I am willing to take your whole career in hand, to find material for you and to build you into a star. You must understand that I am willing to do these things because I believe in your talent and I am willing to back my belief, but I will not compete with the theater for your services. The theater is not my business, and indeed I don't think it is a business any more."

"You know I can't agree with you, Irving," I said. "It is a wonderful business for some people and always has been."

He slipped the coin in his pocket and sat facing me on the edge of his desk. Although every minute of his day must have been taken up with work, he always behaved as if he had plenty of time; I remembered that Sir George Arthur had told me that this is the mark of a genuine top man.

"It may have been, Brian," he said. "But it is no longer. It has been killed by the talking picture. Every big city in the country used to have a theater, but now it is a motion picture theater, and now every little town has one. You know yourself that legitimate plays are restricted to a few theaters in London and New York, which are kept open solely by the power of the metropolitan press, which devotes whole sections to the theater and writes about it in a way that is out of all proportion to its importance, simply because of the vested interests — the jobs, the real estate and tourist and hotel and restaurant trades — that are involved, but even these cities are becoming poorer every year as they are drained of talent by the talking picture, which goes everywhere and reaches everyone. Now you think, because you and Miss Cornell had a big success with *The Barretts* you can find another, don't you? Well, I wonder. Perhaps you may, in five or ten years' time, or you may not; and while you wait you grow older and are forgotten by the public. The odds are in any case heavily against you, because the writers are all here in pictures, making big money with no risk and living in great comfort. When a new man writes a hit play for Broadway, he automatically comes here. He must; this is his market. And so it is for the actor. The theater, Brian, is a good place for a young man to learn his trade and to get some experience, but it cannot provide a career, or even a living. If you are honest, you will tell me that you know these things as well as I do. That is why I ask you again — what else would you do, other than be a movie star?"

Well, I thought, perhaps I might become a doctor. That would be a proper job, a real job, a job to be proud of. With an effort I brought my mind back to Irving Thalberg, waiting patiently for an answer. Would he really be my friend, or was he only seeking to exercise his power over me? There was something about him that frightened me. His gentle manner concealed a brilliant mind and, I well knew, ruthless determination.

"Thank you, Irving," I said. "Let me think about it."

"What — again?" he cried. He picked up the phone and called his wife. "Darling, I have a job for you," he told her. "I want you to find Brian a nice house out here and a nice wife who will tie him down a bit!"

I heard her laugh. I greatly admired Norma Shearer. "Find me a wife like yours," I said, "and I will do more than think about it!"

I went back to my house in Coldwater Canyon and did some very serious thinking, as a result of which I got myself an agent, a charming and most un-Hollywood type named Bill Hawks, who also represented Ronald Colman, Herbert Marshall, Robert Montgomery, and other important actors. To him I told my story. He at once pointed out that my contract was not with Irving Thalberg personally, but with the Metro-Goldwyn-Mayer Corporation. It appeared that there was a tremendous subterranean battle in progress at the studio between the forces of Thalberg and those of Louis B. Mayer, and he thought it possible that we might find the other faction easier to deal with. He went to see them, while I waited anxiously for the result. Next day, he called me.

Good news, he told me. Not only had they a picture for me, but a wonderful one. I was to play Sidney Carton, the lead, in *The Only Way*, which was to go into production later in the year, with David Selznick producing. I was overjoyed. Based on Dickens' famous novel, *The Tale of Two Cities*, this play had brought fame to Martin Harvey, one of the greatest actors I ever saw, who had been acclaimed in the part all over the world. My sister Elana had toured Canada with him some years before, playing Lucy Manette, the ingenue. Two generations of theatergoers had wept as he stood at the foot of the guillotine in the final scene saying, "It is a far, far better thing that I do now than I have ever done. It is a far, far better life I go to than I have ever known."

This was the chance I had been longing for. This would

make up for all the months of waiting, all the disappointment, indecision, and uncertainty. I didn't care when they
started the picture, in that year or the next. Fate had unexpectedly tossed me a glittering, golden prize, and I would
make the most of it. I went straight out to the airport and
bought myself an airplane on which I had my eye, a used,
open-cockpit Waco F.3. biplane, black and red, with a
checkerboard pattern on the tail which was to become well
known in the next few years on California flying fields. To
this day, I am sometimes hailed by airplane captains in various parts of the world, captains who in their youth maybe
earned a buck for pushing her into the hangar, gassing her
up, or wiping her down.

"Hi there!" they cry. "I remember your black Waco with
the checkerboard tail!"

She was stressed for aerobatics and, important to a novice,
very stable; indeed it was difficult to put her into a spin and
even more difficult to hold her there — an attribute surely
more masculine than feminine — and this stability, combined with positive, easy controls, was to help me greatly in
my early flying days. Some of the later planes that I flew,
cleaner and faster, had to be watched all the time. I bought
her, as I remember, for something under $4000, and then,
greatly daring, I bought a used Packard Super 8 convertible
car, painted iridescent blue, for about $2000 — after all, I was
on my way to riches — and these two machines shared my
love for some years. They stand in my memory like old and
valued friends, and no other cars or planes have given me the
kick that they did.

In due course, I passed my written and practical examina-
tions, took my physical, and became the proud possessor of a

"License To Carry Passengers. Private Pilot. Single Engine. Land."

Autumn came before I received the long-expected summons to David Selznick's office. A powerful man, he was reputed to be a formidable opponent in business, but was capable of exercising great personal charm when he wished. He received me kindly and came straight to the point. He regretted, he said, that he had to make a last minute change of plans. He had just heard that it would be possible to get Ronald Colman for the part of Sidney Carton in *The Only Way*, and he knew I would realize that this would mean a million dollars in the box office. He would therefore be unable to use me. There was nothing I could say. Colman was a great star, whom we all admired. He was also a fellow Englishman and one of the very few close friends I had in Hollywood. It so happened that I was to dine with him that night. As we drank our scotch at his bar, he told me of his new engagement, about which he was not too enthusiastic because it would necessitate his shaving off his mustache, and he felt his public might not like that.

This was not the last time I was to lose a fine part to Ronnie, though I doubt if he was aware of it. Frances Marion, the writer, was once kind enough to arrange a small dinner party at which I was to meet Frank Capra, who was to offer me the lead in *Lost Horizon*. The evening passed and he said nothing. Years later, he told me he had been deeply embarrassed because he had found, only that afternoon and too late to cancel the dinner, that Ronald Colman would be available for the part. These were two of Ronnie's finest performances.

At first, I was inclined to blame Bill Hawks for the loss of

The Tale of Two Cities, as it was finally called, but this was unjust. Almost immediately, he told me that Sam Goldwyn would like me to play opposite Merle Oberon in *Beloved Enemy,* a story of the Irish Revolution, but would not make me a firm offer while I was tied to MGM. As my negotiations with Thalberg had reached an impasse, we decided to ask for my release, which he, tiring of the struggle, reluctantly agreed to. Could he have made me a great movie star, as he had made others, and would he if he could? I shall never know, but I shall never forget the slim young figure, the strange, compelling personality, the soft brown eyes, and gentle voice of Irving Thalberg. Still in his thirties when he died, his name is a legend in the motion-picture industry.

Hank Potter directed *Beloved Enemy,* in which David Niven played a small part. Arriving in Hollywood a young and penniless unknown, Niven had quickly become enormously popular with the movie world. I have heard it said that he went through the town like a knife through butter, which is more than I was ever able to do. His gaiety and his apparently inexhaustible fund of hilarious stories amused everybody and made him welcome everywhere. He was perhaps the most charming companion in Hollywood, and I doubt if any of us realized that his canny, Scots mind was even then planning the course that has since led him to fame and affluence.

Early in the year 1936, *Beloved Enemy* finished shooting, and about the same time I received a letter from Gertrude Macy to say that the McClintics were putting on Shaw's *Saint Joan* and inviting me to play the Earl of Warwick. I had always thought this play Shaw's masterpiece, and I had long urged Miss Cornell to do it, but with its tremendous

cast and many scenes it was of course a very costly production, especially as the shadow of rising costs was even then
beginning to fall over Broadway. I knew that Miss Cornell
would not wish to play such a demanding part for long, but
altogether I felt they were showing great courage in doing it,
and I wanted to be with them. Was I perhaps glad, too, of
the opportunity of showing Thalberg that I didn't need him
as much as he thought? After all, I had a picture under my
belt which would come out in the spring. Happily, I made
preparations to leave.

Scene 5

Golden Opportunities

THE SUN was setting over the Pacific, as Gus and I pushed the Waco into the hangar after my last flight, a daring trip over the Hollywood Hills to Burbank and back. As I patted the fuselage of my black beloved, I said, "Gus, look after her till I come back from New York. Start her up occasionally, and fly around a bit if you like, but don't let anybody else touch her."

He straightened the propeller, stepped back, and looked at the Waco admiringly, for he shared my love. "New York?" he asked. "Well, how are you goin'?"

"On the Santa Fe, as usual."

"Gee!" he said. "If I owned a plane like this, I wouldn't do nothin' but fly!"

The idea startled me. "Oh, Gus!" I said. "It's more than thirty-five hundred miles!"

"So what? You've been to Palm Springs alone, haven't you? That's one hundred miles. Goin' to New York would be just about the same, only farther, that's all."

All the way home to Beverly Hills I thought about it. All night I thought about it. The next morning I called Paul Lukas, another actor-pilot, who had flown for years. Can it be done, I asked him? Oh yes, he said, he had done it. It would take as long as the train, three or four days, and one slept in motels near the airports at night.

"You'll find it a great experience," he said, "but I advise you to take a pilot with you."

I canceled my train reservation and went out that afternoon to buy a series of the excellent sectional flying maps put out by the Coast & Geodetic Survey in Washington. I spread these all over my living room floor and, with the aid of my faithful Frank, I laid out a course across the U.S.A. in a thick pencil line, marking off each twenty miles and calculating the changing compass headings. Drift, caused by crosswinds, would have to be calculated in flight, but I was a bit hazy about how to do this, and I figured on sticking closely to the pencil line, as I had when going to Palm Springs. I didn't know any pilot I could take on such short notice, and Bob Blair was away with Ruth Chatterton on a cross-country. I didn't want to ask a friend because, despite my license, I didn't feel sufficient confidence to accept the responsibility of a passenger. Hollywood friends didn't want to fly with me anyway, either then or later; they all thought I was crazy. I could imagine the horror on the face of Ronald Colman or David Niven if I had asked them to come on this trip. I was to find that private flying was, at least in California at that time, poetry and loneliness — two things that appealed to me.

Before I went to bed I called my friends and fellow-aviators Alfred (Abby) and Connie Wolf who live in a wonderful house on the edge of a private airfield — Wings Field — in Pennsylvania. Abby is now the leading expert in aviation law in the country and a full general in the Air Corps Reserve, and Connie is the holder of all the women's world records in a free balloon, while I fly no more, but in those days we were fledgling pilots together. I told them to look out for a black and red Waco biplane landing at Wings some four days later, and they greeted the news with whoops of delight. One more call to the Weather Bureau, from whom I got a favorable forecast, a final reassurance to Frank, and I turned in for a few hours sleep.

Very early next morning, Gus and I wheeled out the Waco and loaded the front cockpit with my baggage, while Frank sat in the Packard watching me with apprehension. I strapped on my parachute, climbed into the rear cockpit, and fastened my seatbelt. Gus reached up and took hold of the propeller.

We went through the starting routine.

"Gas on?"

"Gas is on!"

"Switch off?"

"Switch off!" He gave several lusty pulls to the prop to charge the cylinders and then stood to one side.

"Contact!"

"Contact!"

I switched on and pressed the starter button. The Continental motor burst into sound. I adjusted my goggles, checked the gas tanks, released the brakes, and signaled to Gus who ran to the tail and helped to push the plane around. Faintly, I heard him shout, "Good luck!"

I waved in answer and taxied slowly out to the end of the runway where, after a brief warmup, I took off toward the sea, making a half turn at 1000 feet to bring me back over the airport. As I passed, I saw Gus standing on the tarmac, shading his eyes to watch me. I set a compass course of east-northeast which would take me out over Arrowhead, slightly to the north of Mt. San Gorgonio. When I looked up, there, sure enough and slightly to the right, was the bulk of old St. George, sharply outlined against the rising sun.

Now I watched the U.S.A. slowly unrolling beneath me like a giant, many-colored carpet. My eyes moved continuously from my instruments to the ground, to the map on my knee and back to my instruments, with occasional quick glances around for landmarks and passing traffic, of which, however, I saw practically none. As I crawled along over the deserts, the mountains, and the plains, I felt completely alone, suspended in time and space. The regular beat of the engine, the rushing sound of the wind, and the vast distances around me combined to produce a dreamlike illusion. I had never flown so high before, and the thin air made me feel a little drunk — or was it excitement? Sometimes I sang to reassure myself, but always I watched the map and the ground intently, for of course I had no radio and I knew a little slip in navigation, a little mistake in recognition of a landmark, can have serious consequences. I marked each checkpoint as it slid beneath my wings — a small town, only a few shacks, maybe, but marked on the map if one knew how to read it, a copper mine in the side of a desolate mountain slope, a lonely water tower, a tiny black train crawling along a thin line of rail that snaked away into the distance (the Iron Compass as pilots called it, always reliable, always there to be followed), the highway, our other friend, running across the California desert in a straight line for many miles, perhaps a bridge over which I must change course a little to correct for variation in magnetic north — every landmark noticed and checked.

I was flying the old Transcontinental & Western air route over California, a bit of Nevada, Arizona, and New Mexico;

this was also the route of the Santa Fe railroad, but at times, flying a direct course, I was over trackless desert. Every three hours or so I made a careful approach to an airfield and landed for gas, to stretch my legs, change maps, inquire about the weather, and perhaps eat a sandwich at a lunch counter. The guys were always helpful; I was among fliers and we understood each other. That first night I spent in Winslow, Arizona, and I was very tired.

Next morning I crossed the Painted Desert and climbed to 11,000 feet to go over the Great Divide to Albuquerque. This gave me only 1000 feet clearance over the rough, mountainous country, but without oxygen I did not dare go higher. This, is the area in which Mike Todd's pilot, flying east in an overloaded plane on a winter's night, ran into a snowstorm; not having oxygen, he could not climb above it and had to watch his wings pick up ice until the plane lost flying speed, stalled, and spun in. I once took my Waco without oxygen up to 16,000 feet by way of experiment, but I became light-headed and breathless, and the plane wallowed off into a spin in the rarefied air, and I dived a long way before I was able to pull out. No such troubles bothered me now; the sky was clear and unlimited and I was enjoying myself, except for the fact that my behind was becoming paralyzed from sitting on a hard parachute. At Amarillo, Texas, I decided that as the mountains were behind me I needed it no more, so I mailed it back to California and relaxed on my cushion.

East of the Divide, navigation becomes curiously easy on a clear day, thanks to the early settlers who laid out the country in square sections so that the roads all run either north and south or east and west.

It was a long flight to Jefferson City the next day, and it was near sunset when I landed at a little field with one hangar and three or four planes. Louisville, Kentucky, the following night seemed very grand. I visited Cornelia Otis Skinner who was playing there that evening.

Rather late on the fourth day, I took off for Pennsylvania. The weather was clear and unlimited as it had been most of the way, and indeed in subsequent transcontinental flights I never seemed to have it so good. The dreaded razorback mountains of the Alleghenies, known as the Pilot's Grave-yard, seemed quite innocuous after the Rockies, and I landed without trouble at Harrisburg, in the late afternoon, to gas up and have a cup of coffee. When I came out of the lunchroom it seemed to be quite a bit darker.

"What time is sunset here?" I asked the line boy as I climbed in.

"Five o'clock," he replied.

I looked at my watch. Ten minutes past four. Better perhaps if I had left Louisville an hour earlier, but nothing to worry about. I had figured as I drank my coffee that it would take me about thirty-five minutes to fly to Blue Bell. I was very tired and glad it was the last hop. I looked back at the sun again just after takeoff and it seemed to have gone behind a cloud, but that did not alarm me. I still had a full hour's daylight, and there is always quite a bit of afterglow. In half an hour I would be waving to Abby Wolf at Wings Field. I set my compass and settled down to watch the ground.

This was quite different country to anything I had passed over. No obvious landmarks were apparent, no mountains, broad rivers or straight railroads, and no section lines. The roads wound in and out of countless little villages and towns

below me, getting lost in woods and reappearing in different
directions or disappearing altogether. Pretty soon I didn't
know where I was. Twinkling lights came out on the ground
and as I peered at my map I began to form the conviction
that my compass had gone wrong — the old pilot's illusion,
had I but known it. That mass of lights over to the northeast
must be the town which, according to the map, should lie
straight ahead due east. I altered my course and flew from
one group of lights to another, hoping to recognize some
landmark. Looking behind, I saw that the sun had gone, and
daylight, even at my altitude, was fading fast. Then, as if I
had been struck on the back of the head with a hammer, the
truth struck me. I had crossed a time line at Pittsburgh and
had forgotten to alter my watch; the sun had set while I was
still on the ground at Harrisburg!

Cold fear possessed me. My instruments, evidently phos-
phorescent, began to glow in the darkness, but the compass
was now invisible. I was alone and hopelessly lost at 3000
feet over strange and difficult country, with no parachute, no
flares, and no landing lights — none of which I knew how to
use anyway. I could not see the map any more and I had
never flown at night. What should I do? I'm going to die in
a few minutes, I thought.

Far away to my right, I became aware of a light which
flashed at regular intervals. An airway beacon! I had seen
them from the window of an airliner and I knew they were
established every twenty miles along the airways for the
guidance of pilots; they were marked on the maps and I had
had fun picking them out in all sorts of odd and lonely places
as I flew over them, but I had not been instructed in their
operation. Still, that flashing light meant that the aviation

world was speaking to me, and, although its direction seemed completely improbable, I made a tight turn and flew toward it, easing off on the power and sinking slowly to 500 feet by the time I reached it ten minutes later. I hoped fervently that it marked the site of an airfield, though I seemed to remember that if that were so each alternate flash would be green, but at least there would surely be a cleared strip or a bit of service road on which I could land, and light by which to land. There was not; as the plane rushed by I saw the beacon clearly, fixed to the top of a tall pylon, revolving slowly and lighting the tiny rocky space in the woods where it stood. No place to land there. I pulled into a tight left turn and made a couple of circles around it, my head out of the cockpit in the slipstream and my eyes glancing back apprehensively at the airspeed indicator because I knew this to be a dangerous maneuver close to the ground as numbers of inexperienced — and even experienced — pilots have discovered too late, as they made tight circles low over the girl friend's house, their eyes glued to the porch rather than to the airspeed indicator which dropped unnoticed until the plane stalled and spun in.

As I circled and stared, I saw a large arrow marked on the ground at the base of the pylon, together with the figure 9. What did they mean? Did the arrow point to Philadelphia or to Harrisburg? And nine what? Miles? The number of the light? Of course it is easy to say, sitting in an armchair, that the thing to do was to climb a bit in the direction indicated by the arrow until the next light, probably number 8, came into view, and so to have followed them in to an airfield, but I was in a panic. I had never flown at night and everything was terrifyingly unfamiliar. I dared not climb and lose my shadowy contact with the ground, for fear I would lose with it my ability to keep flying straight and level without visual reference of any kind. The light, which had beckoned me to life, now repelled me, coldly revolving round and round. I straightened out and flew off into the darkness. Removing my tinted goggles, I peered over the side and could see vaguely woods and hills flashing beneath me. I don't know how long I went on like that, possibly a few minutes, but it seemed like hours, and then something happened: somewhere in the back of my head I heard Bob Blair's voice saying casually, "If ever anything goes wrong, just make up your mind what you are going to do and then do it."

I must land, I thought, at the next open space, whatever it is, because in one minute I shall see nothing. Dimly I made out under my wing a narrow opening — it could hardly be called a field — which seemed to run down the side of a hill between trees. I chopped the throttle back and, staring intently at the ground, I made a tight left turn onto a base leg. As I turned on final I saw that the upper half of the field was darker than the lower, probably I thought planted to some sort of crop and — so oddly does the human mind work in emergencies — I remembered stories of infuriated farmers rushing with pitchforks at pilots who had landed inadvertently in a cultivated field. I actually gunned the motor a little so as to pass over the dark part and land further down, and this piece of stupidity nearly cost me dear, because when the plane touched the ground she was going much too fast.

Bang! She hit, and bounced high in the air. *Bang!* She hit again. I switched off the engine to avoid the danger of fire on crashing and I held the stick all the way back to my stomach as, with a series of frightful jolts and jars, she began to slow down. I saw a huge black hedge rushing toward me and I applied the brakes, but very carefully, for I felt the tail rise and I feared she might tip over on her back and crush me. Some final horrendous jolts and she stopped, the propeller within a few feet of the hedge.

I could feel my heart beating as I sat there in the sudden silence. Somewhere in flight I had switched on my navigation lights and now I became aware of them, tiny points of green and red at the end of either wing and white on the tail, glowing brightly in the darkness. I reached down and turned off the gas, unhooked my belt, and climbed stiffly from the cockpit in which I had spent so many hours. I was unsteady on my feet and my hands shook as I got out my map, laid it on the wing, and studied it with the aid of a small flashlight. A lantern came bobbing through the trees and a farmer with his family crawled through the hedge.

"Hi there!" called a friendly voice. "Where have you come from?"

"Los Angeles," I quavered.

"What — today?" He sounded astonished.

"Oh, no," I said. "I've been several days getting here." All of a sudden I couldn't remember how many; it seemed like years. "I do hope I haven't damaged your crop," I said.

"Oh, no," he replied. "But why didn't you take the alfalfa at the back? This field is full of rocks!"

"Yes, I know," I said. "I've hit every one of them!"

I asked him where Philadelphia was and that seemed to stump him. A couple of farm hands who joined us allowed as how they thought "t'were about ten mile t'other side of Gradyville." By the glow of my little flashlight they stared and scratched their heads, but evidently maps were unfamiliar to them, and Philadelphia quite beyond their ken. They couldn't even spot Gradyville. A small knot of people gathered and, after some discussion, a jockey turned up who not only confirmed my belief that the city was about thirty miles away but offered to drive me to Blue Bell in his car. It wasn't long before I was downing a large slug of whisky with the Wolfs.

Next morning we loaded a truck with a mechanic, a spare propellor, and all kinds of equipment for the repair of fabric-covered airplanes, and set out to find the Waco, which we did with some difficulty. There she stood in the sunshine, her nose against the hedge, miraculously without a scratch on her. With the aid of the farmer we hauled her back over the rock-strewn field and up to the top of his alfalfa, and as I looked down the steep narrow slope I marveled that I ever got into it. I would never have attempted it in daylight and I secretly quailed at the idea of a takeoff, but Abby Wolf climbed confidently into the front cockpit. I spoke into the gosport, a system of tubes, mouthpieces, and earpieces by which we communicated in open planes.

"Don't you think you'd better take her off?" I asked. My nerves were still a little shaky.

"No, no!" his cheery voice came back. "Take her off!"

I gave her full throttle, released the brakes and started a lurching rush downhill through the alfalfa. Two final bumps and we were off. It took only a few minutes to fly to Blue Bell.

Another fine cast assembled on the stage of the Martin Beck Theater to rehearse *Saint Joan,* including Maurice

Evans, whom I had persuaded McClintic to bring over from London, as the Dauphin, that fine actor Arthur Byron as the Inquisitor, Kent Smith as Dunois, irascible George Colouris as Brother Martin, the unknown Tyrone Power as Robert de Beaudricourt, Charles Waldron and John Emery once again, and all the usual efficiency of the Cornell-McClintic organization. As usual Jo Mielziner designed a stunning production and Guthrie directed with fervor. Cleveland and Pittsburgh greeted us rapturously, heralding our opening at the Martin Beck which was packed to the rafters at every performance. Katherine Cornell has given many great performances in a wide range of parts but none, I think, better than her Saint Joan for which her gifts and qualities seemed ideally suited. It was a buoyant spring for us all, except perhaps for Guthrie McClintic who faced once again the prospect of closing a great big smash hit on Broadway after a few weeks. Miss Cornell was firm in her resolve not to get tied up again in a long run and we had opened so late in the season that there was indeed barely ten weeks left before the withering heat of the New York summer hit us.

One night, as I sat making up, there was a timid knock at my dressing room door and young Tyrone Power came in to ask my advice. A Hollywood talent scout had seen him and Twentieth Century Fox had made him an offer of the standard seven-year optional contract, with six months guaranteed. Should he take it? I was hardly the person to ask this question of, but he couldn't know that.

"Ty," I said, "you are the son of a famous actor. You have talent and a wonderful appearance, but you are very young. I think you have plenty of time, so why not take a few years to gain your experience and to make your name in the theater. You will then get better offers from Hollywood and, if you want to go out, you can go as a star." He thanked me.

Making up in the next dressing room Maurice Evans, that shrewd Welsh realist, overheard the conversation and shouted "Rubbish! Don't listen to him, Ty! Take your chances when they come. Get out to Hollywood fast. You never know — a good-looking fellow like you — why, you might hit and go up like a rocket!"

Ty heard him, loud and clear. He went straight down to Miss Cornell, smiled at her shyly with his soft brown eyes, and asked her to release him from his contract. To my amazement she did, and it is hard to imagine any other great actress-manager giving up her hours of rest to rehearse with a replacement in order to let a youngster leave in the middle of a run and go off to Hollywood. Her faith in him was more than justified however, for he did indeed go up like a rocket, and was soon established as one of the great stars of the Hollywood firmament. Ty never forgot her kindness and years later, when she wanted him to play a difficult part in *The Dark Is Light Enough*, he dropped everything and came to New York at once, playing for a small fee to cover his expenses. He was a most lovable fellow, as all the Hollywood beauties soon discovered, and his early death while working on a picture in Spain was a tragedy.

When I was a little boy of around five or six years old, our governess, Miss Halden, used to take Patrick, Elana, and myself for daily walks and drives in the lanes of Worcestershire. From time to time, we would meet two other children, a boy my own age and his sister, two years older, walking with their governess. The girl's name was Dolly Bate and she had long, blond hair which seemed, to my eyes, of the purest gold. She was the most beautiful thing in the world, and I thought about her quite a lot. I used to look forward, with a beating heart, to seeing her, but when she appeared round the corner, carrying her doll or rolling a hoop, she seemed so beautiful, so radiant, that I couldn't look directly at her. I would blush deeply and look at the ground instead, faint with happiness and embarrassment.

Something of this romantic feeling has persisted all my life; Dolly Bate, in the person of a pretty, feminine young woman, has only had to look at me with smiling eyes to arouse the old Adam in me — and Dolly Bate has always known it. They say the woman always pays, but if she is clever she often gets quite a lot of change; anyway, she always has out of me. In the course of my long career, I have played with a great many feminine stars and I have usually fallen a little bit in love with them while we were working together; indeed I believe it is hardly possible to play convincing love scenes without doing so, and a leading actor's wife has to realize this unless she wants to live in a constant ferment of jealousy. After all, while an actor is playing a role, especially if it is well written, he is to some extent possessed by it, and if the role is that of a lover it is inevitable that he should be affected by the fact — and I am not referring to the Method which, as far as I can gather, is something quite different.

Actually, great theatrical stars are rarely lovable people. The mere fact that they have rejected a normal life of security, a steady job, marriage, children, and a happy home, in favor of the uncertainty, the bright lights and tinsel of a stage career is evidence that they are devoted primarily to themselves, and if they are successful they soon learn to become self-centered and ruthless beyond the belief of non-theatrical people. They become public people, not private people. Ellen Terry was beloved by everybody, it seems, but even she cannot be called a successful wife. Henry Irving, the greatest of English actors, when driving home in a hansom cab with his wife after the opening night of his gigantic success in *The Bells*, was so upset when she made a critical remark about the performance that he stopped the cab at Hyde Park Corner, got out, raised his hat to her, bade her good night, and never spoke to her again. My own mother, an actress by instinct, spending her life rehearsing before a mirror and dreaming pitiful dreams of theatrical glory, could not function well as a wife, though she tried with all her heart.

I have always referred to the great women stars as the Monsters, and monsters indeed they most of them are, but if I have not admired their characters it has not meant that I have been insensible to the charms which affect the rest of the world. I even found Bette Davis attractive, when I played Maximilian to her Carlotta and, brilliant actress though she is, surely nobody but a mother could have loved Bette Davis at the height of her career. Evidently I failed to make my admiration clear, however, because in her lively and self-revealing book, *The Lonely Life*, she says I looked at her with loathing.

The star of whom I was most wary was the one of whom it was said "She's *so* sweet — you'll love her!" I got on better with the hellions. Constance Bennett, for example, had a difficult reputation, but I found her wonderful to work with, a true professional — intelligent, humorous, kind, and cooperative. Katharine Hepburn, whose trenchant mind and outspoken manner frightened some actors, struck me as a fascinating and extraordinarily attractive girl.

During my visits to Hollywood, I had lived for the most part almost as a recluse, but slowly my youth and my romantic nature had begun to assert themselves, surrounded as I was by world-famous beauties. I came to realize that life must be lived and that I must come to terms with my grief, and though it was always with me and sometimes engulfed me, I forced myself, as it were, to put it underneath. In 1936 I had fallen into a tempestuous affair with a fascinating but fiery little lady whom I followed rather as a traveler, lost in the darkness, is said to follow a will o' the wisp. *Saint Joan* had no sooner closed its short, but enormously successful run, than she beckoned to me from England. Well, I thought, why not? I was becoming a pillar of the Cunard Line by now.

Just as I was about to sail, J. Robert Rubin and Irving Thalberg made a last determined attempt to persuade me to play Romeo, opposite Norma Shearer's Juliet. I had done some work with her on this while I was in Hollywood, and I knew that she would make a delightful Juliet, as indeed she did, but I felt myself too big and too mature for Romeo. We had actually made a test together, directed by George Cukor, and they had all been enthusiastic, but when I had seen it, my own misgivings had been confirmed. Get a younger fellow, I said, so they got Leslie Howard, years older than myself.

By late September, I was following my will o' the wisp, with stumbling feet, over the mountains of North Wales when one night, in a remote country inn, I received a phone call from America. It was Max Gordon, who was in trouble.

"Brian," he said, "I've got Walter Huston out in *Othello,* directed by his brother-in-law, your good friend Robert Edmond Jones. He opens in New York in three weeks, and the show is dying on the road. Now we all agree that everything will be fine if we can replace the Iago. Will you rush here, study it fast, and take over in Philly for the week before the New York opening?"

I relayed the message to my fiery one.

"Certainly not!" she said. "You're staying here with me!" I thought of the phrase which, they say, is used by Buckingham Palace to convey a tactful but negative answer.

"Oh Max!" I cried. "What a lovely idea! — but I'm afraid it might be a little difficult."

A couple of days later, we had returned to London and lunched with friends in Hampstead, where I was delighted to meet Douglas Fairbanks again. As we strolled on the lawn after lunch he asked me, in his usual charming way, what I was up to, and I mentioned the *Othello* offer. He stopped in his tracks, his eyes wide with amazement, and then he hit me in the chest, quite hard.

"You bloody young fool!" he said. "When are you going to get wise to yourself? Get on the phone to Gordon at once and tell him you will do it! Don't you realize it is one of the great parts of Shakespeare? I'd give my eye teeth to play it! God! How can anybody be so stupid!"

He launched into an excited description of the character of Iago who, he said, was not senselessly malevolent as he is usually played, but a highly intelligent man, gifted with mordant humor, whose bitterness about having been passed over by the promotion of the much lesser man Cassio was perfectly valid and whose scorn of the barbaric Othello was understandable in the times in which he lived.

" 'I have looked upon the world for four times seven years,' " he quoted. " 'And since I could distinguish between a benefit and an injury I never found man who knew how to love himself!' " "What a thing to say!" cried Doug delightedly. "And what a phrase — 'since I could distinguish between a benefit and an injury!' "

He paused and took my arm.

"I tell you what!" he said. "Think of Iago as Rhett Butler in *Gone with the Wind!*"

I cabled Max that I would sail two days later and I did, pursued by feminine recriminations and swearing blind that I would return the moment the play closed. I holed up in my cabin to study a part which seemed to me as long as Hamlet, and almost as difficult.

Arriving in Washington, I went straight to the National Theater to see the show, and as I sat there my heart sank like a stone. Robert Edmond Jones — Bobby Jones — the greatest designer of them all, the man from whom even Jo Mielziner will tell you he learned his trade, had done a magnificent production with imaginative scenery and sumptuous costumes, but as a director I knew he had failed. The play was a beautiful, tedious bore. The cast was good and I thought the Iago adequate if uninspired. Nan Sunderland was distinguished, gentle, and touching as Desdemona. The real trouble lay in the casting of Huston as Othello. I knew his work in American parts, such as O'Neill's *Desire Under the Elms* and *Dodsworth,* and had greatly admired him, but here he was out of his depth and had not been helped by direction. The speech to the senators was very well delivered; he looked impressive and conveyed the essential nobility of the Moor, and I had hopes for him, but as the play progressed it became fatally apparent that he lacked passion, without which no Othello can succeed. Indeed in my lifetime none has, with the possible exception of Godfrey Tearle, until Laurence Olivier shook the theater with his towering performance in 1965.

I did not go backstage or risk speaking to anybody that night. I went straight to my hotel room and there I came to a hard decision; I would give Iago a bravura performance, with all the flash, fire, and humor that I could, and the devil take the hindmost; I was in, and there was nothing else I could do. I also came down that night with a severe and certainly psychosomatic attack of my old sinus trouble.

Ten days later I staggered onto the stage in Philadelphia, feeling more dead than alive, and it was there that Max Gordon told me that Huston had put up all the money for the production, a piece of information which shocked me, because I knew only too well what he would suffer at the hands of the New York critics. Max also told me that Huston had insisted on my co-starring with him. Such generosity was a part of his nature and a lesser man would have resented my performance. Poor Bobby Jones was reduced to despair by it and used to leave little notes on my dressing room table saying "Brian — Iago is *evil, slimy* and *dark*. He must *horrify* the audience, not fascinate them and make them laugh as you are doing! It is not fair to the play!" It was perhaps not fair to the play and it was certainly not fair to the character of Othello, but I knew what Bobby was apparently unable to see, that poor Walter would fail anyway. I knew that if Othello fails and the play is to go at all, Iago *must* succeed, and I determined he should do so. I believed in Douglas Fairbanks, and I stuck to my guns. An actor can't do that in movies. Walter and his wife Nan Sunderland never complained, never faltered, and helped me in every way they could. We moved to New York where, for some strange reason, Gordon had booked us into the New Amsterdam, a huge musical comedy house which had long been relegated to a place among the cheap movie houses of 42nd Street.

The headlines were even better than I feared: "Mr. Aherne in Walter Huston's *Othello*"; "Triumph and disaster at the New Amsterdam Theater"; "The greatest Iago of our generation." All next day I wondered if I should telephone to him, but what could I say? I was still wondering as I sat at my dressing table, that evening making up as Iago. The late papers were out with more of the same. The moment is coming, I thought, when I must go down and see him; what can I say? I heard steps on the stairs, there was a knock on my door, and in came Walter, fully dressed and ready for the performance. Sitting down, he gave me a shy smile and said with a rueful laugh, "Well — I'm afraid they didn't like me!"

In that moment we became firm and devoted friends and remained so until the grievous day of his death, some twelve years later.

Othello ran for only three weeks, losing Walter's money and shattering a dream. Not long ago, in a book called *Actors on Acting*, I read an article he wrote about the experience, which had saddened and perplexed him. His sister, Mrs. Carrington, a very remarkable and artistic woman who also became a close friend of mine, had married Robert Edmund Jones quite late in life, and it was she who felt that the family should get together and do something really worthwhile in the theater. Bobby had written a book about the theater, *The Dramatic Imagination*, in its way a little masterpiece which deserves the attention of all who love the craft, and she was confident that if given the opportunity he could establish himself as a great director as well as designer. She also thought *Othello* could establish Huston and his wife as great stars of the American theater; their success in *Dodsworth* seemed to indicate that this was possible and there was then nobody else who was doing classical work. The result of these dreams was so distressing to them all that they might well have found it hard to forgive my personal success, but it was not so and we were, on the contrary, all drawn closer together in bonds of warm and loving friendship. Such people are very rare in show business.

I have dwelt on this episode because its personal implications were very important to me, but it had an amusing sequel. My notices were easily the best that I ever received, and as usual, I only glanced at the headlines to get a general impression of success or failure, and did not read them carefully until some time later, because I have found that they affect one's performance, whether good or bad. A kind person collected them all, underlined them in red, and sent them to me. A few years later, I married a very young girl who suddenly and unexpectedly became a movie star. Discovering the *Othello* notices on my desk one day, she was so overcome by jealousy that she destroyed them. Sic transit gloria.

While *Othello* was still playing, *Beloved Enemy* opened on Broadway to great success, and for a moment I was at the top of the theatrical tree. Bill Hawks now wrote me that Sam Goldwyn, David Selznick, and Walter Wanger would like to sign a three-way exclusive contract with me. They were the three leading independent producers of the day, and as I think of it now, this must surely have been one of the most astonishing and flattering motion-picture offers that a young actor can ever have received. I relayed the news to England.

"You get on the boat as you promised and come straight back here!" said my fiery one.

"What shall I tell them?" I asked.

"Tell them you will discuss it when you get to Hollywood next year!" she said.

I did just that: I turned it down, got on a boat and went back to London. Poor Bill Hawks was left holding the bag, and as for me, I was soon to regret my folly. "Absence makes the heart grow fonder," or "Out of sight, out of mind"? These gems of human wisdom always have their counterpart. My return to wintry England was a mistake from every point of view, personal and professional, and was to lead to a still graver mistake.

Charles Laughton, wearying like myself of Hollywood, had decided to attempt something worthwhile in the theater. Gathering together a group of distinguished English players and enlisting the services of Tyrone Guthrie as director, he had asked Lilian Baylis, the old dragon who for so many years had presented Shakespeare at the Old Vic, if she would allow him to do a season at her theater. The story ran that Miss Baylis received him with suspicion.

"We don't want stars at the Vic," she snapped. "We make our own stars here!"

Charles was used to very different treatment in Hollywood, but he controlled himself with difficulty and spoke earnestly to her. He was the slave of Shakespeare, he said.

Why, God, in heaven! he slept every night with Shakespeare under his pillow!

"That doesn't mean you can speak his verse," replied Miss Baylis.

This was too much for the well-known Laughton temperament.

"Jesus Christ! Just give me a chance!" he cried.

Miss Baylis looked at him, horrified.

"Young man," she asked, "are you blaspheming, or are you saying your prayers?"

Tyrone Guthrie intervened and poured oil on the troubled waters, so that finally, though grudgingly, Miss Baylis agreed to receive the star-studded company. Plans for the season were almost complete when I arrived.

Laughton and I had started in the theater at approximately the same time, and although we had never been friends, there existed between us a mutual professional admiration which, however, we were of course both too English and too reticent to put into words. Even now, he did not speak to me personally, but deputed Guthrie to ask me if I would join him. Unfortunately, the only parts left uncast were small ones which could hardly be attractive to me. As we mulled over this difficulty, which Guthrie perfectly understood, he suddenly said, "What about *Hamlet?* I think I could persuade Charles to do the King, and the other parts would suit the company well."

Of course every actor wants to play Hamlet, and I was no exception because I had long believed that it would be the perfect part for me. I asked him for a couple of days to think it over. My mind was in a turmoil because I was living, at that moment, on top of a volcano in my personal life which might erupt, and my one thought was to escape. My heart, as usual, governed my head. I wrote a hasty note of regret to Guthrie, packed my bags, and left surreptitiously for the South of France, where I joined my mother and father.

When I told Lulu that I had turned down Hamlet, she was appalled. What in the name of heaven could have prompted me to do such a thing? I didn't like to tell her the truth, so I said I felt I didn't have enough experience for the part.

"My poor boy," she wailed, "by the time you have enough experience, you will have to play Polonius — because you *won't look it!"*

It was a bad time for me, and nobody to blame but myself as usual. It is small comfort now to reflect that not many actors can have had the opportunity to turn down Romeo, Hamlet, and a combined offer from Goldwyn, Selznick and Wanger, all in the space of a few months. I never had another offer to play Shakespeare, and I never had another offer from Goldwyn, Selznick, or Wanger.

Over twenty years later, Katharine Cornell and myself played Mrs. Patrick Campbell and Bernard Shaw in the play *Dear Liar,* constructed from their famous correspondence, in sixty-seven cities across the U.S.A. and Canada, and I am reminded that Shaw once wrote of her, "Stella Patrick Campbell had beauty, wit, talent, and temperament. At one time, she had the ball at her feet; she kicked it away; it rolled out of her reach, and she was never again able to touch it."

I too had the ball at my feet after Iago, but although from time to time I returned to the theater, I never again had a great part until I played Higgins in *My Fair Lady* across the country with the National Company in 1957–58.

Scene 6

Important Discomfort

I WAS with my mother and father in Rome when a cable from Bill Hawks brought me an offer from Mervyn Leroy to star in *The Great Garrick*, by Ernst Vajda, author of *Fata Morgana* and other successful plays as well as a number of motion pictures.

A short time before I had left Hollywood, Vajda had come to my house to tell me this story, which he proposed to write as a play for me. Hawks and myself had been delighted with it and he, encouraged by our enthusiasm, had acted the various parts with gusto, keeping us laughing with his witty dialogue and heavy Hungarian accent. I had agreed at once to take the play, and he had rushed home in great excitement to put it down on paper. Unfortunately, on the way he stopped in at a cocktail party where, after a couple of drinks, he had a fine time retelling the story, with embellishments no doubt, to Mervyn Leroy. Without hesitation, Mervyn offered to buy it for a movie, and without thinking, Vajda accepted. Time went by and he failed to deliver a script to either of us. Mervyn pressed him until he finally produced an outline which bore little relationship to the story we had all enjoyed. It seemed he had forgotten it! We all had to remind him of pieces of his own dialogue. I lost my play, and while Mervyn did manage to make a picture for Warner Brothers, the story was never as good as it had been at the first telling.

Co-starred with me in *The Great Garrick* was the young
and entrancing Olivia de Havilland, to whom I gave a cake
at a party on the set for her twenty-first birthday. I little
thought that I would one day marry her younger sister, Joan
Fontaine. James Whale directed, and Edward Everett Horton
exhibited his great comic talent as my valet, but the picture
was to flop at the box office — so badly, in fact, that Jack
Warner told Hawks he never wanted to see me on the lot
again. He did, however, in the following year.

The old dilemma now faced me; to stay in Hollywood or to
leave? This time I had no doubt of the answer; I would
leave. Let them send for me if they wanted me.

The evening before my departure, I gave a small cocktail
party — a most unusual thing for me to do at that time —
and among the people who floated in was a young actor
whom I had not met before. Chatting over a drink, he confided to me that he was practically broke, but if only he
could get to New York he believed he had a chance of marrying a rich girl. So sure was he of this that he was thinking of
working his way round on a freighter. Now I have always
felt a deep sympathy with out-of-work actors who have no
money, so I asked if he would care to fly East with me,
though I warned him that I had planned a dawn takeoff on
the following morning, in the hope of reaching Albuquerque
by sunset. Immediately he begged me to take him, though
he said he couldn't be ready before 9:30, as he had to give up
his room, pack his things, and so on, and to this I agreed,
mentally calculating courses and distances to airports closer
than Albuquerque.

I had sent off my trunks by rail some days before, but
when I arrived at his address next morning I still had a suit-

case, golf clubs, tennis racket, a couple of overcoats, a parcel or two, and a small attaché case which I used to fit into a compartment behind the pilot's seat. I found my young friend sitting outside on a pile of baggage even bigger than my own. All except one suitcase, I told him firmly, must go by Railway Express. This upset him, and he wanted to know why I could take golf clubs if he couldn't.

"For three reasons," I told him. "First, the plane won't carry the weight. Second, it is an open-cockpit job and the rear cockpit has only room for myself and the controls, so all the baggage has to be jammed into the front cockpit with you, where you will have to sit with it for four days. Finally," I said, "it's my airplane!"

He had probably assumed, as I was to him a big star, that I had a big plane with lots of baggage space, a couple of pilots, and all the comforts, so this revelation rather staggered him, but he braced himself and we went off to the Railway Express.

It was around noon when we took off, and the Waco climbed slowly with the heavy load. We passed over the San Bernardino Mountains and the Mojave Desert and made a stop at Needles, on the California-Arizona border, for gas and a sandwich. From there, I set a course for the small grass airfield on the south rim of the Grand Canyon. We could make it by sunset, there was a good hotel and one of the wonders of the world to show my young friend.

It is high at the Canyon, nearly 6000 feet, and the air is thin, and although I came in fast we landed rather hard, and I made a mental note to use the whole runway for takeoff. The sun was setting and I taxied up to the little deserted hut which served as an office. I cut the motor, shut off the gas, set the brake, took off my helmet, and prepared to tie down the plane for the night, there being no hangar. Suddenly I became aware that my passenger, having extricated himself laboriously from the pile of baggage, was attempting to climb out of his cockpit, suitcase in hand, on the wrong side of the plane.

"Hey!" I cried. "Not that side! There's no step there!"

Too late — he tried to turn, slipped, and fell onto the lower wing. There was a smashing, rending sound, as he disappeared from sight. I ran round the tail and stared in horror. He lay on the ground while the suitcase, which had penetrated the fabric of the wing, stood on end in the gaping hole it had made.

The culprit picked himself up, yanked the suitcase out of the wing, and said coolly, "I'm awfully sorry. I hope it can be mended."

Mended. Where? How? By whom? I couldn't speak. I felt as if I had been stabbed. As far as I knew, we were hundreds of miles from the nearest aircraft mechanic, and I had neither the tools nor the knowledge to repair a fabric-covered wing. I knew nothing about such things. My voice came back to me, and I said weakly, "I am booked to sail on the *Normandie* from New York on Tuesday next!"

We were sitting on the ground in silence, when the lights of the hotel car picked us up. We drove to the Canyon and ate our dinner in silence. The disaster was too great for words. But I was thinking, thinking.

Next morning, I was in the drugstore as soon as it opened. I bought several rolls of the widest adhesive tape I could get. I had heard that airplane wings, in those days before the use of aluminum, were covered with fabric to which "dope" was applied before painting. What dope was, I had no idea, but necessity is the mother of invention and I determined to experiment. I cut up lengths of the tape and laid it back and forth across the gaping hole in the wing, the underside of which was fortunately still intact. I knew that the lifting effect of an aircraft wing is provided, for a technical reason which I won't go into here, by the upper, rather than the lower side, and my fear was that the force exerted would, in the absence of dope, lift my ungainly patch from the wing, admitting the onrushing air which might quickly tear the fabric off the whole thing.

I stowed my passenger — by now thoroughly chastened — in the front cockpit, surrounded and covered him with baggage, and gave him strict instructions that he should never take his eye off the patch and should tell me, over the gosport system, if he saw any movement. I then taxied to the far end of the rough, grass runway and carefully warmed the motor for takeoff. This is a moment I don't like to think of now, but fools rush in where angels fear to tread.

Pushing the throttle all the way forward, I waited a few seconds for the motor to wind up and released the brakes. The Waco lurched forward and slowly gathered speed. The field at Grand Canyon is surrounded by scrub pine, and the trees were uncomfortably close by the time I was able to ease her off the ground; she climbed slowly in the thin air, and I saw the trees passing just below me as I applied gentle back pressure on the stick. I was so much occupied with the effort to gain altitude that it was a few seconds before I became aware, over the noise of the engine, of the shouts of my passenger who, in his agitation, forgot to speak into the mouthpiece of the gosport. Turning round, I saw him pointing wildly at the patch. The ends were lifting and fluttering. Gingerly, I made a shallow turn, with the trees whipping by just below my wheels, and landed.

Out came the adhesive tape, and this time I passed it right around the wing, around and around till it looked like a great bandage. Again we took off, and this time miraculously it held, all the way to Albuquerque, where a T.W.A. mechanic effected a proper repair — dope, paint, and all — with no charge.

Next day we reached Springfield, Illinois, landed in a heavy rainstorm and were weatherbound for two days. One can never be sure about weather across the vast American continent. A year later, I was to fly from Los Angeles to Miami and back in midwinter, and apart from a few hours delay occasioned by a wind shift in Mississippi, I had nothing but clear weather all the way. Finally we were able to get out of Springfield and, by following the Iron Compass of the railroad, I groped my way through the murk of St. Louis and got to Pittsburgh. There the weather shut down in earnest, with the forecast offering little hope for the next few days, and in order not to miss the *Normandie* I had to take the airline on to New York. My young friend was difficult about this; I had promised to take him to New York, he said, and the least I could do was pay his fare.

Poor chap, when we got there he found that his bird had flown; her mother, hearing of his imminent arrival, had spirited her off to London. He turned up there later, and I found him waiting outside Claridge's Hotel in the hope of catching sight of her. Taking pity on him, I asked him to lunch, in the course of which I discovered he had seen nothing of London beyond the outside of Claridge's. I offered to spend the afternoon showing him the sights — Westminster Abbey, the Houses of Parliament, the Thames, Whitehall, Trafalgar Square, and so on. With a patronizing smile, he patted my arm and said, "Oh, no thanks. I'm not civic-minded!" I got on a bus and left him. But he was a good-natured fellow, he had courage, and he had faith in me as a pilot. I salute his memory.

Human life is a chancy thing. I nearly died in the darkness over Pennsylvania. I nearly died twice, and possibly three times, during my flying days — and nearly took others with me. I nearly died, like everybody else, countless times on the roads. I nearly died on a hot summer's afternoon in the middle of the Bay of Naples, in 1944, and in my opinion I nearly died twice in hospitals. One of these near misses took place in the American Hospital in Paris that summer of 1938. I had left London to spend a few days in Paris en route to join Reggie Reixach in Antibes. As I remember, I had an assignation with a charming English lady — or was she Australian — but she didn't turn up and I was left to cool my heels in the little Hotel France et Choiseul. I went to bed one night with the intention of leaving in the morning, but awoke in the early hours with a very painful throat which grew rapidly worse. Looking in the mirror, I saw two white boils, or quinsies, one on either side, and I began to run a temperature. The poor old hotel doctor had no idea what to do, so I got myself somehow into a taxi and went to the American Hospital in Neuilly, where I was put to bed and attended by an arrogant, stiff-necked specialist who barked commands in French to his staff and turned to go. Speaking with great difficulty and in imperfect French, I asked if he was going to lance the quinsies.

"Non!" he replied. "Je refuse!"

Well, I said, what did he intend to do? He had prescribed a number of " piqûres," he said.

What would be their effect, I asked painfully.

He lifted an admonitory finger. "Important discomfort!" he said.

"You speak English?" I croaked in astonishment.

"Certainly," he replied. "I speak it as well as you do." And he turned and left the room. The French take little care to conceal their dislike of foreigners, and indeed they don't seem to like each other very much, but I felt this was going a bit too far.

The *piqûres* more than lived up to his description. For several days I ran a very high temperature indeed and at times, I think, was a bit delirious. As the temperature subsided and I came back to life the poison seemed to go into my bloodstream, and I was wracked by agonizing pains in my back and joints. At one point, when I really felt I couldn't last much longer, I sent a message to my family. My brother arrived, went out on the town and didn't turn up again for three days, when he appeared at my bedside with a sheepish smile and a large black eye. I sent him home. My father and mother came, looking old and frail, tenderly concerned about me, and bewildered by the rush and noise of Paris. We had grown so far apart that it was hard for us to communicate, and after a day or two they went back to their nest in Birmingham. I was alone and sick and very low.

I was in that hospital for six weeks and I had plenty of time to think about my life; the more I thought, the less I liked it. Here I was, at the age of thirty-six, more than halfway through my "three score years and ten," and what had I to show for it? A few successes, a lot of failures, no wife, no children, and no home. I had accumulated at one time around $50,000 in savings, but then I had yielded to the advice of the vice-president of my bank, of Walter Huston and others, and had entrusted $40,000 to the management of a firm of investment counsel in New York. At our interview in Wall Street they had spoken to me gravely about the necessity for diversification, and other aspects of investment policy which I didn't fully understand; nor did they, I think, because they lost half my money within the year. I took the balance away from them, so then I was left with $30,000 and this did not seem à great reward for so many years of working, scrimping, and saving, of living alone with a wardrobe trunk in cheap hotel rooms, eating cheap meals, taking a bus instead of a taxi or walking instead of taking a bus, watching pennies and doing without. It didn't seem much to show for all the jobs I had done either, though at least I could say that I owed nothing to anybody, including the U.S. and British tax-gatherers, and that was perhaps more than could be said of most other actors.

What had I gained from this heartbreaking profession to compensate me? Precious little, it seemed. My Packard and my Waco, a set of golf clubs, a large wardrobe such as all actors accumulate, the respect perhaps of some of my fellows, but a reputation among managers and producers and agents as an unpredictable, arrogant actor who might at any time come up with a stunning performance but who had never seemed to build a career, either on stage or screen. My few friends were genuine and loyal but of numerous acquaintances I had made in America how many could be counted as friends? It seemed that I had made more enemies

than friends in the motion-picture industry. The more I
thought, the less I liked myself. At nineteen, in Liverpool, I
had believed that I would be a successful shipping magnate
by the time I was forty, though I could hardly have imagined
getting that old, and at that age I had planned to go into
politics and make a brilliant career in the House of Commons. What was I now? A rolling stone which had gathered no moss and was going nowhere.

I thought of Sir Gerald du Maurier, the king of the London stage, saying to me bitterly, "So you want to be an actor,
eh? Tell me — have you a private income?"

I thought of the great motion-picture stars I had met, Fairbanks and Pickford, Talmadge and Swanson, Gilbert and
Novarro, Rod La Rocque and Vilma Banky, Dick Barthelmess, Monte Blue, Colleen Moore, Edmund Lowe, Alice
White, Conrad Nagel, Milton Sills, George Bancroft and so
many others, all swept away by the talkies — not just having
a bad year, like people in other professions, but out, finished,
waking one morning in a beautiful home and calling an agent
to be told that the studio has not taken up an option, or has "no
suitable pictures in preparation," and hearing in the tone of
the agent's voice that this phone call is really wasting his
time. "Let's have lunch one day . . . Don't call me; I'll call
you . . . Well, let me know if there is anything I can do for
you." These are the phrases by which the agent intimates to
the actor that he is washed up, out of the business, that he
can go and drown himself in his swimming pool for all anybody in Hollywood cares. And who pays the bills now?
Who pays the servants, the secretary, the gardener, the business manager, the whole entourage of a movie star? Where
is the money to come from to meet the life-insurance premi-
ums, the various family allowances, and those frightening

sums of back taxes? A few, a lucky few, might have saved enough to continue to live out there on a reduced scale for a time, and one would continue to see them at the houses of friends, looking jealously at newcomers in the business, but gradually they all drifted away and sank out of sight. Hollywood was a company town, like Detroit, and there was no place in its society for those not actively involved.

I thought of a grand party at the Jack Warner house, one Saturday night, when I had found Frances Marion, the famous script writer, sitting alone. I had always enjoyed talking to her.

"Well, Frances," I had said, "why are you looking so sad and lonely?"

"I am thinking of all the years I have been coming to these parties," she had replied. "Not many people here tonight were here ten years ago, and I think almost none were here twenty years ago."

Had I been right or wrong to turn my back on Thalberg and his long-term contract?

I thought, as I so often did, of Clare Eames, to whom England had refused a work permit. It seemed she had come to the end of her career, and I realized now the wonderful courage and dignity with which she had faced disaster so early in her life. She was grateful, she had said, for everything the theater had given her, and if she was not to act any more she would be content to fill her life with devotion to me and my career. I thought sadly of the wasted years, and of the way in which I had betrayed her burning faith in my ability. She could not have been proud of me now — and yet, in a way, it was her doing, because after she left me I hadn't been able to care any more.

Then and there I determined to change myself and my life.

Like a card player, I looked at my hand and saw that I held
only low cards; how should I play them? I was, I decided,
finished in the acting profession. London had forgotten me,
or thought of me vaguely as an emigrant. New York was occupied with American plays which seemed to provide no
parts for me, and, in any case, after the easy life of California
I hated New York. Hollywood had washed its hands of me
after *The Great Garrick*. I could blame nobody but myself
for my situation, for I had certainly had the ball at my feet.
Now more then ever I needed to find a proper job, a real and
satisfying occupation.

As I sat one afternoon in a chair on the hospital terrace, a
blanket over my knees, I watched a small plane droning
slowly across the sky and suddenly the answer came to me.
Aviation would solve my problem! There was my opportunity, there was a field in which I could find occupation and
absorbing interest in some form or another. To hell with the
theater and to hell with the movies! I would get well, go
back to California, buy a little home with a bit of garden,
marry a nice, good-natured girl who liked to fly, and set myself up in the aviation business, perhaps as a fixed-base operator with a small charter service, or better still a regular
flight service to Palm Springs, which had none in those days.
Doctors everywhere had told me that the only cure for my
recurrent sinus trouble was dry desert air. "You ought to live
in Arizona," they all pontificated. Well, the desert was only a
hundred miles from Los Angeles! I saw it all clearly, and in
my excitement I got up and took a few shaky steps along the
terrace, which surprised and pleased my sweet little White
Russian nurse when she came out to wheel me back to my
room. She was so kind, so gentle and so very good to me.

We stood for a minute, looking at the first hint of sunset, and then, as she took my arm, an idea came to me. I turned and looked at her.

"Do you like to fly, nurse?" I asked her. Her charming smile faded. Oh no, she said, she hated it! Regretfully, I ruled her out.

On the day I left the hospital I didn't see my doctor to say goodbye, but a young American intern, who was standing on the steps, helped me into the taxi and, as he was about to close the door, said, "By the way, did they ever find out what was wrong with you?"

"No," I said, "I don't think so."

Before sailing, I stayed a few days with dear P. G. Wodehouse and his wife, who wrapped me in peace and kindness at their delightful house on the golf course at Le Touquet. I said to them, "You know there's another war coming. You should leave here as soon as possible."

"Oh no," they replied comfortably, "Munich has settled all that. There'll be no war, and if there is we shall be well behind the lines, as we were last time."

From my hospital terrace, I had seen a grand fly-past of the French Air Force, and I had no confidence in it. When the German breakthrough came, the Wodehouses were giving a cocktail party. The local gendarme arrived on his bicycle to say that the Germans were down the road, and a few minutes later the Wodehouses were prisoners of war.

Scene 7

A Banner Year

ARRIVING in New York, I felt so ill that I went straight back into hospital, where I was visited by Walter Huston. After talking about this and that, I came to the usual question, what was the latest news about John? Walter's son, John, was a charming but feckless young rascal whom Walter loved, but whose wild adventures had long been a sore trial. Mention of his name was generally Walter's cue to look at the ceiling and sigh, but now his eyes opened wide and he smiled in wonderment and delight.

"You'll never believe it," he said, "but John has written a script and Warner Brothers are so thrilled with it that they have taken him out to Hollywood and put him on contract as a writer! They think he is wonderful! He is now writing on a picture called *The Phantom Crown*, all about Maximilian and Carlotta. Say — there's a great part for you!"

Upon his urging, I sent a telegram to John, who arranged a test for me as soon as I could get out there. I knew indeed it would be a great part for me because, on my visit to Mexico some years before, I had seen all the Maximilian relics and photographs and I knew that with the aid of a good make-up I would look uncannily like the tragic Emperor. A couple of weeks later I made the test, was signed for the part, and went back into hospital once more to undergo a painful operation for the removal of old tonsil roots, which had been poisoning me. Not only that, but through the agency of Bill Hawks, who very decently forgave my former treatment of him, I signed a contract with Hal Roach to make two pictures, one of which, a successful zany farce with Constance Bennett called *Merrily We Live,* I made before the start of the Warner picture.

On my first day's work on *The Phantom Crown,* I was informed that the title had been changed to *Juarez;* I thought then and still think that this was a very unfortunate idea, because the name could mean little to the American public, most of whom couldn't even pronounce it. I was told that it had to be so because Paul Muni had a clause in his contract which said that every picture in which he played must be named after his character — Pasteur, Zola, Juarez. In my belief it was a pity to insist on this because it undoubtedly affected the business at the box office, and Muni's performance was so fine that he didn't need it; furthermore Juarez, despite the emphasis which was placed on his scenes, could never overshadow the tragic, romantic figures of Maximilian and Carlotta. I also think it was a mistake not to have shot it in color, but it was and still is a great motion picture. Bette Davis was at her brilliant best and the supporting cast was drawn from the cream of Hollywood actors. I sometimes wonder why this wonderful story has never been remade.

I was nominated for the Academy Award for Maximilian, but beaten out by Thomas Mitchell in *Stagecoach.* Frankly, I think I should have won it, but I must admit that on the night of the Academy banquet, which was much more a family affair than it is now, I was in Havana, Cuba, and this can hardly have contributed to any popularity with the voting members.

It is always interesting to actors to watch directors at work
and to see how differently they go about it. *Juarez* was directed by William Dieterle, a very tall, precise German with
dark, burning eyes and strictly formal manners, who had a
fixed belief in numerology. On the day of my test he asked
my birth date and did some rapid calculation on a bit of
paper, which made me apprehensive because my agent had
warned me that if the numbers didn't come out right I
wouldn't get the part. It was said that he refused to start
shooting on an inauspicious day and once, when the studio
insisted, he had brought the crew in a few days earlier and
made one unimportant shot so that the picture could have
its official start on a day favored by the numbers. His script
was a Bible, of which not one syllable could be changed, and
he always wore white cotton gloves on the set in case it
should be necessary, in getting the exact angle he wanted, to
touch the face of a player. Most directors say "Camera!" or
"Action!" to start a scene, but I can still hear Dieterle's classic actor's voice saying, "Here we . . . *go!*"

By contrast, I worked for Hal Roach on *Captain Fury*, immediately after *Juarez*, and on his set things were entirely
different. Hal, who had come up from silent movies with his
Laurel and Hardy series and the Our Gang comedy shorts,
was used to more free and easy ways. He set out to make a
picture from the famous Australian novel *For the Term of His
Natural Life*, but, shortly before starting, discovered that he
didn't have the rights. Nothing daunted, he improvised from
day to day a somewhat similar story which he called *Captain
Fury*, giving the cast dialogue out of his head as he went
along, line by line. He would point at us in turn, "Now you
say this, you say that, and" — pause for thought — "what
could you say then?"

This was rather startling after Dieterle, and I was not often ready with an answer, expecially as I didn't know what was going to happen next. One day the whole unit of nearly a hundred people, with horses and cowboys, technicians and trailers, was on location in the hills above Malibu.

"Now," says Hal, "you ride in here, Brian, and you see Victor McLaglen, riding through the trees. You meet here and both rein in your horses. Victor, you say (pause for thought), 'Now listen you! I'm the boss around here, so you lay off, see!' Then Brian you say, 'You can't get away with this!' Victor, you say, 'Oh can't I? I'll soon show you!' " A little more of this high-class dialogue and Hal tells us that's the scene and we'll shoot it.

"Wait a minute, Hal," I say. "How does it end? I mean I don't just sit here do I? Where do I go?"

"Let me think," he says. He thinks for a moment and then his face brightens. "I know! You see the girl sitting on that gate off-camera and you ride out. Your next scene is with her."

All right, after some trouble with the horses, and more trouble getting Victor to remember his lines, we shoot it.

"Cut!" cries Hal, and then he ruminates a bit. He comes over to me and speaks to me confidentially; he is always very polite because I don't think he has ever worked with legitimate actors before, and he is a little in awe of me; also he has to pay me $40,000 for the picture and that is kind of a body blow to him.

"Brian," he whispers, "you smiled when you went out of the shot. That's not right."

"Oh?" I say. "But you told me I saw the girl over there."

"Yes, that's right — but you're mad at her!"

"Am I? Why?"

Hal reflects for a moment and then he gives me a charming
Irish wink. "I'll tell you tomorrow!" he says. *Captain Fury*
seemed such a farrago of nonsense to me that I was very
happy to know that *Juarez* would rescue me by coming out
at about the same time. Well, *Juarez* turned out to be a
highly respected box-office flop while *Captain Fury* cleaned
up and went on playing all over the world for many years,
with countless television runs. I only wish I had had a per-
centage deal instead of a salary for it. When I reached Italy
in 1944, it had just opened in Naples, being one of the first
American pictures shown in years, with Victor and myself
speaking fluent Italian. Crowds of small boys followed me
delightedly down the streets crying, "Capitano Furio!" As
recently as 1966, a waiter in a small café on the Greek island
of Patmos told me he had seen it several times and would
never forget it. "Everybody in Greece knows *Captain Fury!*"
he said.

And so, in the year following my illness and despair in
Paris, I found myself in the happy position of paying enormous taxes to the U.S. Government. It was a banner year for
me. I bought and furnished a charming little house in Beverly Hills. This was the first house I had ever owned, and I
loved it dearly. I put in a small swimming pool and at last I
had a garden, in which I worked with an Englishman's enjoyment. I had not, however, forgotten the roof of the American Hospital in Paris, nor the decisions I had come to there.
I might be doing well momentarily in the theatrical profession, but my faith in it as a job was no stronger than it had
always been. I still looked for a job that would fill my days
with interest and would last my lifetime. I still believed that
aviation would provide this.

One day, I went over to Burbank Airport and took a lesson in aerobatic flying from Tex Rankin, then national champion, who terrified me by turning me on my back for the first time and keeping me there for several minutes, calmly explaining the technique of inverted flight as he did so. I was feeling rather shaken when we landed. Tex introduced me to a debonair and charming French pilot named Max Constant, who laughed at my plight and consoled me with stories of his own first experience. He had been a cameraman, but had lost his job and, feeling disgusted with the movie industry, had taken up flying instead. In the course of a few weeks, we became firm friends and I learned a lot from him. Together we flew in my Waco all the way to Palm Beach and Miami and back, and over much of the western states. I confided to Max my idea of an airline between Los Angeles and Palm Springs, and found he had been thinking along the same lines. We agreed to go into it together and we spent many hours in calculation and research.

I brought my mother and father out from England, and they attended the Hollywood openings of *Merrily We Live*, *Juarez*, and *Captain Fury*. Willoughby de Lacy wore his navy blue, double-breasted old suit on all occasions, in Beverly Hills, wading in the sea at Malibu, in the hot sunshine of Palm Springs, and he mildly disapproved of everything. Lulu, grown deaf and dim of sight, reveled in sunshine such as she had never seen in Birmingham.

I had hoped to keep them both in California, perhaps in a little place on the beach or in the desert, because after Munich I had the conviction that war was inevitable. When Stalin signed his cynical treaty with Hitler, it became certain, and I said so. My father immediately said they must go

home, and no argument could move him. I tried to explain
that they would simply be two old and useless people to
feed, and I told him that I anticipated terrible suffering for
the civilian population, but all he would say was "Sorry, old
chap. We must go home." My mother said she thought he
missed his cat, and I believe he felt unsafe away from his
own familiar surroundings and little possessions — which,
alas, he was soon to lose. He insisted on going home and she,
the dutiful English wife, went with him. "If he wants to go,
bless him, we must go," she said. Useless to regret that I
didn't make them stay. I never saw her again. They were
bombed out of their home and moved to lodgings in Stratford-on-Avon, and there Miss Louise de Lacy gave her farewell performance.

She wrote that she was standing with the old verger by
Shakespeare's grave in the old village church at Stratford one
quiet summer's evening. The setting sun lighted the stained
glass windows, surrounding the chancel, which depict Jaques'
speech about the seven ages of man from *As You Like It*.
Pointing to each of the seven windows in turn, she recited
the famous lines. There was a moment's silence after she
finished, and then her audience of one heaved a sigh and said,
"You seem to know a lot." Pause. "D'you know Adkins, the
butcher? Ah! — Oi've killed 'undreds of pigs for 'im in my
time."

She waited for more. None came, so she left. Her gentle,
gallant heart failed soon afterwards.

In the spring of 1939, backed at last by the security of a
home of my own and by some measure of success, I had become a little more sociable, less de Lacy and more Thomas

perhaps. In Hollywood it seemed that one lived in a world composed entirely of movie people, who moved in intersecting, but not concentric, circles. Except on big public occasions, the artistic side of the industry — always "the industry," never "the business," as in the theater — did not mix with the executive side and people only mixed with those who were roughly in the same income bracket. The executives, being for the most part Jewish, strong in their faith, aware of their power, and proud of their success, were naturally fearful that friendship with the artists might involve them in embarrassment and obligations; if a producer was too friendly with his star, it might be difficult when he didn't take up the star's option. The artists had similar feelings about the producers, and were divided among themselves by a rigid caste system. Stars never invited bit players or extras to dinner, never saw the technical people of the camera, make-up, wardrobe, or cutting departments outside the studio, no matter how friendly they might be on the set; integration was okay within the gates, but never outside. Then there were national groups, such as the French — as everywhere, a tight little circle, meeting on Saturday nights to discuss wine and food, sighing for the superior civilization of *La Belle France* and shrugging their shoulders at the antics of the American barbarians; or the Germans — mostly refugees from the Nazi persecution, clinging unhappily together and struggling with the English language; and the English — united by the Aubrey Smith Cricket Club, memories of the old country, and shared beginnings in the London theater. The Ronald Colmans, Roland Young, Leslie Howard, Ralph Forbes, the Nigel Bruces, David Niven, the Aubrey Smiths, Edmund Gwenn, Sir Cedric Hardwicke, Henry Daniell, Ian

Hunter, Laurence Olivier, Cary Grant, Robert Coote, Alan Napier, the Basil Rathbones, Ray Millands, Richard Greenes, Greer Garson, Merle Oberon, Madeleine Carroll, Constance Collier, Dame May Whitty and Ben Webster, the Alfred Hitchcocks, Gladys Cooper and Phillip Merivale — most of us had known each other for years. Some of us became American citizens and others resident aliens; all of us enjoyed the unaccustomed sunshine, the casual dress, the swimming, tennis, and golf, the easy trips to the mountains, the beaches, and the desert. The motion-picture industry brought us all together and established a miniature United Nations in California.

I was moving from one picture to another, *Hired Wife,* with the brilliant Rosalind Russell, *My Son, My Son,* with my old friend, Madeleine Carroll, *Sylvia Scarlett,* with Katharine Hepburn and Cary Grant, some good, some bad. It was a successful and happy period for me, but for one thing — I suffered increasingly from the malady of the stars, loneliness. There is not much satisfaction in success if you have nobody to share it with, as the recent tragic biographies of Errol Flynn, Bette Davis, and Hedy Lamarr have revealed. Almost on impulse, I married Joan Fontaine, sister of Olivia de Havilland, young, pretty, gay, and utterly charming — and no actress, thank God, or at least so I thought until the fifth day of our honeymoon in the Oregon woods, when my dream was abruptly shattered by a phone call from David Selznick, offering her the lead in his picture *Rebecca,* with Laurence Olivier.

Over my despairing protests, the honeymoon was instantly abandoned, and we rushed back to Hollywood, where she was launched into orbit as a big new motion-picture star.

Soon after this disaster — and I had seen too much of the marriages of stars to believe it would be anything else — the Second World War broke out and my life, like those of people all over the world, became filled with new and unsuspected problems.

Scene 8

Before the Storm

MEN OF MY GENERATION could never forget the horrors of the First World War or the miseries of its aftermath. In the 1920s, surrounded as we were by widows and orphans, by cripples on crutches and mutilated men in wheelchairs, and seeing as we did ex-officers of famous regiments standing in the gutter, trying to sell pencils or matches, we were all pacifists. We didn't riot, fight the police or sit around on the pavement, like the young Americans protesting the Vietnam war; we were just grimly determined that never, so help us God, would we fight again, for any cause whatsoever.

We were appalled as we watched the clouds of war gathering again in the 1930s and saw ourselves plunging back into the nightmare through which we had so recently suffered. Those of us who had established our lives in California — and by now I counted myself one of them, because I had at last given up my rooms in London, married a California girl, and moved out West — were faced with an agonizing problem: you may be determined never to fight, but when you are attacked by a madman, what do you do?

My family and friends wrote according to their natures. Sir George Arthur said, "This letter may miss you, as I am sure you are already on your way to offer your hand and heart to the service of your King and country." Reggie and my mother both said the war was madness, and I should on no account return to England until I was sure I was needed. My father referred to it only once; he said, "I take no interest in this phony war."

I decided to ask the British Embassy in Washington for guidance, and received an immediate reply advising me to stay where I was until further instructions.

Months passed and I continued to work as a free-lance star in pictures: *The Man Who Lost Himself*, with Kay Francis, *My Sister Eileen* and *What a Woman*, again with Rosalind Russell, and a remake of *Smilin' Through*, with Jeanette MacDonald. In the summer of 1940, Hitler invaded Norway and launched his devastating attack through the Low Countries, taking our leaders so completely by surprise that France immediately collapsed and it was only by a miracle that we were able to snatch our men from the beaches of Dunkirk. The flap was on in England, and was echoed in Hollywood.

The British consul called us all to a meeting and addressed us. The ambassador, he said, was gravely concerned by an English newspaper campaign villifying the so-called British Colony in Hollywood, who were accused of evading their responsibilities. It was essential to stop this, because the fierce light of international publicity beat upon us all and our actions could be of great importance to the British cause in America. It was not desirable, he said, that we should all rush back to England, which had plenty of manpower for the foreseeable future but no equipment, but the Embassy required that each one of us should submit, in writing, his offer of service, and should hold himself ready to be called when

needed. We would further be required, he said, to contrib-
ute heavily to British war charities and to make ourselves
available, whenever called upon, for personal appearances,
speeches, and appeals anywhere in the U.S.A. Sir Cedric
Hardwicke and Cary Grant were deputed to fly to Washington for an interview with the Ambassador, Lord Lothian. A
lighter note was sounded at the end of the consul's meeting
by Errol Flynn, who said that what we seemed to need was a
good public-relations man.

Our two-man deputation soon returned and reported that
Lord Lothian had been satisfied with our letters, and was
firm in his instructions. He addressed a cable to Lord Halifax in London, and gave Hardwicke a copy.* He asked that
a small advisory committee be formed to assist the consul,
and he sent out a retired British Army colonel to act as its
chairman.

We met once a week, the colonel, the consul, Ronald Colman, Basil Rathbone, Herbert Marshall, Cedric Hardwicke
and myself. We reviewed, and as far as possible controlled,

---

* Aug 31st, 1940. Lord Lothian to Lord Halifax:

"I think the short wave broadcast to the U.S. on Thursday night by
J. B. Priestley, supporting accusations against British actors here made in
Sunday Dispatch on August 25th was very undesirable, and will do our
cause no good.

"Nearly two months ago, after consultation with the War Office, I issued
a public statement to the effect that all British actors of military age, that is,
up to thirty one, should go home, and that older actors should remain at
work until new regulations about military age were issued. I understand
that this ruling has been, to all intents and purposes, obeyed. It is therefore quite unfair to condemn older actors, who are simply obeying this
ruling, as "deserters." Moreover the maintenance of a powerful nucleus of
older British actors in Hollywood is of great importance to our own interests,
partly because they are continually championing the British cause in a very
volatile community which would otherwise be left to the mercies of German propaganda, and because the production of films with a strong British
tone is one of the best and subtlest forms of British propaganda. The only
effect of broadcasts like this is quite unjustifiably to discredit British patri-
otism."

the wartime activities of our British Colony; a couple of them, who shall be nameless, were worth nothing, but the rest behaved extremely well and more than justified Lothian's faith in them. One name I must mention is that of Basil Rathbone, President of the British War Relief Association (West Coast Division), who traveled endlessly and worked tirelessly, all over the West, and deserves a large share of credit for the enormous sums of money and gifts of comforts and supplies that were collected by this Division. Had he been in England, he would surely have received a knighthood.

One of our first efforts was to provide ambulances, which were in very short supply in England. I was myself responsible for a number of these, and I sympathized when some of our contributors complained that they never saw the ambulances, or had any idea where they went, or indeed if they went. British War Relief was able to arrange that the name of the donor was painted in small letters on an inside corner of the vehicle; after that, I got letters from friendly drivers, from Birkenhead to Eritrea, at the foot of the Red Sea.

Another activity of the British Colony nearly ended in disaster for us all. At the height of the blitz, our fellow actors in London wanted to send the children of the Actors' Orphanage to America, where they could be brought up in safety. After all, in their eyes we were a lot of rich slackers, so why shouldn't we be made to take responsibility?

At our end, hurried meetings were held, with Dame May Whitty in the chair, and telephones buzzed with anxious debate. It was easy enough to sign pledges, but few actors really have any money, their own futures are uncertain, and there was no knowing how long the war might last; and what

should we do with the children — take them into our own
homes in California or find an eastern school in which they
could all stay together? The British Colony was badly
shaken. London remained firm, and finally, though hesitantly,
we agreed. Thirty children between the ages of five and fifteen sailed, just before the sinking of the *Athenia*, with the
tragic loss of so many young lives, caused the Government to
forbid such schemes. By the time they landed in Boston,
several months had passed in negotiation and in obtaining
the necessary permits and papers from both countries, and
some of those who had blithely signed pledges of support had
either died, gone back to England, or were out of a job and
couldn't pay — and some just didn't pay — so in the end
about eight of us were saddled with the whole responsibility.

Now a miracle occurred. A few days before the children's
arrival, and while they were still at sea, Gertrude Lawrence
and her New York attorney, Fanny Holtzman, made contact
with a wonderful organization, the Gould Foundation in
White Plains, New York, which came to us as a gift from
heaven. They possessed a beautiful school, with dormitories,
classrooms, gardens, playgrounds, a complete staff, lots of
money — and no children to occupy it! They were delighted
to take the orphanage and supported it, with our help, for
four years, giving the children every kindness and attention.
We never quite knew how this miracle came about, but we
thanked God, Gould, Gertrude, and Fanny.

Hagerstown, Maryland, is a small place, but it has a special significance for me. Clare Eames lies on a slope of the
quiet little cemetery and a bronze head of her stands in the

local art gallery. It is also the site of the Fairchild Aircraft factory, and there I went on a bright spring day in 1940 to pick up my new Fairchild 24 high-wing cabin monoplane, successor to the Waco. With her sleek fuselage enclosing a Ranger motor, her black and red paint job with the checkerboard tail, wheel pants, flaps, landing lights, and pale gray upholstery, she was beautiful to behold. The four-place heated cabin was comfortable and the instrument panel well equipped, including a small radio receiver. I fell in love with her on the spot and, after being checked out by a factory pilot, I flew to Washington where Joan was waiting to join me for the flight back to California. No more helmet and goggles, no more wondering about the weather ahead, no more circling the field awaiting a green light for permission to land; I simply switched on the radio, adjusted the frequency and heard the voice of the tower operator saying, "Black Fairchild north of the field. This is Washington Tower. Rock your wings if you hear me."

I rocked.

"Okay, Fairchild. Permission to land runway thirty. Wind southwest ten. Altimeter setting thirty-four point two."

Not quite the exhilaration of open-cockpit flying, but perhaps that's for bachelors, like most of the fun things in life, and a wife has a right to some comfort and convenience.

Joan was a very good passenger, uncomplaining in discomfort and quite unruffled in emergency, just bored with the monotony of flying. I used to have to lay in a supply of magazines and crossword puzzles with which she could pass the time. We crossed and recrossed the continent in the Fairchild, making personal appearances for British War Relief, Bundles for Britain, and the sale of War Bonds. Sometimes we were able to fit in a few days' vacation. We went up with Abby and Connie Wolf to fish the lakes of the northern Maine woods, glorious in their autumn coloring. Out to Cape Cod and Nantucket we went, down the shores of the Chesapeake Bay to Williamsburg, Virginia, out along the desolate coast of North Carolina past Kitty Hawk and Cape Hatteras, landing on the beach to swim in the rollers and taking off again to reach Roanoke Island and Okracoke, the legendary lair of Blackbeard the pirate. On one exhausting trip across the continent for British War Relief, we had with us Connie Wolf as manager and Robert Capa doing a feature story on us for *Life* magazine, but something happened to the great Capa's camera and when we got to Salt Lake City he discovered that all he had was a series of blurs; he left us in disgust and went off to see Ernest Hemingway.

I wrote to Sherman Fairchild, president of the company, telling him of the excellent performance of his airplane. I said, "You should have seen my takeoff from Parco, Wyoming, at sixty-two hundred feet, with four up, lots of baggage and a strong wind!"

He replied, "I am always happy to hear of a Ranger motor taking off at sixty-two hundred feet. That wind must have been a full gale."

In 1941 we flew to Washington for lunch at the White House with President and Mrs. Roosevelt. The English actors, writers, and directors in Hollywood planned to make a motion picture, with the generous help of R.K.O. Studios, in which everybody would donate their services so that the profits might go to American charities. We thought that in this way we could show our gratitude and appreciation for the truly marvelous generosity of the American people to our suffering country. We asked the President to choose the charities, and at this meeting he told us the money would all go to the Infantile Paralysis Fund.

Like most people, I was bowled over by the personal charm, vitality, and magnetism of Roosevelt, who had the irresistible gift of being able to make one feel like the one person he wanted to talk to. In her quiet way too, Mrs. Roosevelt was a woman of immense sympathy and intelligence. I was to visit F.D.R. again, however, when, after *Forever and a Day* had concluded its first successful run, we handed him a check for over $800,000. I walked into his study and there, in place of the vigorous, vital man I had met before, sat a tired old invalid, gaunt and pale. I don't think he really understood who we were or why we were there, but he still smiled automatically and gave us an imitation of his old handshake. The public was certainly not aware of his true condition, for he had recently won a fourth term as President and was on the point of leaving for Yalta to face Stalin and arbitrate the future history of the world. I was shocked because the poor old chap was to my mind obviously incapable of either task.

I cruised eastward from Los Angeles on my way to the desert, watching automatically the various landing fields as they passed under my wing; Ontario to my left, March Field Air Base to my right, and so into the pass between the mountains of San Gorgonio and San Jacinto which leads to Palm Springs. I was alone. Joan, suffering from the traditional nervous breakdown at the conclusion of a picture, had departed — alone, she said — on a Pacific cruise and was now presumably somewhere between Honolulu and Tahiti.

Emerging from the pass, at which point the cool air from the
seaboard meets the hot, rising air of the desert and can often
provide such violent conditions that pilots have nicknamed it
Hellfire Corner, I saw Palm Springs slide into view on my
right and took a couple of turns forward on the stabilizer.
The nose dropped slightly and the airspeed indicator advanced from its normal cruising rate of 120 m.p.h. I began to
see the effects of irrigation on the dry desert ground —
groves of date palms, long straight lines of early Thompson's
seedless grapes, and flat expanses of alfalfa from which as
much as eight cuttings a year can be made by a good farmer.
I flew low over Palm Desert and cut power to glide through
a gap in the foothills, swooping suddenly and dramatically
over the oasis of La Quinta, one of the most beautiful hotels
in the West and a paradise to me. Making a tight circle
within the surrounding hills, I slowed the plane, put down
my flaps and made a feather-light landing on the little
cleared field of sun-baked earth beyond. As I climbed out,
the hot, magical scent of the desert came to me — sagebrush,
mesquite and oleander. I took several deep breaths of the
dry, healing air and I felt it was good to be alive on such a
day. I was tying down the plane, when a truck drove up and
a small, smiling Mexican got out.

"Hello, Pancho!" I cried.

"Oh, I'm glad you've come Mr. Brian," he said. "I think
I've found it!"

The next morning, Pancho and I rode out from La Quinta
on horses, following a line of telegraph poles which marched
across the sandy dunes of the desert. Today there is a fine
highway beside those poles, a golf course covering the
dunes, and broad acres of cultivated land where we passed

only mesquite, sagebrush, and greasewood, on the dry and dusty hummocks; irrigation canals and the widespread use of water from the Colorado River have tempered the extreme dryness of the air; motels, golf ranges, trailer parks, and shopping centers have changed the Coachella Valley almost beyond recognition; but the warm sun is still there, and somewhere in the blue and violet mountains toward sunset a Lorelei sings, soft and sweet and clear. I hear her and my heart aches, but like Ulysses I have lashed myself to the mast, for I know what I know and I pass her by.

On that memorable day neither Pancho nor I knew anything, though perhaps Pancho knew, but Mexicans are easy-going, simple people and it was some years before I realized that they want you to be happy, so if perhaps there are some unpleasant facts that you should know — well, they just don't tell you.

By and by, we came to an unpaved road along which a piece of ground had been leveled and cultivated; the land rose gently to a magnificent semicircle of mountains. Pancho stopped.

"There, Mr. Brian," he said, with a wave of his arm — he never could pronounce the name of Aherne — "there it is! You can get forty acres for $10,000 including the ranch house over there, a well with plenty of water, and a diesel motor to run the pump, and a good old tractor. If you want more desert land you can buy as much as you want for $50.00 an acre!"

In that last sentence, had I but known it, he offered me a fortune for nothing; farming is finished in the Coachella Valley, but desert land sells today for $2500 an acre and up.

I had first seen Pancho a couple of years before, up in a

date palm at La Quinta; the next time we met he was lying under a grapefruit tree. We had struck up an acquaintance based upon love of the desert and a shared dream of a farm which I would own and he would work; alfalfa to start with, followed by Thompson's seedless grapes which, coming from the earliest ripening area in the United States, were then fetching high prices in the eastern markets. He saw in it an assured future, and I health, profit, and at long last a fascinating occupation.

We rode across the desert toward the mountains. A rattlesnake hissed as we passed and a covey of quail skittered out of the brush, breaking the silence. When we reached the highest dune we stopped and looked around, enchanted by all we saw. This is the place, I thought. On this spot I will build my hacienda, round a courtyard in Mexican style, approached by a winding road lined with yellow flowering paloverde trees. In my imagination I saw below me my vineyards, through which I would ride every morning on a tractor, or perhaps on a white horse, with maybe a silver-studded saddle and a big sombrero, greeting the smiling ranch hands as I passed. No more sweating under the lights of sound stages, no more traffic with the labyrinthine politics and intrigue of Hollywood, no more anxiety and nervous strain in the theatres of filthy, crowded cities. Here I would make my home and invest my savings, and fill my life to the end with happiness and interest. A proper job, an absorbing job at last, and in surroundings of marvelous beauty. My heart glowed as I rose in the saddle and, changing the well-remembered lines a little, I cried:

"Under the wide and sunlit sky,
Here let me live, here let me die!"

Pancho laughed delightedly. He thought that was very nice. To a watching coyote, we must have looked like Don Quixote and Sancho Panza.

In the next few days I bought 160 acres of land, including the existing farm. I hired some local "desert rats" to clear and burn the brush and contracted for a couple of big trac- tors to level the land, a drilling team to sink another well, and a cement company to lay irrigation pipelines along the sides of each ten acre plot — carefully excluding twenty acres of the highest ground for my hacienda. Late on a Sun- day afternoon I shook hands with Pancho, climbed into the Fairchild and took off for Los Angeles.

Over Riverside I set a course for Glendale airport, instead of my home base at Los Angeles Municipal, because I wanted to leave the plane for some work to be done on it, and I had arranged with my man Frank to meet me there. It was getting dark as I approached the field and I calculated that I would just make it with a few minutes to spare, but I had no qualms, as this was a municipal field with airline serv- ice and a well-lighted runway. Switching my radio to the tower frequency, I waited for a call. None came, and as I had no transmitter I could only wait and circle the field. As I turned on the crosswind leg of my pattern I suddenly saw a red light glare at me from the tower and, thinking that per- haps some other aircraft was before me in the pattern, I hast- ily pulled up and went around. Again I got the red light, and now I began to be disturbed because it was practically dark and I saw that I had allowed myself to get pretty low on gas; I went around again, straining my eyes to see the lights of any other aircraft or any obstruction on the ground, but I could see nothing in my way. Three or four times I circled and each time I got the red glare. Finally I looked at the black night sky over Los Angeles and I looked at my gas gauge and, remembering Bob Blair's advice, I decided what to do and I did it. Figuring that I would claim an emergency, I broke the law, chopped the power back and came on in with the red light glaring at me indignantly all the way. As I drew up at the hangar and cut the switch, a couple of mechanics ran out, seized my struts and pushed me hastily inside.

A man ran excitedly from the office. "Hey!" he shouted. "The Tower says get that pilot's name and number!" And then as I climbed out of the plane, "Hey, you! How come you pay no attention to a red light? You are to report to the Tower at once! This field is closed to all aircraft!"

"Now look," I said indignantly, "where am I supposed to go? What do you mean, the field is closed?"

"Man," he said, "every airport on the West Coast is closed!"

"*What? . . . Why?*"

He stared at me. "Oh my God," he said, "haven't you heard? The Japs bombed Pearl Harbor this morning!"

It was Sunday, the 7th of December, 1941.

Scene 9

America at War

ALL FLYING was stopped within a hundred miles of the coast and the Army took my beautiful Fairchild for the transportation of senior officers. A few weeks after she went, my friend Abby Wolf, now an Army Air Force pilot, was in a hangar at Chanute Field Air Base, Wyoming, where he caught a glimpse of a black and red checkerboard tail sticking out from behind some old packing cases and an empty Coca-Cola machine. "I know that plane!" he cried. "What happened to it?" Please don't ask, they said; they didn't like to think about it. He insisted. Well, they said, a pilot of the Ferry Command had delivered it one morning for the use of the commanding general and a small crowd had gathered to admire it. Whose was it, they asked? The pilot knew no more than that it had belonged to a movie star. They all went in to lunch. As the weather was clear and calm, nobody thought to tie the plane down and, while they were inside, a sudden local cyclone developed which completely demolished it. All that was left, when they came out, was the checkerboard tail — and the wrath of the commanding general.

America's entry into the war changed the focus of our activities in Hollywood. The British Consul's Advisory Board faded away, replaced by the Hollywood Victory Committee, under whose auspices I was to travel all over the nation, visiting camps, hospitals, and other military installations. I really believe this is the hardest kind of war work, unless one has a special kind of talent like Bob Hope, and in the next war I am determined to be in a uniform in any capacity, whatever my age. In World War II, I carried both English and American draft cards, but neither country called me, and that is an invidious position for a man who is still reasonably young and active.

I can never forget the first camp tour on which I was sent — alone. Just talk to the boys, I was told, they like to see you. After a long, overnight flight in an Army C47, I arrived very tired at a camp in Georgia. A Special Service lieutenant met me and drove me directly to the huge mess hall, where we joined the chow line with hundreds of young soldiers. As soon as we finished eating, he rose, banged his tin dish on the table for silence, and introduced me. The noise died away for a moment as the astonished GIs, knife and fork in hand, looked up expectantly, waiting for the show to begin. I stood up and swallowed, for this is the actor's recurrent nightmare, to be up there, on stage, with no material.

Somehow I found a few words to say to them about Hollywood. I apologized for not being Betty Grable or Alice Fay and I asked for questions; none came, so I sat down. It was one of my poorest performances. All afternoon I was taken around and lamely repeated myself on the drill grounds, the firing range, in the machine shops, the car pool, the hospital, and every part of the installation, and when at long last I got to my bare little room at night, I took pencil and paper and cudgeled my tired brain for a joke, a story, anything to entertain, or even to justify my presence.

Next day, I was flown to Fort Benning, Georgia, where a cowed Special Service officer told me he had orders to take me immediately to the office of the Commanding General. After a long wait, I was ushered into the presence of a tough, imposing warrior with piercing eyes and cropped, gray hair. He regarded me suspiciously for a moment and then he said, "I shall be glad if you will explain to me what you are doing here?"

I said I wasn't too sure myself, but that I had been sent by the Hollywood Victory Committee, which believed that the boys were getting tired of being entertained by a singer with an accordion and would like to meet some of the male stars from Hollywood. The general listened, and his steady gaze was far from friendly.

"Entertaining the boys is not my business," he said. "My duty is to train these very young men to kill or be killed. I have exactly eleven weeks in which to do it. All I want to know is, can you help me?" No, I said, frankly, I thought not. All I could do was to bring a comforting presence and a kindly word to those kids, many of whom must be frightened and lonely.

He thought for a moment and then, still severe, he said, "Very well. We shall see. Please be here promptly at eight tomorrow morning." He turned to the Special Service lieutenant. "Deliver Mr. Aherne here," he ordered. "I shall myself accompany him round the camp."

The frightened lieutenant sprang to a salute and for an instant, despite my civilian clothes, I had an impulse to do the same.

The pencil and paper came out again that night, but alas, my mind was a blank. Oh, for an hour with Jack Benny's gag man! I cursed the Hollywood Victory Committee which, with such a great pool of talent to draw upon, had not supplied me with a word of material.

It was the kind of winter morning that I had almost forgotten, dark and freezing cold, with the trees barely visible through the thick mist, and I shivered in my thin California clothes as the lieutenant drove me to the general's office. We were five minutes early but the great man was already sitting with his driver in the front seat of a jeep when we arrived. I climbed into the back — I was to become very familiar with the hard contours of the army jeep in the next couple of years — and in silence we bumped slowly along the camp roads through the trees until we came to a platoon which was doing some exercise in a clearing. They seemed paralyzed when the general stopped the jeep and called out,

"All right, Sergeant! Stand easy and fall your men out for a few minutes!"

He turned to me and gestured toward them. Unsteadily, I climbed out and started up the slope. I could feel his gimlet eyes boring into my back.

"Oh, what am I, an unknown English actor, doing here!" I thought.

I needn't have worried. The moment I mentioned my name, the boys greeted me with surprise and pleasure. I was astonished to find they all knew me, and I was quickly surrounded by that warm friendliness which I had always found so charming in American people. They laughed gaily at my feeble jokes and asked eagerly about their Hollywood idols.

For the next hour or so, we moved from one group to another, and each time the general stopped the jeep and motioned to me in silence. Each time my knees shook a little as

I climbed out, but each time I was received with warmth. Nowhere did I entertain the boys; they entertained me. Finally the general spoke. "I must go back to my office," he said, and he motioned to his driver.

The Special Service lieutenant was congealed with cold and fear but still waiting on the steps and ready with a snappy salute when we drew up.

"Lieutenant," said the general, "take Mr. Aherne out to the range. I shall expect you both for lunch in my dining room at noon." As he went in, he threw me a quick smile.

The lieutenant's eyes goggled.

"My God!" he said. "Fancy the old bastard asking us to lunch!"

Off duty, the general and his staff proved to be very amiable, and I was much encouraged when the lieutenant and I resumed our tour of Fort Benning in the afternoon. The army continued to welcome and entertain me; they gave me their arms to fire, drove me in their tanks, and enthusiastically explained the operation of everything. At night, under the glare of searchlights, they took me to the top of the tower from which paratroopers jumped in training. If I would stay an extra day, they promised, they would arrange to fit me out and to smuggle me aboard a plane with a bunch of trainees so that I could have the fun of a real parachute jump! I remembered Buckingham Palace and said, "Oh, what a lovely idea! — But it might be a little difficult."

The general wrote a very nice letter to the Victory Committee and I sent him a box of dates from the Coachella Valley.

I was to make other camp tours that carried me all across the nation, and always I was greeted as an old and valued friend. I was also sent on bond-selling tours, addressing crowded theaters and auditoriums, though why the people of America should have been expected to take my financial advice I was never able to understand. In the event, as I later discovered to my personal cost, they would have done better to have ignored it because the Government E Bond turned out to be a singularly poor investment.

Between tours, I did *First Comes Courage* for Columbia, playing a British spy in Nazi-occupied Norway, with Merle Oberon again. It was a weak story directed without enthusiasm by Charles Vidor. This was one of four pictures I made with Vidor, the others being *My Son, My Son, Lady in Question,* and, years later, *The Swan,* Grace Kelly's last picture, with Alec Guiness and Louis Jourdain. Of them all, I enjoyed *Lady in Question* the most. Vidor had somehow got hold of a flickering print of an old French film called *Gribouille,* starring the great actor Raimu, and he persuaded Harry Cohn to let him make it and to use me for the lead, a comical but oddly touching old French shopkeeper who sold bicycles and had a lot of trouble with his family. Of course I was thrilled to play a character part, to pad myself out, to wear a big, weeping mustache and bushy eyebrows, and to lose for once the suave, romantic hero who was boring me so much. Irene Rich came out of retirement to play my wife, Rita Hayworth and Evelyn Keyes were my daughters, and Glenn Ford my son. I doubt if many people have ever seen the little picture, but I loved it and so, I think, did Vidor, though he was always a prey to deep Hungarian doubts and depressions. A successful man of great talent and personal charm, he was, poor fellow, too moody and temperamental to enjoy anything for long.

I was also much in demand on the big radio shows of the time — Lux, the Kraft Music Hall, Kate Smith, Gertrude Lawrence, and others, both in Hollywood and New York — and between all these activities and the strain of coping with the problems of my young wife, now rocketed into orbit as a movie star, I longed for peace and quiet. I found it on my desert ranch.

With the limited help available in wartime, I had leveled about 140 acres of my land, drilled two more deep wells and installed concrete pipelines for the irrigation of crops, there being literally no rainfall in the Coachella Valley. By using electrically driven pumps, we could shoot a big column of water down the pipes, distributing it where we wished, and a pale green carpet of alfalfa began to appear; such is the effect of water and hot sun, within a month this was over a foot high, ready for cutting, baling, and hauling to the barn, where it was loaded and taken away monthly by the hay buyers.

I had inherited an old tractor from the previous owner and had been able to buy a used hay baler before wartime restrictions made equipment impossible to obtain, and these machines constantly broke down. The baler, being an old model, required four men to run it, instead of one, as it does today, so Frank Bito and myself had to complete the baling crew, getting up before sunrise and working in clouds of dust to bale as much as possible before the hay would get too dry and begin to shatter, forcing us to stop.

I had been delighted to discover, when planning the first of my new wells, that I had apparently inherited my father's ability to "witch" the correct spot with a hazel wand, though I had to substitute tamarisk for hazel. Pancho and the drilling crew walked up and down, wand in hand, with no result, but when I took it I felt it bend perceptibly toward the ground as I passed over water, and the crew cried out in astonishment. They immediately set up their derrick and rigged the drill which, driven by a motor, was destined to run day and night until the indications were that they had hit a good head of water. I watched the operation anxiously, because I had to pay for it by the foot, with no guarantee — other than my witching — that it would be successful. It was estimated that about 600 feet would suffice. Down and down they went, hour after hour and day after day, until at 1500 feet they hit rock and could go no farther.

What should they do, they asked me, pull up and try elsewhere, or buy a rock bit for $198.00 and attempt to pierce the obstruction? What were the chances, I asked, but to this there was of course no answer; they stared at me, with expressionless Oklahoma-Indian eyes, spat in the sand, and waited.

"Hold it, boys," I said finally — I always tried to conceal my English accent when talking to the natives. "Just goin' down the road a pace."

Eddie Burnett, a pioneer in the Valley, an old desert rat, a staunch Republican, and my good friend, was sitting on his porch looking gloomily at his date trees when I drove up. I told him the story.

"Eddie," I said, "I'm in deep on this thing. What'll I do?" He scratched his head and cogitated; then he allowed as how he seemed to remember that over on the Coral Reef Ranch, many years ago, they had run into the same situation. They went on, and after eight feet of rock they ran plumb into all kinds of water. But, he added, it was a waste of money, for them damned Democrats in Washington were hatching a crazy scheme to bring water by canal all the way from the Colorado River to our valley. The taxes we would have to pay for it would ruin us farmers. I went back to the drilling crew.

"Okay boys," I said, "give Howard Hughes a hundred and ninety eight bucks, and let's go!"

Just about eight feet later, water gushed from the hole, but that well cost me around $6000 and, after the crew had packed up and left the Valley, I discovered they had taken the rock bit with them, according no doubt to their custom, to sell to other unsuspecting ranchers.

Every hour that I could spare, I worked out in the sunshine, a shovel in my hand, the sound of the running water around me and the song of the redwing blackbirds overhead. I planted long hedges of pink and white oleanders, with here and there the higher tamarisk, to act as windbreaks, and cottonwoods to shade the ranch houses, glorying as I did so in the soft, dry desert air, scented with sagebrush and oleander. There was a special magic in the dawns and sunsets, and I would stand out there, in the quiet evenings, enraptured by the blazing colors of the western sky, until the last tattered banners faded over the mountains. I bought, for a song, a little adobe house backed by a date grove, built with no money but much love by a local schoolteacher with the aid of some Mexicans, which I found on the edge of my property. There I would go whenever I could, with my faithful Frank to care for me and occasionally, when she could spare a day or two, my wife.

Perhaps the most wonderful moments were those spent in an old chair on the porch when, tired from my day's work, I

would sit with a long, cool drink in my hand, looking at the
night sky — "fretted with golden fire" — and listening to the
small desert sounds, the hoot of the owl who lived in the date
palms and the distant howl of the coyotes on the sand dunes.
As I planned the future planting of my vineyards, I began to
lose interest more and more in the uncertain, heartbreaking
profession of acting, and to contemplate a new and better life
in those lovely surroundings.

Alas, there is always a serpent in the Garden of Eden. The
whole world was in conflagration by 1943. Other men were
suffering and dying everywhere. Max Constant was killed
when the Northrop Flying Wing, which he was testing for
the Army, got into a flat spin which he was unable to stop
before he hit the ground and broke his neck. Not only did I
lose a rare and loyal friend, but this was the end of our plan
for a Los Angeles-Palm Springs Airline. In spite of a lifetime's aversion to the very idea of warfare, I yearned to be
more directly a part of the war effort. The crowds might acclaim me on my camp and bond tours, but I felt these were
activities for an old man, and I was ashamed to be living a
life of ease and comparative luxury at such a time.

One day, I could stand it no longer. I packed a bag,
jumped in my car and drove to Mesa, Arizona, where I presented myself at Falcon Field, a training center for R.A.F
cadets. I had heard that they needed civilian instructors for
primary students, and I offered my services. I was interviewed by the head flight instructor, who made no attempt
to conceal his dislike of a God-damned movie star, and I
sensed at once that I would never win him over as I had the
Commanding General at Fort Benning. Soon after dawn the
following morning, he gave me a ride in an open Stearman
biplane.

"Okay!" he barked over the gosport. "Start the motor and warm her up!" I did so.

Soon the voice came again. "Is this the way you warm a motor?"

I was startled. "Yes, sir," I replied meekly.

"Not in the Army, you don't!" he snarled.

It appeared I was facing the wrong way.

"Now taxi her out for takeoff!" I complied. A moment later, I heard, "Is this the way you taxi an airplane?"

"Yes, sir."

"Not in the Army, you don't!" I should have been making constant turns to clear the visibility ahead. This went on with each maneuver — takeoff, climb, turns, everything I did.

"Is this the way? — Not in the Army, you don't!"

As he climbed out of the front cockpit and walked away, he said over his shoulder, "It'll take you fifty hours to pass the test — if you're lucky!"

I felt lost and lonely as I sat in my motel room that night. I had burned my bridges behind me in Hollywood. I had a signed contract with Harry Cohn of Columbia Pictures to make several pictures with him, but had notified my agent that I was leaving and would not be available while the war continued. I had done the unforgiveable in Hollywood — walked out on a contract. Parenthetically, the next time I was to see Cohn was fifteen years later, in a gaming room at Las Vegas. I went up to him and said, "Harry, I did a bad thing to you years ago, and I want to say I am sorry."

He looked at me quizzically. "I don't know what you are talking about," he said.

"That's all right, Harry," I said. "There is no reason you

should remember me at all. I just have to do this to ease my own conscience. I just have to say I'm sorry."

"Still don't know what you're talking about," he said gruffly, but he took my hand and pressed it. I am glad I did that, for he died soon after.

Falcon Field had many cadets and was short of planes, so I spent most of my time sitting on the flight line, waiting my turn for a half hour's instruction. The summer had come, with temperatures often over 100, and I found the heat exhausting. The Flight Commander's dislike of me increased daily, the air was thin, the Stearman trainer slow and heavy, and I seemed to make little progress with the advanced aerobatics I was required to perform with such precision. After a month of misery, I developed one of my old sinus attacks and felt very ill just as I was about to take my physical; the doctor, becoming suspicious, suspended my training and referred my case to an Army Medical Board which, after some delay, rejected me. I crawled back to the ranch.

Life in the desert, so lovely from October to May, is almost insupportable in summer, and we had no air conditioning then. Suffocating heat, gnats that settle in the eyes and ears, cockroaches, scorpions and snakes that get in the house, the pervading desert dust — all combine to destroy the magic. The few people left around seem exhausted and sullen. Life slows in the blood. I stayed there, swatting the gnats and sweating.

The previous November, Pancho had planted carrots on sixty acres of my ground and, after several months of watering, fertilizing and cultivation, they had stood green and high in the spring. I had looked forward to a handsome

profit from them in the Los Angeles market. Trucks and
tractors had been gathered, extra help secured, and a small
army of itinerant carrot-pullers had moved their trailers and
their families on the place; these people, poor white trash
for the most part, seem quite content with their rootless lives
and move slowly with the sun each year, northward from
the Mexican border to Canada and back, leaving a trail of
trash and empty cans and bottles behind them. They squat
on the ground, men, women and children, and tie the carrots,
which are dug for them, at five cents a bundle. When everybody had left, I had seen millions of good carrots lying all
over the ground, and I had hastily called the produce buyer.
No, he said, those were all too small for the market, where it
is only size that counts. Mine, it seemed, were unfortunately
a little undersized this year, and anyway the market was
swamped with bigger, cheaper carrots from Texas — too
bad. Sadly, we had disked them all under and I had written
off the loss on my books.

Pancho, undaunted by the carrot disaster, had immediately planted the sixty acres of sweet corn which, he told me,
would be costly to raise and harvest but would be assured of a
big price in the summer. This beautiful crop was now ready
to harvest and again we made elaborate preparations to pick,
pack and ice the crates, which were then loaded on a truck
and driven by me to the railhead, six miles away, all day
long. For several days we all sweated and strained, and then
a call came from Los Angeles, telling me to stop shipment at
once — the corn was too wormy to sell! What was this, I
asked Pancho, had he not oiled the corn for worms? Yes indeed. He had hired a gang which went along the rows of
standing corn and squirted anti-worm oil into each ear by

hand. I had paid for that, so I knew it to be true. The answer came that the worms at the end of the ear were not too bad, and could in any case be cut off, but nothing had been done to prevent another type of worm, the Corn-Borer Worm, which appears from nowhere and bores into the middle of the ear, making it unsalable.

Again I wrote off a huge loss on the books, and this time I fired Pancho. Jose took his place, another amiable Mexican with a large family to slip on the payroll, and this beguiling old rascal stayed with me for twelve years, until I gave up the place. Many times I should have fired him, but he always knew how to get around me. He had a lot of woman trouble in the town, like most Mexicans, and when I would go down to his house to bawl him out for some piece of laziness or folly, he would lead me behind the barn, out of ear-shot of his wife, and whisper to me earnestly,

"Mr. Brian — man to man — I've got to have $300 today!"

"Jose!" I would thunder, "you are a scoundrel! You've got to stop all this and put your mind on your work!" But he was irresistible, and of course in the end I would give him the money.

"Ah," he would say, his voice choked with emotion, "that's what I always tell the boys — Mr. Brian has a good heart!"

It was he who persuaded me that if I would invest the large amount of capital necessary to plant vineyards of early Thompson's seedless grapes we would be guaranteed a steady market with a handsome income for many years. He had spent his life working in grapes, he said, the land was ideal for them and we could not miss. I decided to do it as soon as the war was over.

Joan appeared briefly from Oregon, where her picture had

been on location; she now had a few days off before resuming work in the studio.

"How long have we been married?" she asked me.

"Nearly four years," I answered.

"What?" she cried. "My God! I never meant to stay married to you that long!"

Standing outside were my new pale green convertible Buick and her old Packard. With a wave of the hand, she jumped into my Buick and drove off. Two days later, I read in Louella Parsons' column that she had decided to divorce me. She would keep the Beverly Hills house, she said, and I would keep the ranch.

As I sat, dumbfounded, with the paper in my hand, the nice old hay buyer from Riverside appeared in his car. He had come down, he said, to ask me if there could be anything wrong with the water on my place. The water? Why? Well, it seemed that his customers had been losing valuable horses and cattle which had unaccountably swelled up and died, and he was pretty sure they had been fed hay from my place. There might be a big claim against me.

Hastily I sent for the County Farm Advisor, who checked the water and walked over the alfalfa fields. Then he shook his head. If this went to court, he said, he could not stand behind me. He produced some dead oleander leaves from his pocket. These, he said, were deadly poison to animals. The oleander hedges had frozen in winter and the spring gales had blown the leaves into the alfalfa, where they had been baled with the hay. A couple of years later I had to settle this claim for several thousand dollars.

At this moment, I received a letter from the British consulate, referring to my written offer of service, still held by the embassy. Although it had not been possible, the letter said, to utilize my services in the armed forces, there was now a shortage of truck drivers in England and volunteers would be accepted. Transportation to England could be arranged, but would not be paid for. The consulate would be glad to know if I was interested.

Bert Allenberg, my agent, called to persuade me to return to Hollywood. The younger men, he said, were all going into the forces and MGM, which had so many big female stars, would like to sign a contract with me. Yes, I thought, and the moment the young men come back, they drop me. Besides, how could I crawl back to Hollywood now? It seemed my life had again reached an impasse, that I could go neither forward nor back.

Scene 10

Overseas with The Barretts

THE PHONE RANG. It was Katharine Cornell, in Washington, D.C. While playing there, she said, she had met General Marshall, who had told her that the Army, which was then in North Africa and Sicily, could provide theaters and opera houses if some of us would be willing to take out a complete Broadway production to entertain the troops. It would be necessary to guarantee at least six months. She wanted to know if I would go with her. Yes of course, I said at once. What play should we take? To my surprise, she suggested *The Barretts of Wimpole Street*, despite its large cast, many costumes, and elaborate set, because, she said, it had always been successful, wherever it had played, and she felt that the GIs were, after all, only a cross-section of the audience. I would have preferred a straight modern comedy, but I bowed to her judgment. Within the next few days, she was able to tell me that the American Theater Wing had undertaken to pay the entire cost of the tour, leaving to the Army only the responsibility for transportation and housing.

I made hasty arrangements at the ranch, turned my back on my problems, and flew to New York. On my arrival, Kit looked at me with a smile and said, "I always come to your rescue, Brian, don't I?"

It was true; she always did. Our relationship, both professional and personal, has been one of the enduring pleasures of my life. Together, we appeared in six productions, all under the Cornell-McClintic management, and only one, *Lucrèce*, was a failure. When in 1959–60 we played *Dear Liar* from coast to coast and border to border, many nice things were said about us, but one line, written by the distinguished old critic of the *Los Angeles Times*, pleased me more than any other. He closed a brilliant and appreciative notice by saying, "We must be grateful to them, for through the years, together and apart, they have been faithful to us."

We took a complete production of the play to the American, and on occasion the British, forces in Italy, France, Belgium and Holland, and we were away six months. One special performance was given, by permission of General Mark Clark, for members of the Italian theatrical profession, who packed the Teatro Elyseo in Rome at ten o'clock on a Sunday morning to see it. The Army was at first very doubtful that a romantic play about two Victorian poets could appeal to the GIs, and there must be no doubt because we would take up vitally needed shipping space and would require very special attention. It was therefore decided that we should give a special trial performance at a huge camp on Long Island where, shortly before the curtain, a Special Service captain put his head in my dressing room and asked, "How long does this show run?"

"It's very long," I replied. "About three hours." His jaw dropped.

"Jesus!" he gasped. "You'll have to cut it!" Not possible, I told him.

"But you don't know these guys like I do!" he groaned. "There are twenty-five hundred of them out there, and few of them have ever seen a play — they've seen flat actors maybe, but not round actors. After an hour they'll get up and leave you!"

Not a man moved, and had he done so there would have been two to take his place. The next day we got our orders, put on our uniforms, packed our kit bags, and entrained for Norfolk, Virginia, under strict instructions to tell nobody where or when we were going. After a few days' indoctrination, we were stuffed aboard a troopship with 3000 soldiers where, after buffeting my way below decks, jammed with struggling men, I was trying to stow my kit bag under a berth, when a little man in civilian clothes, wearing a peaked cap and some sort of badge, touched my arm.

"Mr. Aherne?" he inquired politely.

"Yes?"

"I believe you are a British subject, and you are leaving the country. Could I see your income tax clearance please?"

Squashed by struggling soldiers and bashed to and fro by bulging kit bags, I stared at him, speechless. In American uniform, traveling under Army orders, I felt completely American. My affairs were all in order, my taxes paid, and my will freshly drawn, but the idea of a foreigner's tax clearance had never even occurred to me. He put his hand quickly on my shoulder.

"Oh, I know you have it," he said. "It's in the bottom of that kit bag, isn't it? I couldn't ask you to unpack that now, could I! So just tell me you have it."

"Yes," I quavered, "yes, I have."

"That's fine!" he said. "Good luck and thank you." He squeezed my hand and vanished.

One wonders if an English or a French official would behave so well — one can wonder, and one can hope.

Running at high speed and zigzagging to avoid enemy
subs, we crossed the Atlantic alone, until we picked up a de-
stroyer escort off the Azores, passed through the Straits of Gibraltar in the night, and awoke to find ourselves lying in the
harbor of Oran. Three thousand young soldiers were excited
at the prospect of seeing North Africa, but were all kept below decks until darkness fell, when we slipped out to sea
again. Scuttlebutt named first one destination and then another, but the following afternoon I recognized Capri on our
starboard side, and we were soon edging our way through
the wreckage that choked Naples harbor.

Army Headquarters were at that time in the old Royal Palace of Caserta, a smaller edition of Versailles, and we were
assigned to comfortable billets in the grounds. We quickly
began to prepare for our opening in a small but beautiful
Opera House in the nearby town of Capua. No electricity
was available, but Gertrude Macy proved to be as adept at
handling the Army as she had been with the Shuberts on
Broadway; an Army generator on wheels was secured, and
rolled behind our bus throughout Italy; a lovely Aubusson
carpet was mysteriously "liberated" from the Palace; all
kinds of other things appeared as if by magic. Facilities at
the Opera House had not improved in two centuries, and we
had to obtain water in our helmets from the one tap which
trickled coldly in the basement. The small, whitewashed
cells which served as dressing rooms were encrusted with
dirt, and the walls were covered with the scrawled signatures
of actors of the past; in mine, someone had stuck a piece of
glass over a name in a corner —

Enrico Caruso
Tenore
Rigoletto. 1907

The heat was intense, we worked hard and *The Barretts*
was acclaimed vociferously by packed houses of GIs, but by
the time our first day of rest came, we were all exhausted. I
dreamed of a cooling swim in the sea, so when a sergeant
offered me a ride into Naples in his jeep I accepted with
alacrity.

I found that the whole seafront of the town had been
wrecked by Allied bombardment and German mines, but, as
I picked my way through the rubble, I saw a sailboat,
moored in what was left of a little harbor. Approaching the
Neapolitan bandit who was sitting in it, I made signs indicating that I would like to go for a sail; after some haggling and
counting in sign language, a price was agreed upon and we
set forth. A steady breeze was blowing and we were soon
dancing over the brilliant blue water of the famed Bay of
Naples. I looked around at the old city, climbing over its
surrounding hills, at Vesuvius, Sorrento, and Capri, with a
hint of Ischia on the horizon, and memories of my first visit,
with Reggie and Eastwood nearly twenty years earlier, came
flooding back to me.

After about an hour, I judged we were in the middle of the
Bay, and this was the moment I had been anticipating. I
made signs to my helmsman that I was going to swim. No
expression passed over his face as I took the tiller and
showed him that I would want him to bring the boat up into
the wind while I was in the water. I was quite familiar with
the difficulty of reentering a boat, so I took a rope and tied
one end securely to the mast and threw the other into the

sea, where it trailed about twenty feet behind the stern. I then took off my clothes and dived overboard into the sparkling, translucent water.

Down, down I went, instantly cooled and refreshed, and for a few minutes I luxuriated in swimming slowly underwater; then I surfaced and floated on my back in the golden sunshine. The discomfort of the troopship, the heat, the exhaustion and nervous strain, all magically disappeared as I lay, suspended in heaven and rocked gently by the waves.

Suddenly, a thought struck me — sharks! I had read that the Bay of Naples is infested by sharks. Convulsively, I rolled over and looked for the boat. It was gone! I looked desperately around and at last I saw it, far away it seemed from my position at water level, sailing directly back toward Naples. My heart stopped. I, the enemy soldier, had dived naked into the sea, leaving behind an American uniform, a wallet full of money, a P.X. card, and a British passport, all worth a fortune in Naples then. My bandit had only to sail home and I would never be traced. Nobody would ever know what had become of me; I would simply disappear!

Keep calm, I told myself — don't panic — your life is at stake. Treading water, I looked around. The nearest land appeared to be about four miles away, west of the city; my swimming is of the English type, good for about four lengths of the pool at most. I must try, I thought — swim a bit, float a bit, swim again — but I knew it was useless. If the sharks don't get me, I thought, I shall shortly drown. This is the end. This is where I die.

I turned slowly, searching the horizon in vain for some hope of rescue, but not a boat was to be seen. Suddenly I stopped, for I saw my bandit had come about and was now sailing a course which, while not directly toward me, would take him a few hundred yards to the east of me. The boat grew bigger, until I could distinctly see him, crouching over the tiller and apparently staring in my direction. As he passed, I splashed awkwardly toward him, tried to wave my arm, and shouted as loud as I was able. He kept on going and my heart sank, but a few minutes later he came about again and passed me on the other side, this time within a hundred yards or so. Several times he did this, always staring at me, and each time, like a bull in the ring, I made desperate, futile efforts to intercept him. I grew very tired. Finally, still moving at a good pace, he passed so near that, swimming with all my might, I managed to grab the trailing rope. Hanging on — literally for dear life — and being dragged through the water, I somehow hauled myself, hand over hand, through the wake, looped the rope round my foot, reached up, grasped the stern and, with the last remnants of my strength, lifted myself and fell into the boat, where I lay for a long time, utterly exhausted and gasping for breath.

The bandit made no movement through all this, but sat looking at me impassively and silently. I, too, was silent. He set a course for Naples, and after a while I crawled forward and slowly dressed. As I stepped shakily from his boat, I gave him the whole contents of my wallet.

"Addio," I said, "e grazie!"

"Grazie signor," he replied.

The sergeant was waiting in his jeep and we drove back to Caserta.

After Capua, we played Naples, Foggia, Bari, Lecce, Rome, Siena, Leghorn, and Florence. Much has been writ-

ten about the wartime odyssey of *The Barretts,* so I will tell
only one story. In November 1944, we were playing Florence for the Fifth Army, which was stuck in the snow
and mud, high up on the Futa Pass which crosses the mountains between Florence and Bologna; the Forgotten Front,
they called it. The long struggle up the length of Italy had
been fought, every step of the way, against a powerful and
resourceful enemy who knew how to exploit the unique defensive possibilities of mountainous country on a narrow
front — possibilities which had apparently not been foreseen
by our leaders. As they slowly withdrew from one mountain
range to the next, the Germans had destroyed roads and rail-
ways, torn down telephone and power lines, mined the valleys and slopes, and carefully ranged the ground for their
artillery, so that every time our boys moved forward it was at
fearful cost, as we saw in the crowded hospitals we visited
each day. When they abandoned Florence and made their
final stand before Bologna, it was along a line of almost
impregnable mountain tops. The winter of 1944 brought bitter cold, snow, heavy rains, and seas of mud. The Allied
Command gave up the idea of breaking into the Lombardy
Valley, and transferred the bulk of men to the offensive in
Southern France, leaving the Fifth Army up in the mountains to hold the Forgotten Front. It was these boys we had
come to entertain.

One can imagine the feelings of the GIs who were hauled
out of the muck of a foxhole, stowed in a truck, bumped
down winding, potholed roads to the outskirts of Florence,
given a hot shower and a good meal, and handed a ticket to a
show in town. Our performances were in the middle of the
day, because the boys had to be back in the line by dark, and

we hardly expected many of them to come; after all, that
ticket was a pass into the big city, and the GIs were young!
But the theater was always packed.

One afternoon, as they were streaming out after the show,
our manager overheard a tough, burly paratrooper say to his
buddy, "Well . . . What I tell ya! Told ya it'd be better'n
goin' to the cat house, didn't I?"

We regarded that as the supreme tribute.

From Italy, we flew in a crowded C47 to Marseilles, keeping an anxious eye open for possible German fighters, coming
in from the direction of Genoa. We were stranded in the
wreckage of Marseilles for three weeks, because the freighter
carrying our scenery and generator went aground on the
coast of Corsica and the Navy had to be called to haul her
off. Eventually we got going again and followed the advanc-
ing armies, playing Dijon, Vitel, Versailles, Paris, Rheims,
Maastricht, and Heerlen, on the border of Holland; there our
tour closed in late February 1945. On the day before we
were due to say goodbye to the 9th Army, we were invited to
lunch with General Simpson, who was in command. We had
just received our traveling orders and knew that we were to
be taken back to Paris, whence we would cross to England
and immediately board a troopship for transportation to the
U.S.A. In the course of conversation with General Simpson,
I spoke of my sadness that I should be unable to see my old
father, living alone in Stratford-on-Avon. Immediately he
turned to an aide. "Have my plane ready to take Mr. Aherne
to England this afternoon," he ordered. "He has forty-eight
hours' leave, so arrange that he shall report to his unit in
London."

It was a gesture of such kindness that I shall never cease to be grateful to him. Could I take Brenda Forbes, who yearned to see her sister, I asked him?

"Take anybody you like," he said. "The plane is yours."

Kit bags and equipment packed, and a case of champagne hastily procured, Brenda and I climbed into the general's C47 and were flown across the Channel in brilliant sunshine. It was strange to look down on the calm, blue sea and the coast of England stretching away peacefully toward Dover on the one hand and Beachy Head on the other, and to think that here the Battle of Britain had been fought and the young men of the R.A.F. and the Luftwaffe had shot each other down to death. We came in over Pevensy Bay and I saw quite clearly my grandparents' house, Tower Holme, on the shingle beach below; memories of summers long ago came back to me.

Laden with kit bags, helmet, gas mask and the case of champagne, I staggered into my father's room and found him sitting in his dressing gown, old and forlorn, beside a tiny fire of smoky wartime coal. He stared at me as if I were a ghost.

"Good God!" he said. "Where did you spring from?"

He had received none of my letters since I left the States, none of the rare stamps I had sent him from Italy. As of old, we found difficulty in talking to each other, but he made an effort.

"Well," he said gruffly, "what woman are you mixed up with now?"

About nine o'clock, my brother arrived, and Dad seemed relieved.

"You boys go and have a drink at the pub," he said. "It's my bedtime now."

I tried to hint that, U-boats being what they were, I might

not see him again, but off he went. He died the following year, grieving to the end for my mother.

In London, next day, I visited Sir George and Lady Arthur. Sir George struggled to his feet with the aid of two sticks, saying wryly,

"Fifty years ago today, I fought at the Battle of Tel El Kebir. Look at me now — an old cavalryman who can't even walk!"

Reggie Reixach's greenhouse had been destroyed by a buzz bomb, which had also taken away part of his drawing room. It was more than he could bear, and he had died soon after.

We sat up in the train by night until we got to Greenock and the River Clyde, where we boarded our troopship, which turned out to be the *Queen Mary,* and zigzagged to avoid the U-boats until we reached New York. Having passed all through a shellshocked, ravaged, starving Europe, I felt certain that it would not recover in my lifetime, and I had no wish ever to go back. Henceforth, I decided, my life lay in California. California, here I come, I thought, and this time I would stay for good.

Frank met me at Burbank and drove me to the ranch. On my departure I had, in a moment of perhaps misplaced generosity, given my Beverly Hills house and all its contents to Joan, who had obtained a divorce in my absence, so the little ranch house was my only home. In the days that followed, I slowly recovered from my exhaustion and began to take joy again in walking over my land, carpeted now with alfalfa, in planting my young vines, painting the ranch houses, and riding my horse across the desert to visit my neighbors. I had suffered badly from sinus troubles while I was abroad, but now, in the blessed sun and dry air, I regained my health and strength.

No offers came to me from Broadway or Hollywood. As younger men came out of the services, show business changed and actors like myself, in their middle forties, were not in demand. I did not care, for I believed I had found at last the job for which I had been looking all my life. No more stages, no more studios or studio politics, no more scenery, lights, cameras, and microphones, no more foolish lines to learn, no more spoiled female stars or megalomaniac directors to cope with, and no more filthy cities to live in. Born in the country, I had returned to the country, and there I would build my monument, there I would find peace, happiness, and fulfillment.

Standing bareheaded in the warm sunshine, looking at the first tender green leaves on my newly planted vines, listening to the sound of the water chuckling down the rows, and to the blackbirds overhead, I thought I heard the angels sing. I had found my proper job at last, and it was where I belonged, out on the land — the good land — farming.

CURTAIN

EPILOGUE

Epilogue

I WAS INDUCED to start putting down these rambling reminiscences some years ago by Mrs. Hazel Littlefield
Smith, a talented romantic poetess, a loyal friend to
artists, and a practical Michigan farmer. After a while, I
wanted to give up, but Mrs. Littlefield Smith would not permit it. Gently prodding, encouraging letters got me going
again. She pushed me along slowly, with many stops and
starts, until one day I slammed the box of memory shut and
wrote to her:

> I am now twenty-five, and I won't go any further! The
> problems of autobiography are too much for me. Moss Hart
> and Emlyn Williams stopped there, and I now see the reason.
> When one looks at one's early years, one sees them as through
> a telescope — ordered, enlarged, and defined — but as they
> come nearer, they slip out of focus and become disorderly and
> unclear. Furthermore, there are too many living people in-
> volved; too many will get their feelings hurt — and perhaps
> run to their lawyers — if one tells the truth, and if one doesn't,
> one is a bore. Spicy anecdotes are expected from someone in
> show business. It is no good saying "I had the privilege of play-
> ing with that great artist and gracious lady, Miss Blank," it is
> only interesting if one says "I was forced to play with Miss Mon-
> ster, and wait till I tell you what that spoiled, selfish, egocentric
> bitch did to me!" Of course, most of the great stars *are* mon-
> sters, and I was a pretty arrogant monster myself at one time,

but just as there is said to be honor among thieves, there must
be a little among monsters. One can't tell the whole truth
unless one is very old and doesn't care, or Miss Monster is
dead and doesn't care. So I have stopped, dear Hazel. I have
gone back to golf, to varnishing the verandah furniture, and to
painting the window frames.

Mrs. Littlefield Smith gave me a bit of rope and then she
started again, gently prodding, with a little reproach here
and a little flattery there, until I was shamed into going on
with my second act. Those who have had the fortitude to
last this long will not complain if they are spared the third.

I will tie up a few loose ends.

I thought I was through with marriage, which seemed
much too difficult for me, but a couple of years later I married my Eleanor, sister of the well-known Broadway producer, Alfred de Liagre, Jr. Guthrie McClintic came to our
informal wedding reception, gave me a limp hand, and
sighed. "Well, Brian, you're at it again!"

I took my dear and loving bride out to the ranch, where
she too thought she heard the angels sing. That year, a Phil-
ippino crew harvested, in the burning July heat, our first
crop of Thompson's seedless grapes from my young vineyards.
We broke even on our expenses. The following year, to our
amazement and delight, the vines were covered with beautiful bunches. With a picking crew of sixty men, we worked
from the first light of dawn till the noon thermometer hit 110
or more, the heat exhausting the men and softening the
grapes. We selected, trimmed, and packed them in 24-pound
crates, weighed and checked them in the barn, labelled them
with my own label, loaded them on trucks, and drove them
to the railhead at Thermal. There they were packed and

braced into refrigerated freight cars, iced overnight, and rolled off on the Pacific Fruit Express to the eastern produce markets.

As the last car left, I flew to New York and Boston to watch my fruit unpacked and put on sale at 4 A.M. The buyers would pass, examining the various lots with a critical eye, and would call out to the seller, "Hey, Joe! How much for the actor this morning?"

That year, we shipped nearly 30,000 crates of grapes and, after charging every conceivable expense, throwing a big party for the crews, distributing bonuses and gifts, and paying all taxes, I still made a profit of $28,000.

We were enchanted, and promptly set about trebling our planting. I poured my savings into the undertaking, which was very costly because each vine had to have its special 6-foot redwood stake and crossarm, with three lines of wire nailed to each, all down the rows. Big crews became necessary, and housing had to be built for them. Unused to handling labor, I had to cope with many problems arising from my miniature United Nations. Mexicans from over the border had to be imported to do the normal ranch work; Philippinos did the pruning of the vines, thinning of the bunches, girdling the stems, picking, and packing, while Armenians more or less controlled the wholesale marketing of the fruit.

The following year, a sudden late freeze took half the crop, and I lost $30,000. The next year, all the upper bunches of grapes burned from excessive heat a few days before picking, and I lost $18,000. Next, a violent sandstorm in the spring sandblasted the grapes on the vines, and I lost $40,000. We never had another winning year.

Slowly it dawned upon us that our banner year had been a freak. It was not the voice of the angels we had heard, but the soft, sweet, enticing song of the Lorelei, the wicked sirens who lure unsuspecting mariners to destruction upon the jagged rocks. Slowly and reluctantly we perceived that we never could win again.

The Coachella Valley, between 100 and 200 feet below sea level, is the warmest agricultural area in the U.S.A., and was therefore able to ripen and ship its fruit three weeks before its gigantic rival, the San Joaquin Valley. My ranch however, being for topographical reasons — which I had not realized — in the coldest part of the Valley, ripened last and, five times out of six, was swamped in the eastern markets by the lower-priced, better quality San Joaquin fruit.

Mexicans, I discovered, were charming, easygoing folk, procreating enormous families, seeing that all their relatives got on the payroll, and lying down in the shade as soon as the boss's back was turned. The Philippinos were unprincipled little rascals, whose main interest was cockfighting behind the barn, and who knew every trick in the bag with which to cheat me. A deal would be made with their boss at so much an hour, but once the harvest was in full swing and we were struggling to finish before the San Joaquin Valley killed us, the boss would come to me smiling and say, "Mr. Brian" — I was always Mr. Brian at the ranch, since nobody would ever pronounce Aherne — "boys no like the deal."

"What's wrong?"

"You pay piecework?"

"No!"

"You no pay piecework, boys leave!"

Piecework meant payment by the box, and the moment I

agreed to this, the boxes still looked beautiful on top but the pickers stuffed everything, green and rotting fruit, underneath, to move faster and make more boxes.

The other people who consistently won this loaded crap game were the Armenian produce buyers in the East, who, as often as not, sent me back statements in red ink, claiming that it was I who owed them money.

Between the Mexicans, the Filippinos, and the Armenians, it was apparent that one poor, bloody Englishman stood no more chance than a snowball in hell. The final disaster, predicted by Eddie Burnett years before, was the coming of the Colorado River Canal. This water contains salts which, rising to the surface, began slowly to kill the vines, while the cost of the scheme ruined all but the biggest ranches.

Far into the night I would work on my books and grapple with bills and payrolls, using systems I dimly remembered from Liverpool, so many years ago, but the losses continued to mount until I knew I was beaten. Eleanor and I strove desperately to sell the place. There were no takers. Finally, an Armenian offered me less than half what I figured I had in it; early in 1956, sixteen years after I bought the property, I sold it to him and left. He has never had a winning year. My old vineyards have now been bulldozed flat, all the trees cut down, and all the buildings deserted, to save taxes. One night last year in a great burst of golden fire, the old ranch house in which Pancho had lived and raised his big family, burned to the ground. I stood in the darkness and watched it go. Already sandhills are forming, sagebrush and mesquite are growing back, and in a few years the desert will have reclaimed its own, leaving no sign of the empire I built. Occasionally, we spend a few days at the little adobe house, which we still own. I sit in the same old chair outside, looking out over the desolation to the mountains beyond. I hear, unmoved, the soft, sweet song of the Lorelei and, as darkness falls, the owl hoots at me from his date palm. Out on the desert, the coyotes howl derisively.

During those years, though I made little effort to work at my profession, people from time to time came and dug me out for one thing or another. Soon after the war, I did *Vigil in the Night,* with Carole Lombard — an A. J. Cronin story, directed by George Stevens, which turned out badly. Constance Bennett insisted on my playing with her in a picture called *Smart Woman,* which she produced, and largely wrote and directed herself. I was doubtful about that one, much as I admired the vital, friendly, humorous Connie, but when she offered me the highest salary I had ever had in my life, I could hardly refuse. It was a nice, family picture, and should have done all right, but by the time it was finished, Connie had no money left to exploit it, and after a few obscure showings, it died unseen. A couple of years later, she told me she hadn't made a penny from it, and I felt very sad.

At long intervals, there were others.

Alfred Hitchcock called me from Quebec, where he was making *I Confess,* with Montgomery Clift and Anne Baxter. Would I help him, he asked, by coming up at once to play a small but important part which would only take a couple of weeks. Hitchcock is an old and valued friend, and a great director, so I immediately agreed, but when I told my agent Bert Allenberg he hit the ceiling.

"Warner Brothers has overspent its budget," he said. "They can only offer you one tenth of your last salary and of that, after commissions, taxes, and expenses, you will get about half. How can I sell you again as a star?"

He was right. The picture was one of Hitchcock's less happy efforts and my part of no consequence. I took my wife with me to Quebec, and Warner Brothers charged me with all her expenses, even to excess baggage and one twenty-cent phone call, and there was worse to come. The next year, when Jean Negulesco, my old friend and a very wonderful man, wanted me for Captain Smith in his picture *Titanic*, 20th Century-Fox claimed that my salary had been established at Warner Brothers and could not be raised. Allenberg was able to say, "I told you so!" and I was stuck at that little figure for my next three pictures, *Titanic*, in which I played Captain Smith, *The Best of Everything*, with myself as a girl-chasing executive, both of which were brilliantly directed by Jean Negulesco, and a mishmash of *Prince Valiant*. It was not until Charles Vidor insisted on having me for Father Hyacinth in *The Swan* that Allenberg was able to get Metro-Goldwyn-Mayer to raise me a little.

It was during the making of *The Best of Everything* that I got my one chance to write a scene for a motion picture. Jerry Wald, an ebullient and forceful man, was producing. The story, which took place in a big office in New York, was concerned mainly with the problems of young people, although the only real starring names in it were those of Joan Crawford, Louis Jourdain, and myself. I remarked to Wald that it was a pity I had no scene with Miss Crawford, because I felt the public would expect it. He said there was no possibility of such a scene. I said I thought there was.

"Okay!" he snapped. "If you're so sure, write it yourself!"

I did, and I gave it to him next morning. As he read it, he laughed a couple of times and then he threw it across to Jean Negulesco, saying, "Say — that's not bad! I guess we could fix it up and make something of it!"

All at once, I understood how writers feel. Fix it up, indeed! It didn't need fixing!

The scene was only cut a little, and we shot it. "Nice little scene," said Miss Crawford, and I agreed that it was amusing and charming — but she never knew who wrote it.

During those years, I endured a couple of Broadway flops, *The French Touch*, by Chodorov and Fields, directed by René Clair, and *Escapade*, for my brother-in-law, Alfred de Liagre, Jr. I also twice toured the eastern summer theater, but the ranch occupied most of my attention and my acting was done with the object of providing money for the vineyards.

In 1954, I had the honor of playing with Alfred Lunt, Lynn Fontanne, and Edna Best in Noel Coward's *Quadrille*, and this was one of the most exciting experiences of my career; indeed at one point it was almost too exciting for me. I was in California, about to start shooting a four-day television film, when I had a wire from John C. Wilson, the manager, saying that the Lunts had come steaming into New York and wished to begin rehearsals a week earlier than planned. The television company refused absolutely to release me from my contract at such short notice, but, working overtime, we finished the film in three and a half days, and I jumped on the plane that afternoon. Now such is the brilliance and energy of the Lunts that to be four days late for rehearsal is comparable to getting stuck in the starting gate when the rest of the field gets off in the Kentucky Derby; by the time you get going, they are down the back stretch and rounding the far turn, and you have to be up with the leaders as they pass the stand, first time around. They were understandably anxious, because the play had not been well received in London, and they were determined that it should be played for all it was worth in New York. In the baking heat of August, they worked with dazzling vitality and intensity. I was a little rusty, after my years at the ranch and in pictures, and by the time we opened in Boston I was a nervous wreck. On the Saturday night, having received a well-deserved but rather sharp rebuke from Miss Fontanne, I went all to pieces in the last act, fluffed my lines, and felt miserably ashamed. When the curtain came down, I went to their dressing room, told them of my professional admiration and personal adoration, and begged them, rather hysterically I am afraid, to let me go back to California.

The Lunts were astounded, and seemed shocked. Why, they said, everything was perfectly all right. This was the theater. It was always like this. Had I forgotten? Now, they said, just calm down and take a rest over Sunday, and all would be well. Nothing to worry about.

I stumbled off to my dressing room, feeling lower than a snake's ear. A few minutes later, there was a knock at my door. "Miss Fontanne sent you this," said her maid, and she handed me a large glass of whisky.

I went to a beautiful concert by the Boston Symphony Orchestra on Sunday, took a couple of tranquilizers on Monday, and from then on enjoyed every moment on the stage with those marvelous artists and wonderful people.

In 1956, after the sale of the ranch, I took my wife to Europe, which, with the aid of the U.S.A., had recovered astonishingly fast. While in England, we went to the Derby on Epsom Downs, and there, while walking among the picturesque gipsy caravans which dot the hill in the center of the course, we were accosted by a buxom gipsy woman in traditional costume.

"Cross my palm with silver, kind sir," she cajoled, "and I'll tell your true fortune." Of course we entered her caravan. She laid out her cards, peered into her crystal ball, and clucked her tongue sympathetically.

"Oh, you poor, dear man," she said, "your past has been bad. You've made many mistakes, but your luck has been bad. It seems that you've been shut in like, by four walls, and every move you've made to get out, you've banged your head." She peered again.

"But don't you worry, dear," she said. "Your future is bright. You're going to get a message, dear, very soon, and everything will change for you. I see lights, bright lights, all around you, and there are lots of gay people, and I hear lovely music, and it's all very exciting and wonderful for you! Don't you worry, dear!"

I crossed her palm with silver. "Tell me the truth," I said. "Have you ever seen me or heard of me?"

"Oh, my dear," she said modestly, "I just live in this caravan. I don't read nor write, you know."

A week later, I received a letter from Herman Levin, offering me the part of Higgins in *My Fair Lady* on the forthcoming national tour, and for once I had the sense to accept.

Looking back, it seems to me that I usually turned down the important offers. A Hollywood writer once asked me to explain something to him. At a Warner Brothers studio conference, he said, they were discussing the behavior of

Errol Flynn, which was raising Jack Warner's blood pressure. Suddenly Jack pounded the table in a rage and cried, "Errol Flynn! Errol Flynn! There would never have been an Errol Flynn if it hadn't been for Brian Aherne, damn him!" What on earth did he mean, asked my writer friend? It was true, I told him. I had repeatedly turned down *Captain Blood*, until at last they took the unknown Flynn, who was made a star overnight by it.

All good things come to an end and, although I didn't realize it at the time, my flying days became numbered when I married my Eleanor. She says now that she had no idea that I was a pilot or had any interest in flying, and it never occurred to me to tell her, because I thought everybody knew. On our return to California, one of the first things I did was to buy a new Beechcraft Bonanza plane and, knowing how much they loved an adventure, I invited my old flying friends, Abby and Connie Wolf, to pick it up at the Wichita factory and fly it out. Eleanor was appalled when they arrived. It seemed that, like many women, she had a horror of flying, especially in a private plane. It was a major crisis in our newly married life. She would burst into tears on takeoff and be terrified every moment in the air, whereas to me it seemed infinitely safer than the crowded freeways below. I asked her to give me a hundred hours in the air, thinking that she would become accustomed to it, and she bravely did so, but it was no use. Finally, I flew so little that my technique grew rusty and I felt my judgment was impaired. After a few small but disturbing incidents, due to faulty judgment on my part, I realized that I was no longer maintaining competency at a level where I could feel I was a safe pilot. I sold my plane and gave up flying. It was a hard decision to take, but disappointment and I have walked hand in hand for many years, and we are old friends. I play golf instead, but sometimes, on a clear day with perhaps a few fleecy clouds in the sky, I look upward — and my heart aches a little.

Abby Wolf is now a general in the U. S. Army Air Force Reserve, while Connie is the only licensed woman pilot of free balloons in the U.S.A., holding many world's records, including three which previously had been held by the Russians — for distance, altitude, and elapsed time in the air. In 1968, she gave me my first balloon ride. Ascending from Blue Bell, Pennsylvania, on a clear October day, we covered 120 miles in two and a half hours, finally landing in a patch of trees, to avoid being blown out over the Atlantic. It was quite an experience and I can't wait to repeat it.

Now about show business. I have worked for many years in the theater, motion pictures, television, and radio; I have traveled the lecture circuit — universities and women's clubs — with my own program of dramatic readings; I have recited Shakespeare with the San Francisco and Philadelphia Symphony Orchestras, under the baton of Pierre Monteux; of all these, from my point of view, the best was radio, though I hardly realized at the time how good it was. No long runs, no repetition, no memorizing of lines, no make-up, no traveling or living in discomfort, nothing whatever required but talent, an actor's training, and the ability to read well on sight. The script is too long or too short? All you need is a blue pencil. Cut it to any length you wish, or write more in, right up to show time, and if, as often happened, there was an audience, one had all the fun of a theatrical performance with none of the anxiety. One got paid whether the result was good or bad, and there were no critics to bother about.

Many an actor whose name was unknown to the public made a good living by running from one broadcasting studio to another, reading in different dialects on various shows. Once, in New York, a little man popped up on the other side of a microphone, playing a taxi driver with wit and a perfect Brooklyn accent; within the next two weeks, he faced me twice again, as a Greek waiter and a Mexican bandit, both perfectly done. I stared at him in amazement.

"My, you're a good actor!" I said. He smiled modestly.

"I'll bet you don't even know my name," he said, "but I don't care. I have a wife and four happy children at my home in Connecticut, and I drive a Continental. I never have to make a public appearance, or head a subscription list, or take any responsibility like you. All I have to do is to run from one studio to another, playing any nationality or accent they ask of me, and I make around $50,000 a year!"

If radio was good to actors, it also was good to listeners. Imagination is usually better than realization, and some of the great shows done on the Lux Radio Theater, for example, gave more pleasure than most of the TV "spectaculars" of today, added to which it was possible to listen to them while playing cards, sewing, carpentering, doing the household chores, or driving a car, without having to stay glued to a TV set, watching endless soap and cigarette commercials. Radio is gone, and I, for one, regret it.

The motion-picture industry, as I knew it, has also gone. The winds of change have blown through Hollywood and left destruction in their path. Battered by the government's Divorcement Decree, which shut off their lifeblood by taking away their theaters, and by television, which gives entertainment to the public for nothing, the great studios no longer are able to offer continuous employment to artists. Hoping to stimulate business, they have turned to sex and violence. There are no glamorous and beautiful women on the screen today and no legitimate actors like myself, because we can't use sawed-off shotguns or hit each other convincingly, and we don't care to take off our clothes in public. Hollywood no longer entertains the world; its unrivaled studio facilities are occupied by an army of workers who grind out the commercial television pap with which the great American public drugs itself.

Anyone, anywhere, can produce a picture. All you need is an idea, a star, a hand camera, some gambling money, and a lot of luck, and to judge from some of the foreign films which have recently been acclaimed by critics and public alike, the only essential is the luck. Meanwhile, actors of my style and generation are at liberty — professionally known as "resting."

Television, of course, has been good for certain types of performers, though it tends to burn up their careers in a very few years. I have made many appearances as a guest artist on the leading shows in Hollywood and New York, and have sometimes enjoyed them, but on the whole I am afraid the medium doesn't interest me.

This leaves the theater, and the poor old theater always seems on the point of leaving us! Somehow, it struggles along and there are still occasional shows that make a barrel of money and still people who find it enjoyable, but over all there is not much genuine satisfaction, either in going to it or in working in it. The theater is no longer a vocation; it is rather an activity, best suited to ambitious young girls and homosexual young men. Anyone who dreams of a theatrical career today would do well to ponder the results of a recent survey of the profession conducted by the Actors Equity Association.

"A. In any year, roughly 75% of the Equity membership will earn less than $2,500 in the theater.

B. In any year, only 11–13% of the membership may be expected to earn $5,000 or more from the theater.

C. Median income from the theater currently is unlikely to be more than $1,100 and may even be on the dark side of $1,000."

The chances of making a living in the theater are therefore remote; as for making a comfortable living, they are minuscule. By contrast, the Screen Actors Guild reports that 888 members earned $25,000 or more in 1967, but it is a safe guess that more than half that number made their money in TV commercials.

It was my good fortune that two of the finest parts I ever played, in *My Fair Lady* and *Dear Liar*, came to me, as the gipsy foretold, late in my career.

In the course of these nationwide tours, I played both shows in Los Angeles, and on each occasion I was showered with compliments, and with requests from everybody in Hollywood for aid in securing seats. After this, I thought complacently, all I had to do was to live comfortably at home in Santa Monica and take my pick of motion-picture offers. I was mistaken; months went by and nothing happened. I went to see my agent with an idea I had for a story. He shook his head.

"Brian," he said bluntly, "if you have six million dollars and Gregory Peck, you can begin to think about a picture. Otherwise, forget it!"

When I recovered, I remarked that in that case perhaps I should consider selling my house and leaving Hollywood.

"Yeah, might be a good idea," he said, and then added apologetically, "Oh, you know how it is Brian. The movie business is like the oil business. You were a gusher for us once, but now you're a dry hole."

I thanked him for his advice, which he is now doubtless giving to Gregory Peck, and I went down to Los Angeles to see my man of business. If the time had come to leave Hollywood, I wanted to feel that I could do so with dignity — like Norma Talmadge who, a few years after her retirement from the screen, came out of the smart restaurant of the day in Beverly Hills to find the usual crowd of fans, pushing forward for autographs. With a wave of the hand, she said to them pleasantly, "Run away dears. I don't need you now!"

As I bucked the traffic down to Los Angeles, the memory came to me of a night, twenty years earlier, when I had dined with my friends Ronald and Benita Colman at their lovely house in Beverly Hills. Adolph Menjou had been at the table and, as usual, was holding forth on some burning topic of the day — dear Adolph, so dapper, so faultlessly dressed, so eloquent and so vehement, who loved nothing more than an animated political discussion. After listening to him for some time, Ronnie interrupted the flow of words, saying, "Wait a minute, Adolph! Last week you were taking the opposite point of view!"

Adolph paused and then, in his Gallic way, shrugged his shoulders. "Was I?" he said. "Oh well, I was reading the other book then!" Switching the conversation, he turned to me. "Well, Brian," he asked, "what about you? I hope you are saving your money?"

Oh, I replied, I hadn't much to think about. A couple of bank accounts and a few Quixotic investments in aviation. I knew nothing about money. Adolph was shocked. Pointing a peremptory finger at me, he cried, "I must take you in hand! Tomorrow morning, I shall telephone and tell you what to do!"

He was as good as his word. He picked me up and took me down to Los Angeles, where he introduced me to a firm of investment counsel. Meekly obeying him, I entrusted my affairs to them. It was well that I did so. "Take care of the pence, and the pounds will take care of themselves," Miss Halden used to teach us as children, and my man had helped me to follow that maxim, adding penny to penny and setting aside little sums whenever possible. Now he was able to tell me that, despite the losses I had sustained from farming, divorce, bad investments, and foolish actions, I had somehow managed to achieve that private income — small, but adequate if I were willing to reduce my scale of living — which Sir Gerald du Maurier had told me so long ago was the first essential to an acting career. I don't know which was the greater, my astonishment, my pleasure, or my pride. How did it happen, I asked him, although of course I knew that the credit was his.

"It is quite simple," he answered. "You have lived well, but, unlike so many of our movie clients, you have not been profligate."

Now I live peacefully in part of an old château overlooking lovely Lake Geneva in Switzerland. I am happy there with my dear wife Eleanor. We love to see our friends; to others we say, "Don't come, you won't like it." I visit

America and England and I like to travel about the world, for there is still so much to see and do. Especially I love Ireland. I don't pine to act, though I would be interested in direction. From time to time, somebody persuades me into a studio or onto a stage. I have been in three pictures made in Europe, none successful: *The Waltz King,* in Vienna, for Walt Disney, *The Cavern,* in Rome; and in England I played King Arthur in *Lancelot and Guinevere,* for Cornel Wilde, a very remarkable fellow who not only finds his own material and puts his own money into pictures, but also produces them, directs them, and plays the starring roles — and very good pictures they are too.

In 1967, clever Rosalind Russell and I came together for the fourth happy time, to make a nice comedy, *Rosie,* for Universal in Hollywood. I have never advertised in trade papers, as many actors do, but if I did, I suppose my ad would read:

(William) Brian de Lacy Aherne, professionally known as Brian Aherne, having signally failed to find a proper job in life, is still available to show business. Not arrogant or difficult any more. Has wardrobe. Will travel.

Honors come with age. I hold an honorary LL.D. degree from Baylor University, and Syracuse University has asked for my memorabilia. A cigarette case, inscribed with my name under a coat of arms, bears the words *Canada thanks you for your generous help,* and a lighter says, *Canada thanks you again.* A wall of my study at the Château de l'Aile in Vevey is hung with the usual citations and testimonials. Details of my career fill several pages of *Who's Who of the American Theater.* The oddest tributes of all were paid to me in Hollywood, where an enterprising fellow built a nightclub on Sunset Boulevard, near Vine Street, and wrote that he wished to decorate its front with forty cement slabs, each bearing the signature of "A Hollywood Great." Flattered by being included in this category, I went along and, with a pointed instrument, signed my name in the wet cement. Afterwards, whenever I passed the place, I would stare and wonder, because on my slab was scrawled, in illiterate handwriting, the name *Byron O'Hearn.* Did the workman drop and break it, and did he, thinking that the boss would never notice, decide to fix it up for himself? I shall never know, and apparently the boss never noticed.

I had more hope of the Hollywood Chamber of Commerce, which announced that it would inscribe the names and crafts of A Selected List of Hollywood Immortals on the pavement stones of Hollywood Boulevard and Vine Street. I was pleased to learn that my name was on the list, and one day, being in the vicinity, I strolled along, looking for it. I discovered that there were hundreds, if not thousands, of names immortalized beneath the feet on Hollywood Boulevard, and it was not until I turned the corner onto Vine Street that I saw mine. As Beatrice Lillie used to say, you could have knocked me down with a fender. It read:

BRIAN AHERNE
Television Personality

And so *Per Ardua Surgo* — Through Adversity I Rise.

CURRICULUM VITAE

Curriculum Vitae

AHERNE, Brian. Actor. b. Brian de Lacy Aherne, May 2, 1902, King's Norton, Worcestershire, England, to William de Lacy and Louise (Thomas) Aherne. Attended Edgbaston Sch., Birmingham, and Malvern Coll., England. Studied with Italia Conti. Married 1939, to Joan Fontaine, actress (marr. dis. 1943); married 1946, to Eleanor de Liagre Labrot. Relative in theater: brother-in-law, Alfred de Liagre, producer and manager. Member of AEA: British AEA (founding member, on council, 1930–34).

Pre-theater. Architect (Liverpool, Eng., 1921–22).

Theater. Mr. Aherne made his first stage appearance at the age of eight with the Pilgrim Players in *Fifinella* (Birmingham, Eng., April 5, 1910); his London debut in *Where the Rainbow Ends* (Garrick Th., Dec. 26, 1913); subsequently appeared as Jack O'Hara in *Paddy, the Next Best Thing* (Savoy, Dec. 26, 1923); toured England as Hugo in *The Flame* (opened Feb. 1924); and played Langford in *White Cargo* (Playhouse, London, May 15, 1924).

In 1926, he toured Australia as Valentine Brown in *Quality Street,* John Shand in *What Every Woman Knows,* Crichton in *The Admirable Crichton,* Simon and Harry in *Mary Rose,* and Willocks in *Aren't We All?.* He repeated his role as Langford in *White Cargo* (Strand, London, March 7, 1927); played David in *The Silver Cord* (St. Martin's, Sept. 13, 1927); Gerald in *Let's All Talk About Gerald* (Arts, May 1923); Young Marlow in *She Stoops to Conquer* (Lyric, Hammersmith, Aug. 16, 1928); Walter Craig in *Craig's Wife* (Fortune); Wyndham Brandon in *Rope* (Ambassadors, April 1929); Lt. St. Aubyn in *Tunnel Trench* (Duchess, Nov. 1929); Bastien in *S.S. Tenacity* (Arts, July 1930); succeeded Godfrey Tearle as Francis Archer in *The Beaux' Stratagem* (Royalty, June 11, 1930); Marquis de Presles in *An Object of Virtue* (Duchess, Nov. 1930); and Alan Varrey in *A Marriage Has Been Disarranged* (Royalty, Dec. 1930).

He made his N.Y.C. debut as Robert Browning in *The Barretts of Wimpole Street* (Empire, Feb. 9, 1931); followed by Tarquin in *Lucrèce* (Belasco, Dec. 20, 1932); appeared as Mark in *Birthday* (Cambridge, London, Feb. 1934); Mercutio in Katharine Cornell's *Romeo and Juliet* (Martin Beck Th., N.Y.C., Dec. 20, 1934); repeated the role of Browning in a revival of *The Barretts of Wimpole Street* (Martin Beck Th., Feb. 25, 1935); played the Earl of Warwick in Katharine Cornell's *Saint Joan* (Martin Beck Th., Mar. 9, 1936); and Iago in *Othello* (New Amsterdam, Jan. 6, 1937); repeated his role of Browning in *The Barretts of Wimpole Street* (Ethel Barrymore Th., Mar. 26, 1945) and played the same role in the production that toured the ETO (July 1944–Feb. 1945), under the auspices of the American Th. Wing.

Mr. Aherne played Roublard in *The French Touch* (Cort, N.Y.C., Dec. 8, 1945). In July–Sept. 1948, Mr. Aherne toured as Archer in *The Beaux' Stratagem;* played Young Marlow in *She Stoops to Conquer* (N.Y. City Ctr., Dec. 28, 1949); John Middleton in *The Constant Wife* (Natl., Dec. 8, 1951); John Hampden in *Escapade* (48 St. Th., Nov. 18, 1953); and the Marquis of Heronden in *Quadrille* (Coronet, Nov. 3, 1954). In 1957–58, he toured as Henry Higgins in the national company of *My Fair Lady;* played George Bernard Shaw in *Dear Liar* (Billy Rose Th., N.Y.C., Mar. 17, 1960).

Films. Mr. Aherne made his film debut in England where he appeared in several silent films. He made his American film debut in *Song of Songs* (Par., 1933); followed by his role as John Shand in *What Every Woman Knows* (MGM, 1934); *The Constant*

Nymph (Fox, 1934); *Sylvia Scarlett* (RKO, 1935); *I Live My Life* (MGM, 1935); *Beloved Enemy* (UA, 1936); *The Great Garrick* (WB, 1937); *Captain Fury* (UA, 1939); Maximilian in *Juarez* (WB, 1939); *Lady in Question* (Col., 1940); *Hired Wife* (U, 1940); *My Son, My Son* (UA, 1940); *Skylark* (Par., 1941); *My Sister Eileen* (Col., 1942); *Smilin' Through* (MGM, 1942); *Forever and a Day* (RKO, 1943); *What a Woman* (Col., 1943); *The Locket* (RKO, 1946); *Smart Woman* (Allied, 1948); *I Confess* (WB, 1953); Capt. Smith in *Titanic* (Fox, 1953); *Prince Valiant* (Fox, 1954); *A Bullet Is Waiting* (Col., 1954); *The Swan* (MGM, 1956); *The Best of Everything* (Fox, 1959); *Susan Slade* (WB, 1961); King Arthur in *Sword of Lancelot* (U, 1963); Johann Strauss, Sr., in *The Waltz King* (Disney, 1963); and General Braithwaite in *The Cavern* (U, 1964); *Rosie* (U, 1967).

Other Activities. He is a founder of the Aircraft Owners' and Pilots' Assn. and has held a flying license since 1934.

Awards. Mr. Aherne was nominated for an Academy (Oscar) Award for his portrayal of Maximilian in *Juarez* (1938). He is an honorary Texas Ranger, and received the honorary degree of LL.D from Baylor Univ. (Texas, 1951).

Biographical Encyclopaedia and Who's Who of the American Theater Ed. by Walter Rigdon. (James H. Heineman, Inc.).